Art and Crime

Art and Crime

Exploring the Dark Side of the Art World

Edited by
Noah Charney

Afterword by John Stubbs

Praeger
An Imprint of ABC-CLIO, LLC

A B C CLIO

Santa Barbara, California • Denver, Colorado • Oxford, England

Library of Congress Cataloging-in-Publication Data

Art and crime : exploring the dark side of the art world / edited by Noah Charney ;
afterword by John Stubbs.
p. cm.
Includes bibliographical references and index.
ISBN 978-0-313-36635-2 (hard copy : alk. paper) — ISBN 978-0-313-36636-9 (ebook)
1. Art thefts. 2. Art—Forgeries. I. Charney, Noah.
N8795.A78 2009
364.16'287—dc22 2009011639

13 12 11 10 9 1 2 3 4 5

This book is also available on the World Wide Web as an eBook.
Visit www.abc-clio.com for details.

ABC-CLIO, LLC
130 Cremona Drive, P.O. Box 1911
Santa Barbara, California 93116-1911

This book is printed on acid-free paper ∞

Manufactured in the United States of America

To the volunteers, trustees, and supporters of ARCA,

without whom none of this would be possible.

Thank you.

Contents

Acknowledgments

By definition, a collection of essays is a collaborative effort. Its editor fades into the background and permits the essayists to speak for themselves. But in the assembly of such a collection, the editor has countless individuals to thank.

First and foremost, thanks go to the essayists, who contributed their chapters free of charge, because they believe in the book's message of strength in unity against art crime. Their wider belief in, and support of, ARCA has been so encouraging to this fledgling nonprofit organization, the one goal of which is to study art crime in order to preserve art for the future. Essayists (and the editor) accepted no fees, so that 100 percent of the profits from this book go to support ARCA's charitable activities.

I would like to thank the board members of ARCA, both its trustees and the Editorial Board of its new peer-reviewed academic journal, *The Journal of Art Crime,* which will continue what this book has begun (many of whom contributed essays). Lord Colin Renfrew, Petrus van Duyne, Matjaž Jager, Bojan Dobovšek, Travis McDade, Ken Polk, David Simon, Erik Nemeth, Liisa van Vliet, Dick Drent, Michael Kirchner, Anthony Amore, Dennis Ahern, Richard Ellis, Giovanni Pastore, Neil Brodie, David Gill, Edgar Tijhuis, Benoit van Asbroeck, Howard Spiegler, Judah Best, and Patricia Garland.

Having lived in Italy, I have developed the Italian habit of doing business only with people I know and like. This results in friendships with colleagues that transcend business, and makes "work" a pleasure. Neither ARCA nor this book would have been possible without the moral support and encouragement of colleagues in the world of art and art protection. Special thanks to Vernon Rapley, Martin Finkelnberg, James Hess, Veronique Plesch, Michael Marlais, Rob and Stevan Layne, Willem

Henkman, Andrea Pizzi, Danielle Carrabino, Louis Burke, Paul Sandler, and to John Stubbs, a great friend, collaborator, and fellow Slovenophile.

Thanks also to the institutions that have hosted me as a visiting lecturer in the past year, and supported the work that this book expresses: Yale University, The Institute of Criminology in Ljubljana, University of Maribor, University of Ljubljana, Amsterdam's Rijksmuseum, The Yale British Art Center, The Peabody Museum of Natural History, Venice in Peril, The National Library of Spain, University of Cambridge, The International Foundation for Cultural Property Protection, the European Society of Criminology and the American Society of Criminology, the Art Loss Register, the French National Institute of Art History, the Union des Avocats, the American Bar Association, ArtInfo and its editor David Grosz, and more.

Great thanks to my editor at Praeger, Suzanne Staszak-Silva, for believing in this project. And to Urška, my sweety, who married me in the midst of this project, and who doubtless hears the words "art crime" far too often.

Introduction

Noah Charney

I stood at the bar of the old Eagle pub in Cambridge, England, the smell of stale pipe smoke in the air, and 20 pints of beer on the scuffed oak bar before me. At the end of the bar to my right, decked in tweed and bow ties, half of my guests stood clustered: a select group among the few professors in the world to have studied art crime. At the opposite end of the bar, glancing furtively over at the academics, my other guests maintained a tight defensive formation: the world's top art police, from the FBI, Scotland Yard, and Italy's Carabinieri.

I was in way over my head. While still a postgraduate student at Cambridge University, I had organized the first international conference to bring together academics and police, to work on the shared problem of art crime. There had been conferences for art police, for museum security directors, and for criminologists, to be sure. But my interest lay in bringing together the various fields influenced by, and working against, art crime; to see what a team effort could produce, combining theoreticians with experts in the field.

I knew that the police and the academics would be shy around one another. The police, without advanced degrees (or, in some cases, any degrees) were wondering what they were doing in the halls of academe. The professors, on the other hand, were terrified of these police who actually *did* something for a living. I had wrestled with how best to break the ice, before I settled on beer—the great unifier. Was it not Aristotle who said, "All men are equal, when they are three sheets to the wind?" Maybe not Aristotle, but whoever said it, it is a point well taken. After a few pints, the coy police and the sweaty professors were slapping each other on the back, buying rounds, suddenly the best of friends. By the next morning, when the conference proper began, there was a general aura of camaraderie in the air, mixed with a tinge of hangover.

I had stumbled into the study of art crime quite accidentally. I began as an art historian. While still a full-time student, I began writing my first novel, the plot of which involves art theft and forgery. As I researched real art crime, to provide context for the novel, I quickly found that there was both relatively little scholarly material on the subject, and that there was no professor who could be considered an authority in the field. The study of art crime straddles different disciplines, combining elements of art history, criminology, sociology, law, security studies, policing, and history—and each subject deferred to the other. As a result, no one was studying the nature and history of art crime with the academic discipline required by other fields. A few years, and a lot of research later, I emerged as an anomaly in the academic world: an historian of art crime.

I founded ARCA as a direct result of the encouragement of participants in the 2006 Cambridge conference, many of whom would become the organization's first trustees. ARCA (The Association for Research into Crimes against Art), a nonprofit organization, is the first interdisciplinary think tank and research group on the study of art crime. Its goal is to inform and educate the public and professionals about the true nature of art crime, its severity, and what can be done to curb it. ARCA uses research and analysis techniques, the academic's arsenal, to suggest practically applicable solutions for policing and art security. We ask and hope to answer the question: what lessons can we learn from historical successes and failures, in order to better protect and recover art today?

Our basic thesis is that academics and theoreticians can help police and security professionals in the future by studying and analyzing past crimes. In addition to acting as a bridge between academics and professionals, as well as bringing together police of different nations, ARCA's projects include the establishment of a new, independent master's program in the study of art crime, the first such program in the world. We are also publishing a new, twice-yearly, peer-reviewed academic and informational journal, *The Journal of Art Crime,* which will provide academics with a venue to publish their studies, and will also contain up-to-date news and information on art crime, so critical for the art trade, museums, security, police, art lawyers, and private collectors. More information on these and other ARCA projects may be found on our Web site, http://www.artcrime.info.

This collection of essays is the first book published under the auspices of ARCA. It is particularly important to us that ARCA is a nonprofit organization, a guarantee against any ulterior motive or prejudice biasing our group's research, activities, and recommendations. I am particularly pleased and proud to say that the money earned on royalties from the sale of this book goes directly to support ARCA. The essayists generously waived any fees, writing for this collection because they believe in its message, and in ARCA's mission.

The essayists for *Art and Crime* come from a wide variety of backgrounds and professions. They range from university professors to police, art lawyers to archaeologists, members of the art trade to insurers, security experts to museum staff, and more. The diversity of the contributors is the book's strength, demonstrating the spectrum damaged by art crime—but also the formidable team working against it. The authors have been asked to write their chapters in the voice and manner with which they feel most comfortable. This collection is of importance to museum guards as well as emeritus professors, and its essays are meant to be approachable as well as enlightening. Some essays read as conversational, while others are more scientific—this is intentional, in keeping with the collaborative nature of work across disciplines and professional fields, and to ensure that the essays are accessible to the broadest spectrum of readers. Overly scientific, and often elitist, style and jargon are not necessary to convey important and useful ideas—and too often, the more formal and academic the essay, the less interesting it is to read for all but the handful of peers in the author's given field. The danger, of course, is that of such a diverse collection, the academic readers and critics will deem it insufficiently academic, and the professional and lay readers will find it too academic to be accessible and practically useful. We hope that this collection will appeal to both groups of readers, who will appreciate the mixed target readership and the attempt to build a bridge in book form to link the two in a common, good cause. This book should be enjoyable, as well as important, to readers of all backgrounds.

The key to the book's success is that all the essayists, in the vocabulary and format of their choice, present vital information and advice, much of which has never found its way to the printed page. Each essayist has been asked not only to provide an introduction to their subject, coupled with expert theoretical analysis, but to end their chapters with practically applicable suggestions based on those analyses.

This book represents the first interdisciplinary essay collection on the study of art crime, and its effect on many aspects of the art world. Essayists discuss subcategories of art crime, including vandalism, iconoclasm, forgery, fraud, peacetime theft, war looting, archaeological looting, smuggling, submarine looting, and ransom. If the essays topics here seem rather broad within the overall umbrella of art crime, this too is intentional. This book is meant as an introduction to a wide array of pertinent topics.[1] In the future, ARCA will publish books focused on the various subcategories of art crime addressed here.[2] The goal of this collection is simply to start the ball rolling, so to speak, and encourage interdisciplinary, interprofessional dialogue and the study of art crime.

This work is of critical importance to anyone involved in the art world, its trade, study, and security. It introduces art crime as a new, interdisciplinary field of study. Both academic and professional authors represent the various spheres damaged by art crime, and present a diversity of complementary views and approaches, working towards the common goal of curbing art crime in the future.

Together, the members of ARCA, the authors of this essay collection, and you, the reader, can present a united front, working together to protect the world's cultural heritage, and to fight art crime. Thank you for your interest and your support of this endeavor.

NOTES

1. If any one aspect of art crime seems under-represented, or indeed passed over, in this collection, this is due to the specificity of the research interests of both ARCA and the essayists in the period leading up to the book's publication. Future ARCA books and *The Journal of Art Crime* will endeavor to fill in the gaps that are inevitably present in this essay collection which, for pure reasons of logistics, could not accommodate more chapters than it currently holds.
2. ARCA is currently working on books covering the history of art crime, the history of forgery, library, and archive security, as well as monographs on historical thefts.

Art Crime in Context

Noah Charney

Art crime has as yet received very little scholarly attention, in spite of the fact that it infects a multibillion-dollar legitimate art industry, with illegal profits running to an astounding $6 billion per annum by conservative estimates.[1] Art crime has evolved from a relatively innocuous phenomenon into the third-highest-grossing annual criminal trade worldwide, run primarily by organized crime syndicates and therefore funding their other enterprises, from the drug and arms trades to terrorism.[2] It is no longer merely the art that is at stake.

Why study art crime? Information and scholarly analysis of art crime is critical to the wide variety of fields involved in the art trade and art preservation: from museums to academia, from auction houses to galleries, from insurance to art law, from collectors to archivists, from police to security. Despite this, most people unfamiliar with the machinations of the art world, including many police and politicians, are under the misconception that art crime is not particularly important—that it only involves the collectibles of the wealthy, and the only victims are members of the elitist art world (with the implication that they probably deserve all they get). This fallacy comes from a lack of understanding of how art crime really functions.

It is true that, until the Second World War, independent of conflict zones, most art crime was perpetrated by idealistic individuals with gentlemanly aspirations. Thefts were nonviolent and elegant, in their use of dexterity and intelligence over force. But after the war, and specifically since 1960–61, most art crime has been perpetrated by, or on behalf of, international organized crime syndicates.

Nineteen sixty-one was the first year in which organized crime, in the person of the *Union Corse* (the Corsican Mafia), began to incorporate art theft into their criminal repertoire. They were inspired to steal art by the new interest of the television media in the prices for which art was selling at auction. The Metropolitan Museum of Art in New York purchased Rembrandt's *Portrait of Aristotle Contemplating a Bust of Homer* for the record price of $2.3 million. That same year, records were broken for the sale of Cézanne and Picasso paintings. The media has always enjoyed both the sex appeal of art crime and touting stratospheric art sales prices. In 1961, the Union Corse was dutifully watching the television news, and they recognized art as a commodity that, to their minds, was highly valuable, highly portable, and underprotected.[3] Not being particularly creative, the Union Corse stole exactly what the television news had said was valuable: Cézannes and Picassos. They began a string of thefts on the French Riviera, including major thefts in 1960 and 1962, culminating in 1976 with the largest peacetime art theft in history, when 118 Picassos were stolen in one night from an exhibition at the Papal Palace in Avignon.[4]

The sprawling criminal network through which crime syndicates function, including the codes of silence, smuggling systems, and international connections, is what permits organized crime to profit from art crime. Apart from the occasional individual thief or forger, syndicates have pushed aside or muscled out the competition and have been behind, or involved in, most art crimes since the early 1960s. They may be responsible for the smuggling, the transport, the design of the crime, the sale of the stolen goods, or the theft itself, but they are there. Organized crime brought to art crime the methods they use for their other activities, namely the threat of violence. And because organized crime is responsible for most art crime over the past 50 years, the sexy museum heist that we love to read about, and think must be relatively harmless, is actually helping to fund the other activities in which organized crime is involved, including the drug and arms trades, and terrorism.

Many people assume that there are only a few art crimes per year. In actuality, there are tens of thousands of art crimes per year, though the general public only hears about the handful of them that make international headlines, because they involve major museums or masterpieces.[5] In Italy alone, there are over 20,000 reported annually, and many more go unreported. Experts believe that more art crime goes unreported than reaches police files.

Most art crime (perhaps as much as 75 percent) involves antiquities, which may be looted directly from the earth or the sea. No record exists of objects that have remained buried until they are dug up by tomb raiders, so looted antiquities are most difficult to track down. They will never appear on any registry of stolen art. Police agencies cannot know what to search for if they do not know what has been stolen. These antiquities may be sold for full value on an open market, with the addition of a forged provenance (the documented history of ownership) to suggest that they have a legitimate pedigree. Looted antiquities are a significant funding source for fundamentalist terrorist groups. The museum heist about which we love to read may be financing terrorism, as we shall see in an example below.

RANSOM, DRUGS, AND TERRORISM: HOW CRIMINALS PROFIT FROM ART THEFT

The most frequently asked question by members of the press and public is how criminals profit from the theft of recognizable works of art, those which cannot be shopped on an open market? For recognizable artworks taken from extant collections, there are three probable avenues for criminal gain.

Ransom

One option is for criminals to try to ransom stolen art back to the victim, or to their insurers. For prominent examples one might refer to the 1934 theft of the "Righteous Judges" panel from *The Ghent Altarpiece* by Jan van Eyck, or more recently, the 2004 Munch Museum theft.

History suggests that certain general rules dictate the way art ransom functions. If a ransom demand comes immediately after a theft, as in the 1934 case, then it may be assumed that ransom was the primary motivation for the crime. If the ransom is not paid, the thieves are out of luck. Unless they have a buyer lined up, it is a highly risky endeavor to shop stolen, recognizable art on even a closed black market, in which buyers are "screened" to ensure that they are not police in disguise. Most recoveries of recognizable stolen art come when criminals grow careless and desperate to turn their art into profit, and offer the goods to an undercover agent. A ransom attempt indicates that there is no buyer, and thus no other recourse for the criminals that can lead to cash profit. Historically, if a ransom attempt fails, much of the time desperate criminals will simply abandon the stolen work, as in both the 1934 van Eyck and the 2004 Munch cases.

If a ransom demand comes after a longer period of time, several weeks or more, it suggests that the criminals had another plan for the art, such as sale, but that this plan fell through. Ransom is therefore the only possible backup plan. But if the victim or the victim's insurance company fails to pay the ransom, the thieves are once more out of luck, and will most likely abandon the stolen goods, when they realize the art is "too hot" to sell without significant risk of arrest.

Threats to destroy or damage art are rarely taken seriously, for the simple reason that the destruction of art is equivalent to setting fire to a suitcase full of hundred-dollar bills. It benefits no one. The art, unlike a kidnap victim, cannot inform on the thieves and reveal their identities. The art loses value dramatically if it is damaged. Only spite or stupidity would lead a criminal to destroy the art they worked so hard to steal—and potential profit will stay their hand in all but the most unusual cases. The moral that history tells us: never pay a ransom for stolen art. Failure to pay will dissuade future attempts, by showing that they do not succeed.

Black Market Sale

The second means to profit from stolen recognizable works is more complicated. While it is dangerous to seek a buyer for stolen art, screening out potential police in disguise, it does happen. Examples include the Sicilian Mafia's attempts to sell works by Caravaggio, Bronzino, Andrea Del Sarto, and more to unscrupulous dealers and collectors, the 1994 theft of Munch's *The Scream*, and the recent recovery of a Rembrandt *Self-Portrait* stolen from the Stockholm Museum of Art and recovered in 2005.[6] It is true, however, that if criminals are willing to take on the considerable risk, they can usually find someone to buy a beautiful and desirable artwork, albeit at a fraction of its market value. But in practice, criminals have learned that the only time they really risked arrest was when they tried to sell the stolen art, inadvertently offering the goods to undercover police.

Barter and Collateral, Drugs and Terrorism

Instead of trying to liquidate and turn their art into cash, criminals involved in syndicates have come up with an ingenious alternative—they use the stolen art for barter or collateral on a closed black market, trading with other members of crime syndicates. Based on the prices for which stolen art has been offered to police and criminal informants, as compared to its estimated legitimate auction value, the estimated "black market" value for stolen art is 7–10 percent of its probable auction value. Criminals will assign the black market value to stolen art: what they could probably get in cash if they were willing to take the risk. The art is then swapped or used as collateral in deals with other criminals for other illicit goods of an equivalent value—goods that would also require a risk in order to liquidate, primarily drugs or arms.

An example from 1986 will best illustrate this point, in particular the link between stolen art, drugs, organized crime, and terrorist groups.[7] Martin Cahill was a notorious Irish gangster, with supposed links to the

IRA terrorist group. Cahill loved to thumb his nose at the police, the government, and high society. He saw art theft as a chance to do all of the above in one go, and to profit along the way. Cahill and a dozen associates stole 18 paintings, including Vermeer's *Lady Writing a Letter with Her Maid* and Gabriel Metsu's *Woman Reading a Letter,* from an Irish country home called Russborough House. At the time (until the 1990 Gardner Museum heist), this was the biggest art theft in peacetime history, in terms of the estimated value of the art involved.

What did Cahill do with the paintings? He had planned to sell them for millions on the black market. But the sales he expected were not forthcoming. He could not seem to find any of those criminal art collectors he had learned about at the movies. Unable to find a buyer himself, Cahill would employ an alternative plan to profit from this stolen art.

In May 1990, the Turkish police in Istanbul interrupted a Scottish criminal trading the Metsu painting, stolen from Russborough House, for a shipment of heroin—a barter of stolen art for drugs between members of two crime syndicates. But what of the Vermeer?

For nearly a decade, Cahill's gang had been selling stolen diamonds to a crooked gem merchant in Antwerp. When Cahill needed cash to buy heroin for resale, he smuggled the Vermeer painting to Belgium. The Antwerp merchant accepted the Vermeer as collateral on a loan of £1 million, with which Cahill would buy the wholesale heroin. The merchant locked the Vermeer in his Luxembourg bank vault. If Cahill failed to repay the merchant, he would keep the Vermeer. If Cahill paid back the £1 million loan, the Vermeer would go on to act as collateral in future such deals.

The police were on to the case and staged an elaborate, multiyear undercover operation, in which one of their detectives posed as a collector of stolen art. In August 1993, an associate of the Antwerp merchant named Niall Mulvihill offered the Vermeer and another painting stolen from Russborough House, Goya's *Portrait of Dona Antonia Zarate,* to the disguised detective. The detective agreed to pay £1.25 million for both paintings, and brought a major international bank in on the sting operation, to help reassure the criminals that it was a legitimate deal. The transaction was meant to take place at the Antwerp airport. Standing in a parking lot, admiring the stolen paintings in the trunk of Mulvihill's car, the disguised detective signaled by brushing his tie with his hand, and the Belgian SWAT team descended upon them, seizing the paintings and the hapless Mulvihill. Four paintings were recovered in that operation, including another work by Metsu.

Over the years, 12 of the original 18 stolen paintings were recovered, all from members of crime syndicates. Six remained missing. The Antwerp gem merchant was never charged. Mulvihill escaped prosecution, as it was deemed that the theft of the paintings took place out of Belgian jurisdiction—indicative of the dismissive attitude and lack of international cooperation that is too often present in art crime cases, even among judges and politicians. Cahill, too, was never caught. (The criminals did not, however, come to happy ends. Cahill was assassinated in August 1994, shot through the window of his car. Mulvihill was killed in a gang firefight in Dublin in January 2003).

All but two of the 18 stolen Russborough House paintings have been recovered. They provide a concrete example of how stolen art is used by organized crime as barter and collateral for other illicit goods. The few such instances that police have stumbled upon show the tip of a great iceberg—this is what is happening with most recognizable stolen art that is not offered for ransom, making its recovery a matter of luck.

The IRA was involved in numerous art thefts, beyond Cahill's, which were primarily for profit rather than for ideology. Under the leadership of art historian Rose Dugdale, the IRA launched a series of violent art thefts from Irish country homes. Profits from these thefts were used to support IRA terrorist activity, and some of the paintings were used in an attempted ransom negotiation with the British government, returning the paintings unharmed in exchange for the release of imprisoned IRA agents. Such incidents involving the IRA are the most overt and best-documented instances of art crime funding a terrorist group. There are countless more, particularly involving antiquities looting and forgery in third-world countries. The careful gathering and presentation of empirical evidence linking art crime to terrorism is one of the best ways to get world governments and police departments to take art crime as seriously as those who have studied it recognize that it warrants.

WHAT IS BEING DONE, WHAT COULD BE DONE

Recovery rates for world police are dismayingly low, often below 6 percent, with an even lower rate of successful prosecution. The fault is not the police's, but rather that of the overall administration—with the notable exception of Italy, most countries do not take art crime seriously, and do not assign enough resources to it. They do not take art crime seriously because studies have not been done to demonstrate the scale and depth of art crime, specifically its extensive links to organized crime and terrorism.

What began as a relatively innocuous crime, nonviolent and perpetrated by individuals for personal profit or ideological reasons, has evolved into one of organized crime's most lucrative enterprises. Running parallel, but lagging behind what is actually happening, is the popular conception of art crime—which has not caught up with reality. What was once the realm of the idealistic thief has become the territory of international crime syndicates. But the general public, and a large percentage of police and government officials around the world, still believe that it only involves the collectibles of the elitist wealthy, and dismiss it as an occasional misdemeanor that occurs a few times a year.

One problem has been the lack of data kept by police around the world.[8] But this issue is made more difficult by the fact that many art crimes go unreported by the victims. Museums and galleries may be loath to admit their own security failures, while private collectors may not have declared ownership of some objects in their collection, in order to avoid luxury tax. The result is that only a fraction of art crimes are reported.

The looting of antiquities is another difficult component. Antiquities tend to be looted from remote sites, jungle tombs, or coastal shipwrecks that may go undiscovered for months or years, if someone comes across them at all. Even if an illegal excavation site is discovered, there will be no record of what was at the site to begin with if the site was never before excavated. Therefore, police may learn that a tomb has been opened, but have no idea what to look for, because the contents are known only to the thieves.

Once word gets to the police, a problem of data management may arise. Most police departments file art thefts with general stolen property, when in fact the nature of the crime is distinct—one might as well file kidnapping cases in with stolen cars. Police tend not to file art crime cases with particular care, because they are unaware of the severity and nature of the crime. They are unaware because good analyses of art crime are rare due to the poor data available, which is itself caused by inadequate filing systems. Thus the problem becomes cyclical: with so little data available, professionals continue to dismiss art crime as a trifling and occasional misdemeanor, making good news stories and thrillers, involving the collectibles of those whose affluence protects them from real misfortune. One of the goals of this book is to take a step outside of that cycle, by informing police and the art world about art crime, explaining how it functions, and why it is necessary to take it seriously.

The first step in the right direction would be for police agencies to file art crime separately from other kinds of offenses and to make the information in their files available to researchers, who can place each incident in both an historical and contemporary context, for analysis.[9] Parallel to this, members of the art world (museums, galleries, collectors) should report all crimes to the police. Failure to report will ultimately result in more such crimes in the future and will certainly not help to recover stolen art or protect antiquities.

This briefly illustrates the uphill hike that the united front of academics and art, police, and security professionals face in order to establish and develop this new field of the interdisciplinary and practical study of art crime. These essayists take a strong first step. One of the goals of ARCA and this collection is to encourage scholars and professionals worldwide to turn their attentions to art crime. The more studies, articles, books, inventions, conferences, and collaborations on preventing art crime, the better off the world will be. Curbing art crime both protects our beloved cultural heritage, and impedes organized crime.

NOTES

1. This sum has been quoted by major sources such as the FBI, Scotland Yard, and Interpol. In truth, no one has any idea of the actual dollar value of art crime, for two reasons. Firstly, so much art crime goes either unreported or undiscovered that it renders specific estimates impossible. This estimate is a "best guess" based on reported crimes only—the actual number is certainly higher. Secondly, the concept of an artwork's value is nebulous and protean. On one day an artwork may be worth $1 million, and the next day $500,000, according to the interest of collectors, perceived rarity and authenticity, and the world's economy. These two factors make it impossible to state accurately the annual criminal income from art crime. Suffice it to say that it is significant, and ranking it as the third- or fourth-highest-grossing annual criminal trade is entirely appropriate, conveying its severity.

2. This statistic is from Interpol, which has ranked art crime as the third-largest criminal trade for many years. For all other statistical references, unless otherwise cited, please see Interpol's Stolen Works of Art CD-ROM and art police conference proceedings, as well as the published information from the FBI Art Squad, the Carabinieri Division for the Protection of Cultural Heritage, and Scotland Yard's Arts and Antiques Unit.

3. This is not the first period in which the media inspired criminals to turn their attentions to art theft. In 1876, the world-record sale of Thomas Gainsborough's *Portrait of Georgiana, Duchess of Devonshire,* made international headlines in the newspaper media, and directly inspired the criminal mastermind Adam Worth, after whom the term "Napoleon of Crime" was coined, to steal the painting.

4. This is the largest theft in terms of quantity of objects taken in a single theft, as opposed to estimated value of objects taken, outside of a conflict zone.

5. For a complete list of reported art crimes by country, please see Interpol's Stolen Works of Art CD-ROM, published annually and available by subscription.

6. For more on the Mafia crimes, please see Peter Watson's *The Caravaggio Conspiracy* (1983). The Rembrandt was recovered by an FBI agent in disguise as a criminal art collector, who worked with international police in an elaborate sting operation.

7. For a good, journalistic account of this case, please see the *Times* (London) newspaper article, July 31, 2005.

8. Even Interpol admits that its data on art crime, provided by constituent national police forces around the world, is incomplete and insufficient. Even with the incomplete data, art crime is still the third-highest-grossing annual criminal trade over the past few decades. In 2008, money laundering overtook art crime for the number three slot—not necessarily because there was less art crime, but rather that more money laundering was discovered.

9. Most countries have no dedicated art police (leaving aside the more opinionated contemporary arts columnists). Only Italy, with its Carabinieri Division for the Protection of Cultural Heritage, seems to take art crime as seriously as they should. They have over 300 full-time agents, and by far the best recovery rate of any country on art cases. In addition to Italy, Spain, France, the FBI Art Squad, and Scotland Yard's Arts and Antiques Division have done exemplary work in this specialty field. The authors of this collection urge other countries to follow suit, establishing their own art squads, or nominating at least one dedicated art detective who can inform the rest of the national police, and act as a liaison to groups like Interpol and ARCA.

PART I

Archaeology and Antiquities

Chapter 1

The Fundamental Importance of Archaeological Context

Derek Fincham

Heritage advocates and nations of origin have an impressive and growing array of legal measures to help protect and preserve antiquities: national ownership declarations, export restrictions, and enforcement of these measures by various domestic and international courts and law enforcement agencies. Supporting these legal measures is a growing body of scholarship and empirical research.

Why has such a grand multinational legal regime and body of scholarship been created? There are a number of reasons, but three predominate: (1) these crimes destroy archaeological context; (2) these objects are often acquired and displayed by museums and institutions with important educational missions—which are of course perverted when theft and destruction are the root cause of the tragic journey of an object from its archaeological context; and (3) the United States gives valuable tax breaks to institutions, and this financing should never be used to violate the laws of other nations.

But at its heart, cultural heritage policy attempts to answer a more fundamental question: why does it matter if *tombaroli*[1] or archaeologists unearth antiquities? Imagine if the Euphronios Krater, a masterpiece of ancient art, was found in a kitchen, or a burial chamber, or a farmer's home, or a merchant's? What if it was found in Spain, Southern France, Sicily, North Africa, or even North America? These different contexts could tell us a great deal about the object, and also about the society that created it.

Archaeologists are currently researching important historical questions. How do the recently discovered mass graves found near Machu Picchu inform our understanding of that ancient city's importance? Was it advancing barbarians from Northern Europe who compelled the first Venetians to construct their fabulous canals? Was it the Romans who introduced the leek to Wales? Was it a shortage of women that caused the Vikings to expand their empire? These important historical questions are difficult to answer, to be sure. But they will be far more difficult if the areas containing the answers to these questions are spoiled by the looting and destruction of archaeological sites.

The widespread and unskilled illegal excavation of objects forever destroys this invaluable archaeological context. Precious information can be learned through careful excavation, which inexpert excavation destroys. In many instances, looters will destroy or toss aside intellectually important objects in search of easily sold objects made of gold or precious metals. Wherever possible, then, the preservation of archaeological information mandates that unearthing antiquities should be done by experts. As Patty Gerstenblith argues "today, ever more sophisticated scientific techniques, as well as interdisciplinary methods of

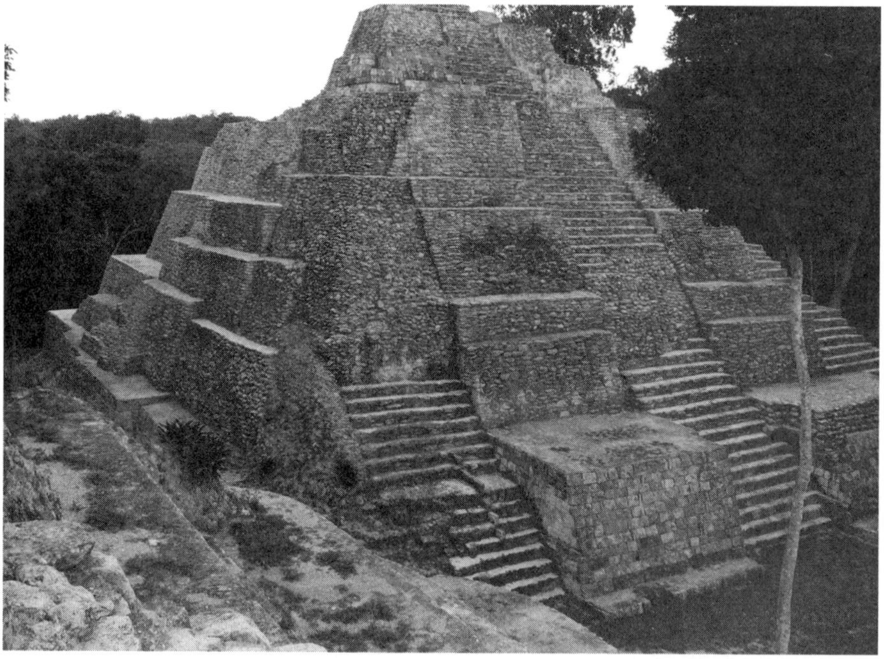

Maya ruins of Yaxha, Guatemala. The West Temple, North Acropolis.
Image source: Wikicommons, http://commons.wikimedia.org/wiki/Image:Yaxha NorthAcropolis.jpg.

analysis, are available and routinely used in the reconstruction of past civilizations."[2]

These excavations continue because a market exists for these objects. The illicit trade in antiquities presents more difficult regulatory challenges than the trade in stolen art. No records exist for many newly discovered antiquities, particularly those that are looted. Nations of origin are justifiably reluctant to sell or lose to foreign institutions many objects that are unearthed legitimately by archaeologists. As a consequence, this only further fuels the illicit trade in antiquities by increasing demand, which can often only be met by the illicit and illegal trade.

In many cases, nations and cultural institutions are unable to devote resources to documenting and cataloguing the stores of antiquities that have been excavated but are not on display.[3] A great deal of the trade in antiquities may include objects that have been illegally excavated, illegally exported, or even stolen from museums or storehouses. Illegal excavations destroy not only archaeological context, but sometimes even the actual objects, which are often chopped up or disguised to hide their value or render them more difficult to recognize. The illicit trade has the potential to remove large parts of a nation's cultural heritage. In 2002, Italy reported over 18,000 objects stolen from its museums, churches, historic sites, and archaeological sites.[4] These objects are valuable for their artistic, cultural, and historical importance. When they are stolen or destroyed, we lose the ability to study and learn about our past.

Antiquities can move easily across borders, and too much enforcement still relies on self-regulation by buyers, dealers, and museums. Adding to the difficulty is the fact that there is no clear consensus on the best laws, policy, and penalties. Many in the antiquities-acquiring community argue that these objects are better served by being purchased, and thereby secured against theft or mutilation. They point out that preservation of art and antiquities is inherent to their "fundamental value."[5] This includes preserving objects against mutilation or destruction, as well as maintaining artistic collections. Future generations will continue to be able to view, possess, or study art and antiquities as a product of their acquisition via excavation and purchase.

But there is also a national political agenda behind the preservation of cultural heritage. James Cuno has argued that the national ownership laws and export restrictions through "accident of geography" allow nations of origin to use heritage and antiquities as political and diplomatic pawns.[6] Much of the scholarly interest in preservation aims to make sure "that the recovered property will be protected by conservation, safety, and security measures that meet international standards, and that the object will be adequately displayed and, normally, accessible to the public."[7] However, this fails to acknowledge the critical role that acquisition may play in destroying archaeological context.

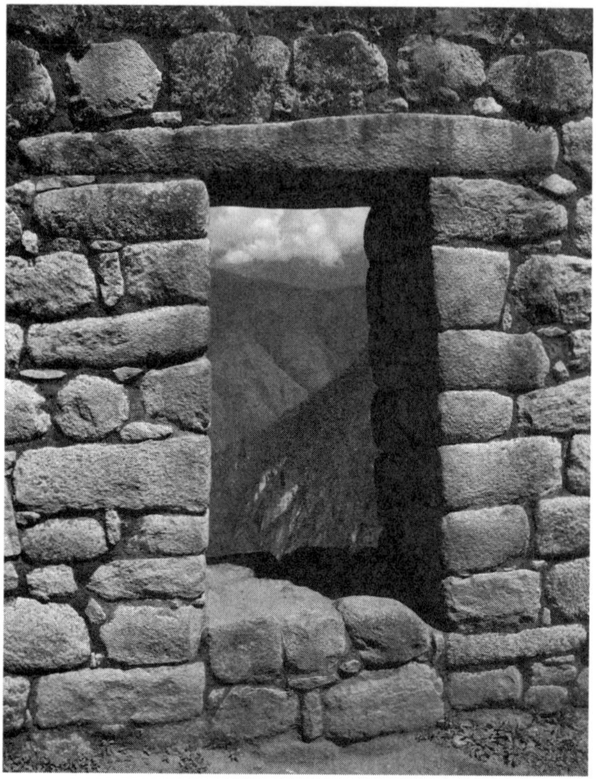

Author's photo of Macchu Picchu in Peru.

Many of the nations with the richest archaeological heritage are unable to support adequate measures to deal with the theft, excavation, or destruction of cultural property because of financial constraints, poor organization, or even corruption.

GUATEMALA: A CASE STUDY

Guatemala provides one such example, as a typical nation of origin with a wealth of cultural heritage. Clemency Coggins decried the damage being done to Mayan sites in Guatemala in 1969, which was among the first of the efforts to raise awareness about the illicit trade in antiquities. Coggins's work helped to usher in a wave of scholarship.[8] Even today, as a result of economic difficulties, civil unrest, and the remoteness of many archaeological sites, national authorities have been unable to devote adequate resources to protecting sites. Guatemala has 5,000 recognized archaeological sites, many of which contain the remains of the Maya and Xinca civilizations. The most-prized Guatemalan antiquities include polychrome artefacts, jade carvings, and stelae fragments.[9]

In his introduction to the history of the "Discovery, Looting, and Archaeological Investigation" of Río Azul, Richard Adams notes with clinical precision that the city "was reported in 1962, partially explored the same year, published in 1964, looted from 1976 to 1981, and investigated by a five-year project between 1983 and 1987."[10] Sadly, such an account is all too typical of many important archaeological sites. This is just one account of one site in Guatemala's Péten region, but it is emblematic of a larger problem. Adams notes that an archaeologist, to reconstruct history and past civilizations, must "[juggle] time, space, and content."[11]

Archaeology is the scientific study of ancient cultures through a number of different techniques. Excavations use scientific methods, history, art, ancient languages and mathematics to create a picture of an ancient civilization. When a stratigraphic study is begun at a site, it relies on a body of context that is painstakingly removed. Soil stratigraphy helps to date finds and features. Phases of human activity can be seen when a trench is viewed in profile. The unskilled and random unearthing of sites by looters destroys or limits this data.

At the excavations at Río Azul, stratigraphic excavation was an important tool. This rests on the principle that older material is the deepest, and the more recent material is on top. Also, ceramics and other objects change over time, and these changes can be documented and used to date other stratified and unstratified material in a room. The ancient Maya also left "another chronometric tool," their calendar system with dates "recorded on stone, in stucco, painted on tomb walls."[12] This data all helps to create a picture of the Maya civilization in this city. When radiocarbon dates were obtained in Tomb 19 at the site, for example, the pottery in the tomb was given a specific time window (roughly when it was created). This sequence could then be used to compare with other sites. When looters take objects, perhaps removing monumental objects such as calendar stele or destroy stratigraphic material, the archaeological record is diminished, and we lose invaluable and priceless information about the Maya civilization and how Río Azul played a part.

Looters take objects and spoil sites so they can sell objects to dealers. Paradoxically, the history of the Maya, and the remnants of this civilization, help give these objects value. Guatemalan archaeologist Juan Antonio Valdes described the looting of archaeological sites as:

> [A] Social phenomenon that reflects the economic state of the nation and the lack of public awareness with regard to the meaning of cultural heritage. In Guatemala, ninety percent of the looting is done by illiterate farmers from the region surrounding the site of the looting . . . The looting networks are becoming increasingly complex and are now involved with bands of drug traffickers based along the border with Mexico and Belize in the north of Guatemala. These people are armed with high-calibre weapons and

> threaten to kill archaeologists and their teams if they refuse to leave the site they wish to rob.[13]

What, then, has Guatemala done to protect this data and its cultural heritage in the face of this tremendous adversity? Its constitution states that archaeological sites should receive special government consideration, and that all monuments and archaeological objects are owned by the state. Private individuals may serve as "trustees," but with the understanding that ownership of these objects rests with the state. Recent efforts have created a multi-institutional commission for the protection of Guatemala's cultural property, which brings together the airport security authorities, Public Prosecutor's Office, Ministry of Culture, Guatemalan Institute of Tourism, and national and international police authorities.

Other initiatives have encouraged advertising agencies and tour operators to promote archaeological tourism. One such measure has been particularly successful. A joint enterprise of Vanderbilt University, the National Geographic Society, and the humanitarian organization Counterpoint International pioneered a sustainable tourism and development project responsible for recovering an ancient Mayan altarpiece from the Guatemalan city of Cancuén.[14] Researchers gained the trust of villagers and showed them how tourism can improve their lives, if these sites are developed. Though that kind of development carries a risk of destruction or damage to the cultural site, it is precisely the kind of private fundraising that must occur, as the budgets of many developing nations do not allow for an adequate response to the illicit trade in cultural property. Responsibly introduced private funding can help to ameliorate this.

Looters commit these crimes with the intention of selling the objects. By concerning themselves merely with the preservation of the most beautiful or desirable objects that make their way to the market states, preservation proponents are avoiding a critical component of the trade in illicit antiquities.

LOOTING IN THE UNITED STATES

We should not make the mistake of assuming these problems exist only in developing nations. In the United States, the illegal excavation of sites is a major problem as well. One estimate indicates that over half of the 6,000 important sites on National Forest land in Arizona have been destroyed.[15] In Virginia, 95 percent of Native American graves in the southwest part of the state have been disturbed. In 1987, the evaluation and investigation arm of Congress, the Government Accountability Office (GAO), indicated that in the Four Corners area (New Mexico, Arizona, Utah, and Colorado), which comprised an area of 100 million acres, a total of only 271 individuals were employed to enforce the applicable laws.[16] Lynell Schalk, a Bureau of Land Management ranger, remarked in 2005 "[w]e didn't exactly have them surrounded," in describing the duties of 13 rangers tasked with policing an area of more than 12 million acres in California.[17]

Most nations of origin attempt to prevent the looting of archaeological sites by vesting ownership of undiscovered cultural objects and restricting their export. These are extremely important regulatory steps for securing the return of looted objects, and the punishment of those who violate these laws. However, these measures do not create a workable or effective cultural heritage policy.

Consequently, at the moment, heritage advocates find themselves in an uneasy position. The discourse during much of the 1980s and 1990s asked whether market states can or should enforce foreign export restrictions and ownership declarations. In recent years, a consensus has emerged: they have recognized and enforced these restrictions and declarations in a myriad of ways, and will continue to do so for the foreseeable future. Having then earned a powerful imperative, Italy and Greece have gained repatriations of some of the most impressive works of ancient art from institutions such as the Getty, the Metropolitan Museum of Art, and the Museum of Fine Arts in Boston.

LAWS AND DISCOURSES

It remains an open question as to whether this increasing recognition of foreign law and the attendant repatriations are adequately protecting and preserving ancient sites. The author looked at the underlying values of the shapers of antiquities policy, to ask whether the current state of American criminal penalties is up to the task of context-preservation in nations of origin.[18] Alex Bauer has expanded on this approach to uncover the inconsistencies in the antiquities trade debate.[19] All too often, heritage scholars have polarized their policy discussions. This is problematic, as it leaves no room for meaningful discourse. Antiquities are a limited resource, and constituent groups must work together to prevent theft and the looting of ancient sites. All members of the policy-shaping community, from archaeologists to dealers and museum directors, share a core set of priorities: they argue against the looting of sites. They differ dramatically, however, on how and what should be done to prevent that looting.

Effective regulation of cultural property requires an effective legal framework, resources to implement that framework, and a desire on the part of a nation's citizens to protect and preserve their heritage. Because of either political choice or the lack of available funding, a well-funded antiquities protection framework is exceptional. The current market for art and antiquities does not inject funds back into developing source nations. When illicit antiquities are sold in market states, profits go to auction houses, dealers, and those who avoid regulations in many source nations.

MODELS FOR FUTURE POLICY

The domestic legal framework for undiscovered antiquities in England and Wales has taken a novel approach to this conundrum. It has resulted in a better cultural policy that leads to less looting of important archaeological sites, allows for a tailored cultural policy, and has in fact produced a massive set of contextual information with which to conduct historical and archaeological research on an unprecedented scale. It has created this system by working cooperatively with finders and treasure-seekers, and rewards certain valuable finds.[20]

There has been an impressive sea change in how shapers of cultural policy, particularly in the North American museum community, have viewed the antiquities trade and their role in the looting of sites. The American Association of Museums (AAM) has recently released a new standard for museum acquisition of archaeological material, which focuses squarely on the provenance of objects and transparency on the part of acquiring institutions.[21] In 2008, the Association of Art Museum Directors announced new guidelines for the acquisition of antiquities.[22]

There has been a paradigmatic shift in the way cultural policy makers view the antiquities trade and how it has led to the loss of our precious collective cultural heritage. Much work remains to be done, but the recent repatriations to Greece and Italy and the new guidelines adopted by the American Museum community signal a dramatic shift. Heritage advocates need to move beyond merely trying to account for antiquities that have already been looted. They must continue to press for public education, novel means of heritage protection, and a renewed effort from all interested parties, including nations and antiquities dealers, to ensure their actions are preserving objects and context.

NOTES

1. The Italian term for tomb-robbers; see Cristina Ruiz, *My Life as a Tombarolo,* The Art Newspaper, No. 112, 36 (2001).

2. Patty Gerstenblith, *The Public Interest in the Restitution of Cultural Objects,* 16 Conn. J. Int'l L. 198, 199 (2001).

3. The Ka-Nefer-Nefer mask on display at the Saint Louis Art Museum was likely stolen from an Egyptian warehouse in the 1980s, where it had been stored since its discovery during a professional dig in 1951 at Saqqara south of Cairo. The Saint Louis Art Museum acquired the mask in 1998, but Egypt has requested its return. Malcolm Gay, *Out of Egypt,* River Front Times, http://www

.riverfronttimes.com/2006-02-15/news/out-of-egypt/full (published Feb. 15, 2006).

4. INTERPOL, *Cultural Property Theft Statistics* http://www.interpol.int/Public/WorkOfArt/statistics/StatPlace2003.asp (last visited Aug. 10, 2008).

5. Paul Bator, *An Essay on the International Trade in Art*, 34 STAN. L. REV. 276, 295 (1982).

6. JAMES CUNO, WHO OWNS ANTIQUITY (Princeton Univ. Press 2008).

7. James Nafziger, *The New International Legal Framework for the Return, Restitution or Forfeiture of Cultural Property*, 15 N.Y.U. J. INT'L L. AND POL. 789, 808 (1982–83).

8. Clemency Coggins, *Illicit Traffic of Pre-Columbian Antiquities*, 29 ART J. 94 (1969) (arguing "In the last ten years there has been an incalculable increase in the number of monuments systematically stolen, mutilated and illicitly exported from Guatemala and Mexico in order to feed the international art market.").

9. *United States v. Pre-Columbian Artifacts*, 845 F. Supp. 544 (N.D. Ill. 1993), in which a Guatemalan Stelae was seized and returned to Guatemala under the *McClain* Doctrine. *See also United States v. Hollinshead*, 495 F.2d 1154 (9th Cir. 1974), in which a dealer was convicted under the NSPA for dealing in Guatemalan antiquities.

10. RICHARD E. W. ADAMS, RÍO AZUL: AN ANCIENT MAYA CITY (Univ. of Oklahoma Press 1999).

11. *Id.* at 21.

12. *Id.* at 21.

13. Juan Antonio Valdés, *Management and Conservation of Guatemala's Cultural Heritage: A Challenge to Keep History Alive*, in ART AND CULTURAL HERITAGE 94, 95 (Barbara T. Hoffman ed., 2006).

14. Sean Markey, *Archaeologists Uncover Maya 'Masterpiece' in Guatemala*, NATIONAL GEOGRAPHIC NEWS, *available at* http://news.nationalgeographic.com/news/2004/04/0423_040423_mayapanel.html (last updated April 23, 2004).

15. Robert Hicks, *Time Crime: Protecting the Past for Future Generations*, FBI PUBLICATIONS, http://www.fbi.gov/publications/leb/1997/july971.htm (published July 1997).

16. General Accounting Office, *Problems Protecting and Preserving Federal Archaeology Resources*, GAO/RCED-88-3 (1987).

17. Lisa Schiffman. *Riding for the Brand*, ARCHAEOLOGY, http://www.archaeology.org/online/features/schalk/index.html (published Aug. 18, 2005).

18. Derek Fincham, *Why Federal Criminal Penalties for Dealing in Illicit Cultural Property are Ineffective and a Pragmatic Alternative*, 25 CARD. ART & ENT. L. J. 597 (2007).

19. Alexander Bauer, *New Ways of Thinking about Cultural Property: A Critical Appraisal of the Antiquities Trade Debates*, 31 FORD. INT'L. L. J. 690 (2008).

20. For a detailed overview of the antiquities policy in England and Wales by the author, *see* Derek Fincham, *A Coordinated Legal and Policy Approach to Undiscovered Antiquities: Adapting the Cultural Heritage Policy of England and Wales to other Nations of Origin*, 15 INT'L J. CULT. PROP. 347 (2008).

21. American Association of Museums, *Standards Regarding Archaeological Material and Ancient Art*, http://www.aam-us.org/museumresources/ethics/

upload/Standards%20Regarding%20Archaeological%20Material%20and%20Ancient%20Art.pdf (approved July 2008).

22. American Association of Art Museum Directors, *Report of the AAMD Task Force on the Acquisition of Archaeological Materials and Ancient Art*, http://www.aamd.org/newsroom/documents/2008ReportAndRelease.pdf (June 2008).

Chapter 2

Homecomings: Learning from the Return of Antiquities to Italy

David W. J. Gill

In the last few years, there have been several high-profile returns of antiquities to Italy from North American institutions: one private collector, and one dealer. A selection of these items were placed on display in the Quirinale, Rome, at the end of 2007 in an exhibition, "Nostoi: Capolavori ritrovati"; a further exhibition with newly returned material, "Nostoi," opened in the Palazzo Poli in Rome in late March 2008. The title, evocative of the Homeric *Odyssey*, captured the idea of random traveling over a long period before returning home. What lessons can be learned from these returns?

A CHRONOLOGY FOR THE RETURNING OBJECTS

There have been sporadic returns from North American museums over the years, such as the 1999 return of an Attic red-figured cup, "signed" by Euphronios and attributed to Onesimos, from the J. Paul Getty Museum, in Malibu, California. However, the present spate of returns started in October 2005, when the Getty agreed to return three antiquities, among them the Asteas krater, to Italy. In February 2006, the Metropolitan Museum of Art (MMA) agreed to return a series of objects. The most prominent was the Sarpedon (or Euphronios) krater acquired in 1972; it was allowed to remain on loan to the MMA until January 2008. Other items included a batch of Hellenistic silver, perhaps found at Morgantina,[1] an Attic red-figured psykter (wine-cooler) attributed to Smikros, and an Apulian red-figured dinos[2] attributed to the Darius painter.

In September 2006, the Museum of Fine Arts (MFA) in Boston agreed to return 13 items, followed in November 2006 by the Getty with 26 objects: this was increased to 40 on August 1, 2007.[3] In October 2007, Princeton University Art Museum agreed to the return of four objects, which were to be transferred to Italy, and the transfer of title of a further four pieces (though they were to be loaned back to the museum). This was quickly followed by the return of eight antiquities from the Royal-Athena Galleries in New York in November 2007; three of the bronzes had been stolen from Italian collections during the 1970s. In January 2008, Shelby White handed over nine antiquities to Italian authorities—a tenth is due to follow in 2010.[4] Finally, in February 2008, two acrolithic sculptures, apparently derived from a site in Sicily, were returned from the University of Virginia Museum in Charlottesville, where they had been on loan from Maurice Tempelsman.

THEMES

It is likely that there was documentary evidence, probably Polaroid photographs, to demonstrate the link between these pieces and Italy. However, even without this information, some of the material is very likely to have come from archaeological sites in Italy. Take for example the Apulian pottery that frequently appears in graves in Puglia (Apulia).[5] The returns include a dinos from New York (acquired in 1984), three pieces from Boston (two acquired in 1988 and one in 1991), six Apulian pots from the Getty (two acquired in the 1970s, four in the 1980s), and two from Princeton acquired in 1989. Among them were four pieces attributed to the Darius painter: a dinos from New York, an amphora from Boston, a pelike[6] from the Getty, and a loutrophoros[7] from Princeton. (The volute-krater[8] acquired by the Cleveland Museum of Art in 1988 was part of the agreed return to Italy in November 2008). It is perhaps significant that in 1993, J. Michael Padgett, had observed that, "Recent years have seen a host of new vases by the Darius Painter."[9] This category of Apulian pottery is recognized as having been widely looted exactly in this period.[10] Elia has suggested that some 94.5 percent of the Apulian corpus is derived from "unsystematic recovery, including looting," that "lacks any archaeological contextual information."[11] Although reservations about Elia's research are said to have been aired in an unpublished (and now reportedly lost) memorandum written by Dyfri Williams of the British Museum,[12] the returns of Apulian pottery confirm the basis of Elia's important work. Other Italian pottery fabrics returned to Italy include Lucanian, Paestan, and Etruscan.

Among other apparent Italian material were two fragments of Roman wall-painting, one from Shelby White and the other from the Getty (formerly in the Barbara and Lawrence Fleischman collection).[13] These

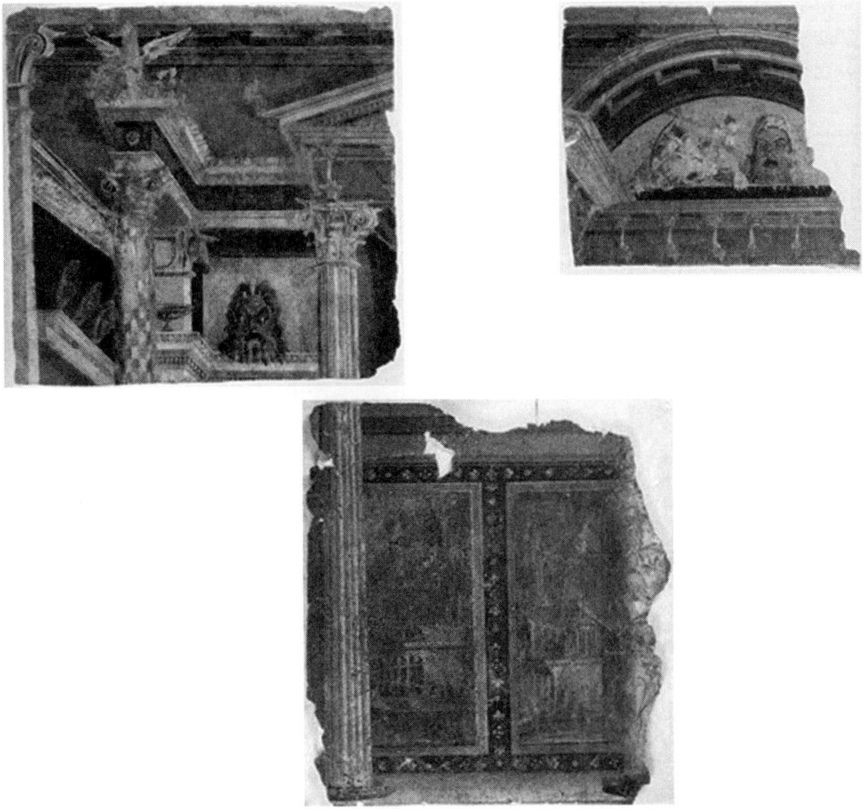

Reconstruction of Roman wallpapering formed by fragments from the Shelby White/Leon Levy and Lawrence and Barbara Flesichman collection; two of the fragments have been returned to Italy.

actually came from the same wall of a Roman villa (probably located in the vicinity of the Bay of Naples)—a third fragment remains in the Getty, though the reasons for its retention are not clear. The polychrome marble figures and painted marble lekanis from the Getty appear to have come from near a villa site just outside Taranto in southern Italy.[14]

There are also polychrome Etruscan terracotta roof fittings returned to Italy from the Getty as well as from Princeton; the one from the Getty was said to have been found at Cerveteri. Sicily seems to have been the find-spot for the set of Hellenic silver as well as the acrolithic sculptures returned from Virginia.[15]

PRIVATE COLLECTORS

Only one private collector, Shelby White, has returned antiquities directly to Italy. White seems to have elected to do this in order to deflect criticism away from other projects, not least of which was the Fall 2008 opening of the Institute for the Study of the Ancient World (ISAW) in New York. Other private collectors represented by the returning antiquities include Barbara and Lawrence Fleischman: 13 pieces from their former collection have been returned from the J. Paul Getty Museum. The histories and archaeology of both these collections were studied in 2000.[16] This analysis suggested that large numbers of the antiquities were unknown prior to the 1970 UNESCO Convention (objects acquired before this Convention were exempt from many regulations implemented by it), and even fewer had any indication of find-spots (the exact location from which antiquities were excavated), making them suspicious items. Yet White has dismissed this study, even though subsequent events have confirmed the suspicion that the lack of secure history was suggestive of possible looting.[17]

Three of the pieces returned from Malibu had been owned by Maurice Tempelsman, as had the two acrolithic statues on loan to the University of Virginia Museum of Art in Charlottesville. The celebrated collection formed by Nelson Bunker Hunt and William Herbert Hunt is represented by an Etruscan antefix[18] from the Getty (once part of the Fleischman collection) and the Attic red-figured calyx-krater attributed to Euphronios at present in the Shelby White collection.

This raises the question about the ease with which a private collection can be formed. Do the antiquities surfacing on the market come from "old collections," or have they been looted in recent years? "Old collections" include the historic collections such as the Hamilton "vases" acquired in the eighteenth century,[19] the Egyptian antiquities gathered by the Reverend William MacGregor in the late nineteenth century,[20] or the antiquities held by Charles Ricketts and Charles Shannon.[21] A university collection like that of the Fitzwilliam Museum in Cambridge has been assembled through the connections with alumni.[22] Contrast this with contemporary collections of antiquities. "The Stanford Place Collection of Antiquities" places itself in the "long tradition of collecting that originated with the Greek and Romans and has endured for over two thousand years."[23] However only 30 percent of the lots in the sale appear to have been known prior to 1970, and the remaining 70 percent included objects purchased on the London, New York and Swiss antiquities markets.

The scandals surrounding the antiquities department of Sotheby's in London, and more seriously the objects that passed through the hands of Giacomo Medici, can leave little room for doubt that the market in antiquities has significant problems and weaknesses.[24] Some of the pieces returned to Italy had been "associated" with old collections, though without any supporting evidence. For example, the statue of Sabina, returned from Boston, was said to have come from "an aristocratic family collection in Bavaria."[25] An Etruscan duck askos[26] and fragments of the Attic

Onesimos cup returned from Malibu were said to have once been in the Samuel Schweitzer collection in Arlesheim. It has been suggested that this collection has been used to launder recently surfaced antiquities, as it was hard to cross check.[27] It reinforces the need for authenticated documentation to support the histories of objects appearing for sale on the market.

DEALERS

The collecting histories of some of the pieces returned to Italy from Princeton, the Royal-Athena Galleries, and Shelby White have not been disclosed. However, it is clear from the material transferred from Boston and the Getty that there are some common threads.

One of the most prominent links was Atlantis Antiquities in New York, owned by Robert Hecht and Jonathan Rosen.[28] Robin Symes handled several of the pieces, including objects from the Maurice Tempelsman collection and a bronze kouros[29] returned from Shelby White.[30] Three pieces in Boston, an Attic black-figured hydria,[31] an Attic red-figured pelike, and an Apulian bell-krater, passed through Palladion Antike Kunst of Basel. This gallery was operated by Ursula "Rosie" Becchina, the wife of Gianfranco Becchina, a rival to Medici.[32]

Many of the pieces in the Getty and the Shelby White collection were identified from Polaroids seized from Giacomo Medici in Geneva.[33] Other returning pieces had been auctioned at Sotheby's (London), such as an Apulian loutrophoros from Boston.[34] Documentation has demonstrated that Sotheby's had received regular consignments from Giacomo Medici and his agents.[35] The resulting scandal caused the closure of the antiquities department in London (though sales have continued in New York).[36]

One possible solution is for museums to buy from galleries and dealers that are members of the International Association of Dealers in Ancient Art (IADAA), which has a clear code of conduct. However, one of the dealers who supplied the Getty was Galerie Nefer, Zurich, which recently resigned from the association.[37] This gallery is owned by Frida Tchacos; her husband, Werner Nussberger, was also a donor to the Getty. It is clear that the IADAA needs to regulate its members.

Another body is the Antiquity Dealers Association (ADA). Yet, as recently as 2007, Bonham's (London), a member of ADA, tried to sell a Lydian silver kyathos[38] that conceivably came from the "Lydian Hoard" (famously returned from New York).[39] The piece was withdrawn, but the incident left many questions unanswered. Bonham's also had to withdraw a fragment of an Egyptian text from its May 2008 auction, as it had appeared to have been removed from the tomb of Mutirdis (TT410) in the Asasif; it was said to have come from the collection of an Australian seafarer. Rupert Wace, the chairman of ADA, had to return a Middle Kingdom Egyptian duck, stolen from the Saqqara store, to Egypt in 2006. It had come from a "French private collection," which turned out to be a syndicate of four French auctioneers.

All these examples suggest that the due diligence processes conducted by members of the antiquities market have been allowing recently surfaced (and stolen) antiquities to enter public and private collections.

THE NEED FOR TRANSPARENCY

Earlier studies of private collections had suggested that a significant percentage of the objects could not be traced back prior to 1970.[40] Exhibition catalogs, hosted by major museums, need to include the full collecting history for the pieces. A good example of this can be found in the publication of the private collection of George Ortiz that was shown at the Royal Academy in London.[41] The same requirement is needed for permanent catalogs of the collections, including the fascicules of the *Corpus Vasorum Antiquorum.*

Museums should aim to show the earliest known mention, and then provide a continuous history.[42] Statements such as "purchased" or "anonymous donor" hide the previous history. Although the acquisition of the pieces being returned to Italy from the Princeton University Art Museum have appeared in the *Record of the Art Museum, Princeton University,* the list rarely provides previous owners or the names of dealers. Of the eight pieces (four returned to Italy; four have transferred their title to Italy but remain on loan to Princeton), four are listed as "museum purchase" and "anonymous gift," two more were purchases (with named donors or fund), and two were named as gifts (Brian T. Aitken; Ali and Hicham Aboutaan). Museum curators need to make such collecting histories public.

TRUSTEES AND MUSEUMS

One of the safeguards on any museum, or indeed organization, is the group of trustees. The board can have the ultimate decision over new acquisitions. There can be a perceived conflict of interests, and the J. Paul Getty Museum, for example, issued a policy document on "Standards of Conduct. Conflicts of Interests—Trustees" on December 3, 1999. It addresses the issue of trustees competing for the same objects as the Trust.

Yet it is significant that objects from trustees have been returned to Italy. Peter Aldrich, a trustee of the Boston Museum of Fine Arts, donated an Attic bell-krater and a Lucanian nestoris.[43] Both had surfaced at Sotheby's in London. The nestoris had appeared on December 13–14, 1982, an auction in which the Attic amphora, attributed to the Berlin painter and returned by the Metropolitan Museum of Art, had also passed. The nestoris had subsequently been on loan to the Borchardt Library at La Trobe University (1988–94), and resold at Sotheby's on December 10, 1996.[44] The krater had been purchased at Sotheby's (London) on December 14, 1995. Aldrich has donated other pieces to Boston, including a Sicilian red-figured bell-krater, first known at Sotheby's (London) on December 11, 1989.[45]

Barbara and Lawrence Fleischman sold or gave their collection to the Getty (mostly) in 1996. Some 13 of these pieces have been returned to Italy.[46] Some had passed through the hands of Fritz Bürki, Robert Hecht, and Robin Symes, and others, such as the terracotta antefix of a Maenad and Silen, had once been owned by the Hunt brothers. Barbara Fleischman realized that there was a possible conflict of interest and resigned as trustee in January 2006.

Shelby White is a prominent trustee of the Metropolitan Museum of Art. The only link with the returned objects from the MMA is the "Morgantina" hoard of Hellenistic silver—the Jerome Levy Foundation helped to support its acquisition in the 1980s.[47] White has been a major supporter of the museum: with her late husband Leon Levy, she loaned her collection in a major exhibition, she donated money for the creation of the "Leon Levy and Shelby White Court," and she loaned further antiquities to the museum.[48] Yet 10 of her antiquities were returned voluntarily to Italy in 2008 (one of them will return in 2010). Few details have emerged about the previous histories of these pieces. Several featured in the Polaroids seized in the Geneva Freeport, and some passed through Sotheby's (London) and Robin Symes.[49] White continues to be active in the MMA and served on the search committee that appointed Tom Campbell to succeed Philippe de Montebello as director. It seems unlikely that she will support anybody who has taken an ethical position on collecting antiquities.

Trustees need to hold public trust in order for them to uphold the good name of their institutions. Trustees who have been shown to have collected recently surfaced antiquities on the scale reflected by the Fleischman and White collections have the potential of compromising the integrity of the museum boards on which they serve.

LOANS

One outcome of the scandal surrounding the returns will be the unwillingness of museums to acquire antiquities that do not have a documented record prior to 1970. This is reflected in the new policy, "Acquisition of Archaeological Materials and Ancient Art," announced by the Association of Art Museum Directors (AAMD) in June 2008. The importance of the 1970 date is also being reflected in the high prices achieved at auction for pieces with good "histories": the bronze Artemis formerly in the Albright-Knox Art Gallery fetching $28.6 million at Sotheby's (New York) in June 2007, and $57 million for the Mesopotamian "Guennol Lionness" at Sotheby's (New York) in December 2007. Histories now give added value.

But what do museums do when they do not have substantial holdings of classical antiquities? They turn to private collectors. The Association of Art Museum Directors (AAMD) issued a "Report on Incoming Loans of Archaeological Material and Ancient Art" in 2006. There is clearly a perceived issue that recently surfaced antiquities could be displayed and provided with a documented history. The report covers short-term loans and recommends that for incoming loans "museums should inquire into their provenance history, seeking to obtain all relevant information from the lender, and an appropriate warranty of their legal ownership of the work" (II.C). As far as long-term loans are concerned, they should be treated with the same criteria as acquisitions. The emphasis must be on documentation and the need for transparency. Lenders who are unable to demonstrate the history of the piece (for example, the invoice from the dealer or auction-house) or who deliberately avoid providing information, should not be able to lend.

It is perhaps significant that some of the antiquities on loan from Shelby White to the MMA have now been returned to Italy (and a 10th, a fragmentary Attic krater by Euphronios, is due to follow). Bronzes from White's collections have also been on loan to North American institutions.[50] The problem with the AAMD guidelines is perhaps illustrated by the long-term loan of an archaic bronze volute-krater of Trebenishte type to the Houston Museum of Fine Art by Shelby White.[51] Although curatorial staff will confirm its presence, they have refused to provide any further information. When was it first acquired? What is its history? Where was it found?

THE ART LOSS REGISTER

The Art Loss Register (ALR) was founded in 1991. It is now commonplace for antiquities passing through the market to be checked against the ALR database to confirm that the item has not been stolen. Indeed, in the sale of the Stanford Place collection of Antiquities at Christie's London in 2006, each entry had the prominent caption: "This lot is accompanied by a certificate from The Art Loss Register."

Yet a database is only as good as the data within it. If an object has been stolen from a recorded museum or private collection, then there is a strong likelihood that there will be images and descriptions can be made available to the ALR. However, a recently surfaced antiquity, perhaps last seen as it was being placed in an Etruscan grave around 500 BCE, will not appear in the ALR database. The ALR is a move in the right direction, but it needs to do more to indicate that there are gaps in the documentation for the object. One way forward would be to introduce a category of certificate that indicates there is certified documentation for an object prior to 1970 (the date of the UNESCO Convention).

The weaknesses in the system are clear from some of the recent returns to Italy. Two of the bronzes, a Nike and an athlete, returned voluntarily by Jerome Eisenberg (of the Royal-Athena Galleries), had been the property of John Kluge, and were sold at Christie's (New York) on June 8, 2004. Their history was known back to the 1980s, when they had been sold to Kluge by Eisenberg. Although the pieces would have been checked against the ALR database, nobody had spotted that the two bronzes had been stolen from Italian collections in the early 1970s. Clearly, the weakness was that the bronzes did not feature in the system.

The database can work. The same sale at Christie's was due to auction a Roman marble portrait of Marcus Aurelius, consigned by Galerie Samarcanda in Paris. The ALR database showed that it had been stolen from a museum collection in Algeria. Yet even objects from a well-publicized theft from the Corinth Museum in December 1997 and March 1998 surfaced at Christie's (New York), where they had been consigned from "an American private collector." They were spotted not by the ALR, but by scholars scanning the catalogs. It should be stressed that in these three cases, the items had been stolen from museum collections.

Although a database is a useful tool, it is also a partial one. Museums and collectors cannot claim to have completed a "due diligence" process if they have had limited searches on incomplete data-sets.

THE LOOTING PROCESS

Have these newly discovered antiquities emerged thanks to chance, perhaps through the construction of new roads, housing developments, or other infrastructure that requires excavation? Some, perhaps, have followed this route. Is this the case for the thousands of Apulian pots that have been emerging on the market in recent decades? Peter Watson described witnessing *tombaroli* at work in an ancient Apulian cemetery:

> What [Sean, the cameraman] saw on the edge of the orchard took his breath away. There in the middle, in the light of the moon, was a huge mechanical digger tearing into the soil, snatching enormous chunks of earth from above the roof of a tomb. . . . It brought home the sheer barbarity of the tomb robbing and desecration that Italy suffers at the hands of the *tombaroli*, and the disgraceful, tawdry nature of the illegal antiquities trade that ends up at auction in London or New York.[52]

It is impossible to provide protection for such archaeological sites. This is particularly true for sites that have yet to be excavated. Large numbers of rural sites are being identified in Greece through intensive field-surveys, and in Egypt by remote sensing.[53]

It also needs to be remembered that for each of the objects returned to Italy, there is a destroyed archaeological context that can never be reconstructed.[54] Were the Apulian pots part of a large group? Did the marble reliefs come from a domestic complex? Where was the Roman wall-painting displayed? Repatriation cannot restore this lost knowledge.

DISPUTED CULTURAL PROPERTY

The return of over 100 pieces from North American collections to Italy perhaps gives the impression that attitudes are changing towards the return of cultural property. Are there wider implications for disputed material?

The Greek minister of culture Mihali Liapis, speaking in the new Akropolis Museum at Athens in 2008, linked the return of the Italian material to a renewed claim for the return of the Parthenon Marbles. Yet the material returned to Italy surfaced after 1970 (the date of UNESCO Convention) and many of the pieces appear to have appeared in the Polaroid dossier of Giacomo Medici. In other words, those museums (and the single private collector) should have known that recently surfaced antiquities were likely to have appeared as the result of looting, and had therefore been removed from Italy contrary to Italian law.

As far as the Parthenon marbles are concerned, they were removed from Athens before the formation of the modern Greek state.[55] And unlike the Italian antiquities, which have lost their archaeological contexts, the marbles in the British Museum come from a known building (and from specific locations on it). Indeed, ancient documentary evidence is such that it is possible to date the carving of the sculptures within a few years.[56] The argument is more moral than legal. Is it better for the Parthenon marbles to be displayed in Bloomsbury, or in a state-of-the-art gallery that makes a direct visual link with the building on which they were displayed? The same sort of issues are raised for the Altar of Zeus removed from Pergamon and now in display in Berlin, the pedimental sculptures of the temple of Aphaia on Aegina and now in Munich, or the Rosetta Stone.[57]

THE ROLE OF THE SCHOLAR

A further issue to emerge from the return of antiquities to Italy is the role of scholars within the system. It seems that some scholars have been willing to comment on emerging pieces, and indeed in the case of Attic and South Italian pottery, individual pieces have been attributed to named "artists."[58] Part of this process has been the publication of newly surfaced antiquities to create a paper trail and ultimately a pedigree.[59] There is a tension here. The publication of pieces from the Barbara and Lawrence Fleischman and the Shelby White and Leon Levy collections in glossy exhibition catalogs allowed Italian authorities to identify a number of pieces. Without the publications, there may not have been any returns.

CONCLUSION

There is now public recognition that recently surfaced antiquities had been acquired by institutions. It is also accepted that attitudes must change. Museums and private collectors need to acquire responsibly and ethically, insisting that there is (wherever possible) clear documentation showing the authenticated history of ownership for the object. Museums in particular need to publish the details of new acquisitions and long-term loans, either on paper or by electronic means, so that the history can be presented in a clear and unambiguous fashion.

NOTES

1. Bothmer 1990, 54–59, nos. 92–106.
2. A *dinos* is a large bowl with a rounded lip.
3. Gill and Chippindale 2006; 2007a.
4. In July 2008 Shelby White agreed to return two items (a fragmentary funerary stele and a bronze calyx-krater) from her collection to Greece.
5. Trendall and Cambitoglou 1978; 1982a, 1982b; 1983; 1991; 1992; 1993. See also Trendall 1989.
6. A ceramic vase with two open handles that are vertical on their lateral aspects, even at the side with the edge of the belly of the vase. The vase has a narrow neck, a flanged mouth, and a sagging, almost spherical belly—similar to an amphora.
7. A vase, also similar to an amphora, but very large, with an elongated wide neck and handles on either side.
8. A large bowl with handles, used for mixing wine with water.
9. Padgett 1993, 114, under no. 41. This area will be discussed in Gill and Chippindale 2009.
10. Elia 2001.
11. Ibid., 151–52.
12. A document clearly known to George Ortiz: Ortiz 2006, 27.
13. Bothmer 1990: 201, no. 142; Exhibition Catalogue 1994, 250–52, nos. 125–26.
14. Gill and Chippindale 2007a, 211–12.
15. For the silver: Bothmer 1984, 54–59, nos. 92–106.

16. Chippindale and Gill 2000.
17. Mead 2007; see also White 2005.
18. The vertical blocks which terminate the covering tiles of the roof of Greek and Etruscan temples.
19. Jenkins and Sloan 1996.
20. Brown 2004.
21. Darracott 1979; 1980.
22. Gill 1992; 1999.
23. The Stanford Place Collection of Antiquities, Christie's London April 26, 2006.
24. Watson 1997; Watson and Todeschini 2006; see also Gill 1997; Gill and Chippindale 2007b.
25. Gill and Chippindale 2006, 314.
26. A vessel used to pour small quantities of liquids such as oil. It is recognizable from its flat shape and a spout at one or both ends that could also be used as a handle. In this case, the vessel is in the shape of a duck.
27. Watson and Todeschini 2006, 95; Gill and Chippindale 2007a, 216.
28. Gill and Chippindale 2006, 314–17; Gill and Chippindale 2007a, 217.
29. Statue of an athletic nude young man.
30. Gill and Chippindale 2007a, 217.
31. A three-handled pot used for carrying water.
32. Gill and Chippindale 2006, 317–19.
33. Watson and Todeschini 2006, 344–54.
34. At least seven of the pieces returned to Italy had passed through Sotheby's in London in 1982, 1984, 1985, 1987, and 1995.
35. Watson 1997; see also Gill 1997.
36. Sotheby's (New York) has sold over $225 million worth of antiquities since the London operation was closed down (and to June 2008).
37. Gill and Chippindale 2007a, 217.
38. A painted Greek ladle with a long, looping handle.
39. Özgen and Öztürk 1996.
40. Chippindale and Gill 2000.
41. Ortiz 1994.
42. See Gill 1990.
43. Gill and Chippindale 2006, 322.
44. Gill and Chippindale 2006, 319, 325, no. 13.
45. Gill and Chippindale 2006, 328n74.
46. Gill and Chippindale 2007. See also Chippindale and Gill 2000; Exhibition catalogue 1994.
47. Bothmer 1984, 54, under nos. 92–106.
48. Bothmer 1990; Pico´n, et al. 2007; Mead 2007. See also Chippindale and Gill 2000.
49. Watson and Todeschini 2006.
50. Chi and Gaunt 2005. The calyx-krater (no. 9) appears to be one of two antiquities due to be returned to Greece in July 2008.
51. Krater, noted in Stibbe 2006.
52. Watson 1997, 124–25; see also Perticarari and Giuntani 1986.
53. Greece, e.g. Jameson, et al. 1994; Mee and Forbes 1997. Egypt: Parcak 2007.

54. Editor's Note: Please note the coarguments in this and Chapter 1 on the importance of archaeological context.

55. Howland 2000; see also Jenkins 2001.

56. E.g. Brommer 1979; Boardman and Finn 1985; Jenkins 1994.

57. Fagan 2004.

58. Gill and Chippindale 2003; Vickers and Gill 1994.

59. Pastore 2001, 157.

Chapter 3

Lack of Due Diligence and Unregulated Markets: Trade in Illicit Antiquities and Fakes in Hong Kong

Toby Bull

> *It is a melancholy observation that, although the UNESCO Convention ... was adopted as long ago as 1970, the destruction of acknowledged sites through looting has increased rather than diminished in the thirty succeeding years ...* [1]

Colin Renfrew made the above statement in his foreword in *Trade in Illicit Antiquities—The Destruction of the World's Archaeological Heritage.* Renfrew was one of a number of experts who expressed their views on the problem of the illicit trade in antiquities. It is a widely held view (both from inside and outside China in documented media reports—many of which have been sourced for this paper) that there is large-scale looting of and trafficking in antiquities taking place in China. According to the NGO Cultural Heritage Protection Center, based in Beijing, the problems of illicit excavation and trade have reached dramatic proportions: whereas in the past, recipients were foreign museums, the demand in recent times appears to come from the markets (dealers and auction houses) abroad. Hong Kong, as will be seen, plays an important part in this movement of antiquities.

A stroll down Hollywood Road in the Central district of Hong Kong enables one to see the thousands of items on display in the windows of the many antique shops that ply their trade here. Many advertise their wares in the glossy magazines—proudly announcing "new arrivals" to their stock. Most people would not give this a second thought, yet the majority of these antiques for sale could never have been exported legally from China, as it has very strict export laws.

The question of historical ownership of cultural artifacts has never been an easy one to answer. For some, they were, are, and always will be the property of the state, while others believe these artifacts should go to whoever finds them and thus be accorded the right to trade them freely. Simon Mackenzie, in his paper for the Australian Institute of Criminology entitled "Regulating the Market in Illicit Antiquities," split the market into three stages: The supply of antiquities coming from "source" nations, the demand created by consumers in the "market" nations, and the transportation routes between the "source" and "market" nations.[2]

J. H. Merryman explains,

> The world divides itself into source nations and market nations. In source nations, the supply of desirable cultural property exceeds the internal demand . . . rich in cultural artifacts beyond any conceivable local use. In market nations, the demand exceeds the supply. Demand in the market nations encourages the export from source nations, when, as is often (but not always) the case, the source nation is relatively poor and the market nation wealthy, an unrestricted market will encourage the net export of cultural property.[3]

China is an example of a source country and the process by which the artifacts arrive to market nations, like the UK or the United States, is of particular interest to this chapter. The focus of Hong Kong as a transit hub and a free port will be discussed at a later point. Of course, not all antiquities that have originated from China, or that are in China now, are necessarily all categorized as having a problematic background. Indeed, antiquities being sold on the open market today fall, according to Mackenzie,[4] into three categories: (1) licit, (2) gray area, and (3) illicit.

1. Licit antiquities: artifacts excavated by authorized persons, their context safeguarded and the object placed in the possession/care of, usually, the state. Very few of these objects enter the market.
2. Gray area: looted artifacts that are out of the ground and known about, perhaps in a private collection or on the market for a long time. These items are tolerated by those with a legal interest in the trade of stolen goods. These antiquities are originally illicit in origin (not excavated by an authorized person) made licit by the operation of time.
3. Illicit antiquities: recently looted artifacts that are accepted by the market as these objects masquerade as category 2 above. If their true identity were known, the law would not tolerate any trade, and such items would be repatriated to its original source country.

For the purposes of this essay, a fourth category has been included: (4) Fakes: those modern reproductions, which masquerade as antiquities.

Christine Alder, a criminologist from the University of Melbourne, in a paper entitled, "The Illicit Traffic in Asian Antiquities," put forward her opinion as to how organized criminal networks facilitate the smuggling of these artifacts:

> Since the traffic is international and since it is illicit, it follows that complex smuggling networks evolve in order to handle the traffic in material . . . emergence of organized criminal activity since if there is a need for movement of material on a regular and systematic basis, this is best satisfied if a stable organization is created to provide the necessary smuggling services. In turn there may be the evolution of generic smuggling activities which move different forms of illicit goods, creating a convergence of illegal market activity (drugs and antiquities, for example).[5]

This chapter also concerned with the number and quality of fakes of antiquities and paintings that are at present flooding both the market here as well as further afield in the afore-mentioned market states. Forgery is hardly a new phenomenon in the art world, and China is considered a leader in the field. According to American journalist Ron Gluckman,[6] up to as much as 80 percent of the value of the goods for sale in Hong Kong are fake, with many pieces ending up in museums, auction houses and high-end galleries.

THE CONCEPT OF "GENUINE" IN CHINA

The concept of a genuine work and an imitation one is by no means as clear-cut in China as it is in the West. As a result, art forgery in China has never carried the dark connotations that it does elsewhere.[7] Copying masterpieces was, and remains, widely practiced. Historically, copying was seen as a stage in the learning process, giving value to the copyist and not, as with Western attitudes, demeaning the act of copying for a lack of imagination. The problem arises when the copies made for the purpose of study and practice merge with the ones that intended to deceive.

Southern China is the world's leading center for mass-produced works of art—with Dafen Village (actually a suburb of Shenzen, just over the border from Hong Kong and certified by the Chinese Ministry of Culture in 2004 as a "Cultural Industry Model Base") exporting millions of paintings a year (most of them copies of famous masterpieces). An estimated 60 percent of the world's cheap oil paintings are produced here, with assembly lines of painters—the fastest "artists" producing 30 paintings a day each! It has been dubbed the "McDonald's of the Art World"[8] and now has hundreds of oil-paintings shops, over

700 galleries, and thousands of artists. In 2006, total oil-painting sales exceeded the 100-million-yuan mark.[9] While previously famous for copying Western art, these workshops have now moved into copying their own local born-and-bred artists—thanks to the huge art boom in Chinese contemporary art.

Some of the painters in Dafen are graduates of China's most renowned art academies, whose skills are exceptionally good, yet who earn meager salaries. The temptation to create or alter art works is ever present. It is in the area of contemporary art where copying activity is at its most frenetic. For every authentic work on display in the city's galleries, hundreds of reproductions are being churned out (often in Dafen) by "artists" who have almost perfected the centuries-old Asian tradition of faithfully copying their masters.

This is not just true for paintings. Modern technology has enabled objects to be reproduced with far greater accuracy. For the last 20 years, copies of various art forms have appeared from China of a quality that was previously unknown—particularly with porcelain and pottery pieces. Counterfeiters (predominantly in southern China) are producing copies of two thousand-year-old pottery items with such skill and sophistication that even experts say they are finding it difficult to distinguish fake from genuine.[10] Especially prevalent is the reuse of "ground-up" bits of ancient clay found at excavation sites throughout China—such as in Jingdezhen, where Ming porcelain was produced between the fourteenth and seventeenth centuries. There are an estimated 150 factories and 100 kilns that are capable of churning out over a million pieces of "Imperial copies" porcelain per day.[11] These items not only look convincing, but can also pass a scientific test (thermo luminescence), which is widely used in dating porcelain and pottery. The thermo luminescence test measures the radiation level emitted by a tiny sample (weighing about 100 milligrams) drilled from the object. When heated, the powder emits a faint light signal, which can indicate when the pottery was last fired in a kiln. If the measurements are consistent with the reported age of the antique, the dealer will receive a one-page certificate of authentication. A wander down Hollywood Road in Hong Kong will see hundreds of such certificates pinned next to their "antiquity" and always given great prominence in the display.

Forgers have learned how to "beat the system." They try to confuse the analysis by incorporating pieces of genuine porcelain into areas where they think the test holes will be drilled. Many of the better quality fakes are made from the same ancient clay and is either re-carved or spliced together (from the shards of ground-down pieces and then rebuilt). As a result, they can pass the test. Forgers are known to irradiate the fake porcelain in an attempt to artificially age them. However, what often seems to be ignored by the buyer of the object is the fact that all the thermo luminescence test pertains to is that the sample is of a certain age, and not that the piece itself is genuine. Under these circumstances, "caveat emptor" is surely wise advice.

So, just how bad is the problem?

"DUE DILIGENCE" EXAMINED

The title of this paper mentions "due diligence" and asks whether a lack of due diligence fuels the trade in illicit antiquities and fakes in Hong Kong. Generally, due diligence refers to the steps taken prior to purchasing an item in order to determine the status of that piece as well as stating to whom the legal title belongs. The purchaser must be able to demonstrate the steps taken in his/her research that would emphatically show that the artifact is not a stolen item and that the title ownership can legally pass between buyer and seller.

A dealer might satisfy his "due diligence" by conducting several checks on known databases—such as with Interpol or a private firm. However, these databases only keep a record of objects reported stolen. For many antiquities, it is very hard to prove their theft once removed from their original source.

Only a tiny percentage of stolen art is ever reported. There are certainly thousands of artifacts that have yet to be documented by overworked and underpaid cultural-relics officials. That means that there are no paper trails, and thus, no database to check them against. In fact, the Chinese government does not have a system for the registration of cultural heritage items, nor a database on stolen art and antiquities. According to the Cultural Heritage Protection Center, there are no plans to develop a registry or database.[12] In Hong Kong, there is no obligation for a seller to prove the amount of "due diligence" he/she has done on an item. Provenance, especially tracing ownership back to a time before certain conventions came into effect (such as the 1970 UNESCO Convention), has become all the more important in terms of the salability of certain categories of Chinese art that are known to be forged to a very high standard.

Despite modest improvements to listing provenance (where known), the historical indifference of the market to this area is still prevalent within the trade. This is certainly the case in Hong Kong, where so many objects have made the short trip across the border. Although there is more information in the market now than ever before, those objects with provenance are still in the minority, and a reason for this is the continuing strong market for unprovenanced pieces.[13]

The market for trade in antiquities in Hong Kong is the same as it was before the handover from the British to the Chinese government in 1997. Indeed, the then-director of the Chinese State Bureau for Preservation of Cultural Relics, Zhang Wenbin, stated, "Chinese laws on the protection of cultural relics will not be applied in Hong Kong."[14] Hong Kong was designated a Special Administrative Region within China with a separate customs territory, free to promulgate its own policy, keeping its status as a free port. That great anomaly of being part of China, yet having separate export laws, is what helps perpetuate the trade in illicit antiquities, both genuine and fake.

HONG KONG AS TRANSITION PORT

As mentioned, Hong Kong is a free port and is also referred to as a "transition port." It gives export documentation to all sorts of imported goods. That is to say, if goods are to be sold legally in galleries or at auction in the market nations, then they must be imported with legitimate export documentation. The status of Hong Kong as a free port means that once the goods are in the hands of a merchant/dealer in Hong Kong, there are few limits on where the goods can be sent so long as these objects are not stolen. Proof of theft is very rare in the case of illicitly obtained antiquities. It is in locations such as Hong Kong where the transition from illicit to licit takes place.[15]

As a way of illustrating this, Mackenzie highlights how an illicit antiquity might be inserted into a legitimate market as follows: The illegal removal of the antiquity from its original context renders it illicit. It then leaves its country of origin in contravention of legal export rules. It can then enter the legitimate chain of supply without buyers being aware they are dealing in stolen property. Thanks to well-established international smuggling gangs and the exploitation of transport networks, the antiquity gains certain documentation. This documentation vouches for the legal export of the goods from a port such as Hong Kong, which then gives the piece an air of legitimate provenance.[16] Thus, it is in Hong Kong where objects first surface as apparently legal goods.

The result of this movement through a transit port is the transformation of objects illegally excavated in, and exported from, their source country into "ex facie" legal and freely tradable goods.[17] However, just because they appear to be legal does not make them so. They are still stolen according to the law of the source country and remain so no matter their subsequent location, although proving this is another matter.[18]

Although the Chinese government formally takes a serious stance in combating illegal excavation and export of Chinese antiquities, many questions can be asked about the sincerity and efficiency of their policies.[19] China has a strict embargo on the export of cultural objects, yet it has struggled to enforce this embargo. Murphy makes the point in relation to China's export restrictions.

> Embargo or retention legislation is toothless without the resources to enforce the laws, and meaningless unless there exists the means to preserve, catalogue and display the relics that the state means to protect.[20]

In 1982, China enacted "The Law on the Protection of Cultural Relics" (amended in 1988 and 2002). This law vested ownership of all archaeological material to the state, and prohibited the export of all such items. However, the 2002 amendments have slightly relaxed this strict retentionist standpoint. It allows for the export of Chinese relics—albeit in very limited cases—mostly for trade and exhibition purposes. There are many categories and classifications involved and, of course, all the bureaucracy that comes with it. No object produced before 1795 is allowed to be exported. The exception to this is for limited exhibition purposes, and then with the approval of the State Bureau of Cultural Relics.[21]

China is a party to a number of legal instruments and conventions that are part of its arsenal in trying to halt the flow of illicit antiquities and cultural property. They are as follows:

1. Convention for the Protection of Cultural Property in the Event of Armed Conflict (The Hague Convention, 1954).
2. Convention on the Means of Prohibiting and Preventing the Illicit Import and Transfer of Ownership of Cultural Property (1970).
3. Convention for the Protection of the World Cultural and Natural Heritage.
4. Unidroit Convention on Stolen or Illegally Exported Cultural Objects (1995).

Hong Kong is the Asian center for the sale of Chinese antiquities and has been since the two main auction houses, Sotheby's and Christie's, set up operations here over 20 years ago. This is due in part to Hong Kong having the best location, geographically, commercially, and in terms of its import/export regulations.[22] The relevant law in Hong Kong is the Import and Export Ordinance, Cap. 60 in particular, Part IV: Unmanifested Cargo and Smuggling, S.14-19, which highlights Hong Kong's relative freedom with regard to its Customs and Excise. It is not illegal, so to speak, to import antiquities into Hong Kong, although importing without a manifest (a document that specifies the nature of the cargo for Customs purposes) is an offense, and it is this offense that is commonly known as smuggling. Section 18 of this law specifies the offense of importing or exporting unmanifested cargo. Penalties upon conviction are certainly not harsh enough to be a deterrent, with suspended sentences and paltry fines often being handed down.

It is interesting to note that the value of Chinese antiquities seized by Hong Kong Customs and returned to China in the five years running up to the handover (1992–96) was HK$15 million. The next 10 years (1997–2006), however, saw only three antiquity cases detected by HK Customs, with a total value of just HK$2.3 million.[23]

Quite clearly, the enforcement action with regard to checking for illicitly smuggled-in antiquities has all but stopped. It does not feature on their list of priorities of top smuggled goods. High-value goods that are deemed worthy of enforcement attention are of the high-tech/digital variety or cigarettes. There is absolutely no pressure brought on the Customs and Excise Department from the Hong Kong government or, surprisingly, from the mainland.

So why is the Hong Kong government not paying any attention to "regulating" the art trade here?

INTERPRETATION OF INACTION

The government's apparent lack of action and general unwillingness to tackle this problem can possibly be traced to its preoccupation with its membership in the Financial Action Task Force of Money-Laundering (FATF): a preeminent intergovernmental body established in 1989 to examine and recommend measures to counter money laundering and terrorist financing.

Hong Kong has been an active member since its inception, and has put in place effective legal and financial systems to counter the problem, affecting the banking, securities, insurance, futures, and leveraged foreign exchange sectors. These industries observe stipulated standards and procedures in their record keeping, customer identification, and reporting of suspicious transactions. The Hong Kong Police Force and the Hong Kong Customs and Excise Department are responsible for enforcing the anti-money-laundering legislation in Hong Kong. The Joint Finance Intelligence Unit (JFIU), jointly operated by the two agencies, was set up in 1989 to receive and analyze suspicious transactions reports, and they work closely with financial regulators and the Department of Justice in investigation and prosecution matters.

Hong Kong has a very well-regulated financial sector, as one would expect of a major trading financial center. However, where it falls short is with regard to other business sectors, where it is possible for money laundering to flourish. Interestingly, Recommendation 20 (of a total of 40) of the FATF states that members should consider applying the FATF Recommendations to non-financial business and professions that pose a money-laundering or terrorist-financing risk.[24] This part was reiterated at the June 2003 Plenary, stating that there should be an extension of anti-money-laundering measures to designated non-financial businesses and professions.

The revised recommendations were to have been implemented immediately by FATF members, yet Hong Kong has been slow to bring in anti-money-laundering regulations to any sector outside the financial one and does not seem to be in a hurry to do so, either. Effectively, what this means is that anyone can buy an antique/work of art from one of the many galleries or auction houses in Hong Kong, pay cash for it, and not be asked for the various facts and details that are mandatory in the financial sector if doing a substantial cash transaction. Of course, companies may have in place their own stringent internal regulations relating to cash transactions. However, the Hong Kong government does not stipulate what these should be.

So, what can be done to help raise awareness to this problem? One of the most vocal NGOs is the Cultural Heritage Protection Center, CHP (formerly known as Cultural Heritage Watch), based in Beijing. It is a private nonprofit NGO, founded in 1998, whose aim is to rouse public awareness to the importance of protecting the nation's cultural heritage. CHP places a lot of emphasis at the local level, where many unearthed tombs or sites of archaeological interest are at their most vulnerable to tomb robbers and antiquity smugglers. While having no direct links to the government, it is given de facto support by the National Administration of Cultural Heritage. As a result of CHP guidance, as well as intervention in certain cases, smuggled cultural relics have been retrieved and the looting of heritage sites has been exposed.[25]

Another well-known, nonprofit NGO is SAFE (Saving Antiquities for Everyone), which is dedicated to preserving cultural heritage worldwide. It works with CHP on China issues, and like CHP, it aims to raise awareness about the irreversible damage that results from looting, smuggling, and trading in illicit antiquities. It creates educational programs and media campaigns in partnership with academia and various professional communities, such as the legal and law enforcement sectors. SAFE is based in the United States and is apolitical. Again, outside of China, the Australian National University set up in March 2005 the China Heritage Project and sends out a quarterly newsletter that focuses on the problems and issues related to heritage protection in China.

One thing that might affect the trade in Hong Kong is China's request to the U.S. government, in May 2004, to curtail dramatically most classes of antiquities/antiques being imported from China under Article 9 of the 1970 UNESCO Convention. The restriction covers all Chinese cultural materials predating 1912. It is supported by NGOs such as CHP and SAFE, although it has elicited objections from both the U.S trade. and museums, and it is by no means a certainty to be enacted.

Opponents argue that China has a deplorable record of protecting its cultural patrimony and does not effectively enforce its own export restrictions.[26] The latter point is certainly true with regard to its rather porous border with Hong Kong. Other opponents simply, or rather cynically, see it as China's way of keeping more of their antiquities on home soil while rapidly building up a large internal auction market.[27] China has not requested any other UNESCO signatory nation to impose similar restrictions. This has led many to believe that China's request will actually have no impact on the looting, so long as there continues to be a growing market inside China, as well as strong demand from market states. This issue has yet to be resolved, with the U.S. State Department announcing a delay in its decision on China's request.[28]

This still brings us to the question that if pressure from the Chinese government to the Hong Kong government is not forthcoming, and with the Hong Kong Customs and Police Force not yet seeing this issue as high priority, who is left to regulate the market and ensure that proper due diligence is carried out?

ENSURING DUE DILIGENCE

Agencies such as Interpol, as well as certain private sector companies like the Art Loss Register and Swift-Find, have large databases of stolen and missing works of art. A dealer can easily check whether an item has been listed as stolen. However, there remains the problem that these databases cannot "red flag" a recently dug-up antiquity for which no records have previously existed. In most cases, no documents or photos exist for these items, which enter the market without any provenance at all. These databases certainly have their place and are useful for searching stolen/looted antiquities and for checking against auction catalog lists. There is a great need of them within the trade to maintain good due diligence, but they are less useful in the case of newly looted antiquities. There is also the possibility that if the private sector takes on a bigger role, competition and secrecy can rear its ugly head between the private agencies.

This is why the issue of self-regulation within the trade is so important in creating the climate that all is above board and in knowing which dealers are the more reputable ones in the trade. The crux of the problem is that the majority of antiquities on the market are without a full and properly documented provenance, and if the method of their original acquisition is unknown, then it should be treated as suspect.[29]

With regards to due diligence checks, one area that has not been resolved, and which needs looking at, concerns how much due diligence constitutes the right amount. Can a dealer check on one database and be satisfied when the item in question is not flagged or does not show up at all? If a dispute on a title arises in litigation, can the dealer use the one check as a rebuttal? One database search seems very inadequate, but there is nothing in the various existing codes of due diligence to specify how extensive a check should be.

Critics of the codes argue that the voluntary nature of the codes defeats its purpose. While not suggesting that they are the solution to solving the illicit antiquity trade, they are surely a move in the right direction. With the best practices of the code being employed, and a thorough level of due diligence conducted, it should enable greater transparency in the art market.

CONCLUSION

To conclude, as P. M. Bator noted in 1983:

> No dealer or auction house will normally reveal the provenance of an object offered for sale; it is assumed that buyers and the public have no business knowing where and when and for how much the object was acquired. Museums (and, of course, private collectors) will also disclose such information rarely. . .Indeed, the tradition is that such information is rarely even sought. . .too much information may spoil the acquisition of a stunning and desirable treasure.[30]

Certainly, for anyone who has had the experience of going into many of the antique shops along Hollywood Road and asking for information about certain pieces, the above would seem to hold true. It appears that there is a certain degree of acceptance within the trade that objects without provenance can be freely bought and sold. So, what of China's request to the United States to restrict imports, as well as their rather draconian export regulations? Murphy suggests that:

> The art world knows that embargo legislation in developing source nations does not prevent export; it only ensures that the traffic goes underground.[31]

Alder goes on to state that the trade in cultural material will continue regardless of any new steps taken to protect heritage sites and objects.[32] As long as demand in the market states remains high, policies such as those used by China, which attempts to restrict the supply, will not have a great deal of impact on the trade.

This would indeed appear to be the case, certainly, inasmuch as the enforcement and prosecution figures show and the fact that new deliveries of stock arrives in the antique shops and galleries on a very regular basis. This, coupled with the Hong Kong government's apparent lack of interest, means that no matter how stringent the export laws of China are, the mere fact that on their doorstep is the laissez-faire unregulated market of Hong Kong means that the trade will continue to flourish.

Education, especially in China and Hong Kong, is, perhaps, the right approach to take with regards to this illicit trade. It is necessary to convince the potential consumers of the damage being done to China's heritage through their purchasing of these unprovenanced antiquities. At the same time, make those same potential customers equally aware of the abundance of fakes in the market and the fact that the certificate of authentication (so prominently offered with the object) merely gives the guarantee to the tiny core sample tested and not the whole piece. The trade does not generally educate the public—caveat emptor—and whistle-blowers on this multimillion dollar industry are unlikely to appear. Greater prominence by the NGOs is certainly needed, as they have an important role to perform in alerting the public to this trade.

If collectors are made aware of the illicit trade going on and refuse to buy unprovenanced objects, together with the public also being made to understand the costs to society in an historical heritage context, then the trade would surely start to diminish.[33] It is through this kind of reform—education—rather than the likes of China's blanket export ban, that results will hopefully be seen. It is a massive uphill battle. O'Keefe has argued that in order to change public opinion, it will be necessary to educate the professionals (such as in law enforcement), as well as the collectors in the market states.[34] The focus has to be at the demand end of the market.

As stated, attention needs to be directed to altering the way people buy antiquities, so that dealers will not sell and consumers will not buy unprovenanced objects. It is crucial to get the trade involved and to realize that ultimately it is up to them to bring about the changes to the way antiquities are traded. Trade codes of practice and trade association codes of ethics need to evolve in Hong Kong—a Hong Kong version of the UK's Council for the Prevention of Art Theft (CoPAT) would be a great achievement. This would hopefully ensure that the illicitly smuggled antiquities would not enter the market and, for those pieces that did slip through, the consumer would have been educated to ask for the object's provenance. No provenance, no sale.

NOTES

1. Brodie et al. 2001.
2. Mackenzie 2002.
3. Merryman 1986, 831.
4. MacKenzie 2005, 4.
5. Alder 2001 3.
6. Gluckman 2002.
7. Luce, 2002, 10.
8. Praetsch 2006.
9. Shenzhen Government Online 2008.
10. Editor's Note: Please note the differences between the concept of forgery in China, as discussed here, and Western concepts addressed by Polk and Chappell in Chapter 7.
11. Gluckman 2002.
12. Soudjin et al. 2003.
13. Mackenzie 2005, 34.
14. Crowell 1997.
15. Alder 2001, 4.
16. Mackenzie 2002, 4.
17. Mackenzie 2005, 140.
18. Mackenzie 2005, 140; and Polk, 2001, 4.
19. Soudjin et al. 2003.
20. Murphy 1995, 155.
21. Lubina 2006.
22. Thompson 1981, 36.

23. Hong Kong Customs and Excise Department, letter dated September 7, 2006, in response to information request by author.

24. Hong Kong Government, "Financial Action Task Force," available at http://www.nd.gov.hk/text/moneylaundering/index.htm2007.

25. China Heritage Project 2007.

26. Kaufman 2005.

27. Ibid.

28. Kahn 2006.

29. Editor's Note: Please see Giovanni Pastore's discussion of a similar theme in Chapter 12.

30. As cited in Mackenzie 2002.

31. Murphy 1995, 155.

32. Alder 2001, 5.

33. Ibid., 10.

34. O'Keefe 1997.

PART II

Thieves and Forgers

Chapter 4

Who Is Stealing All Those Paintings?

A. J. G. Tijhuis

One of the recurring themes in articles and books on art theft is the type of perpetrator responsible for most thefts. Here, I look at the different types of art thieves and try to answer the question: who steals art?

Trying to answer this question can be a rather tricky endeavor for a number of reasons. First of all, the definition of art for this purpose does not speak for itself. Secondly, sufficient and comparable empirical data about art thefts is not available to scholars, police, or governments.

The latter reason is the result of the rather limited interest of most police services in the theft of works of art. Police services are usually the primary source of data on crimes studied by criminologists and other researchers. However, in most countries, no special art theft units exist within the local or national police services. Furthermore, data on art thefts are usually not registered in national or international databases—indeed, no complete databases exist worldwide. Some important exceptions to this general pattern are the efforts of the Italian and French police, as well as New Scotland Yard in London. However, these institutions do not provide data to the general public, nor have they traditionally provided it to researchers, who are in the best position to cull answers from the available data. The same goes for a number of private organizations that have built databases with stolen art. None of the databases are sufficiently comprehensive to provide definitive information.

Given the aforementioned lack of data, in order to study the different types of thieves, I will briefly describe the results of an academic study in which some practical choices were made to circumvent any problems related to definitions or sufficient data. For the purposes of this study, the concept of "art" was restricted to valuable paintings in museums or private collections. The thefts analyzed were restricted to thefts in Europe from 1960 to 2003, for which the perpetrators had been arrested. Finally, the relevant facts of these thefts were taken from the available literature and journalistic accounts, as well as from specialized sources like the Stolen Art Alert from IFAR. These choices resulted in the accumulation of about 50 solved art thefts, about 30 of which will be mentioned in this essay. This selection does not provide a pool of data that can claim to be representative of all thefts of fine art. Indeed, its limited nature is indicative of the problem that students of art crime must overcome.[1] However, this group of thefts can help to draw at least some tentative conclusions as to the different types of art thieves.

Hereafter, the different types of thieves will be described as: (1) the "Dr. No" type, collector-commissioned thefts; (2) the compulsive thief; (3) the thefts originating from the drug trade or more general Organized Crime; (4) ideological thieves with a "higher purpose"; (5) thieves as "art-nappers"; (6) internal thieves; and (7) common thieves.

DR. NO

One of the most popular explanations for prominent art thefts is as follows: mysterious, superrich collectors commission thefts to add unique works of art to their secret collections. Sometimes the name of Dr. No is mentioned in media reports, referring to the character in the James Bond movie of the same name. This character had a famous stolen work of art in his secret hideout—one which will be discussed later. The idea of a malicious rich collector has been in use since the time of the Bond movie, and each era has added its own stereotype. In the 1970s, for example, oil sheiks were the main suspects. During the 1990s, it was the leaders of drug cartels. Postulators often suggest inconsistent arguments as to why thefts have probably been ordered by collectors. When very famous paintings are stolen, the argument runs that the theft must have been to order, because the thieves should know that they can never sell these paintings themselves. On the other hand, when less well-known paintings are stolen, they argue that the theft must be to order because only a collector would appreciate these paintings.

Looking at the solved thefts, little convincing evidence supports this popular explanation. An example of this kind of theft came in a heist from the Museum of Fine Art in Budapest in 1983. In that case, the Italian Mafia was supposed to have stolen the paintings, on order from a Greek olive oil tycoon. The police arrested the Greek businessman, but had to let him go when they could find no evidence at all against him. The paintings were later found in a Greek monastery.[2]

COMPULSIVE THIEVES

Whereas the thefts to order from rich collectors are hard to prove, at least one peculiar example of thieves who are at the same time collectors (though not the stereotypical sort) should be added here. In November 2001, Stephane Breitwieser, a French waiter, was caught after returning to the Richard Wagner Museum in Lucern, from which he had stolen a rare bugle made in 1584. During the investigation and trial that followed, Breitwieser admitted to have stolen over 200 works of art, especially old masters, from dozens of museums and exhibits in Switzerland, France, and other countries, abetted by his then-girlfriend. He kept the objects purely for his own enjoyment, never selling anything. The total value of the works of art stolen by this one man was estimated to be over $1 billion. In a dismaying turn of events, more than a third of the works were destroyed by Breitwieser's mother, after she found them in his house and hoped to eliminate the evidence against her son. In 2006, Breitwieser published an autobiography in France called *Confessions d'un Voleur d'Art* ("Confessions of an Art Thief").[3] Although figures like Breitwieser are uncommon, they are nevertheless important, as they are responsible for an incredible number of stolen art works.

ART THEFT, THE NARCOTICS TRADE, AND ORGANIZED CRIME

At the beginning of 1999, the Spanish police rounded up a gang of art thieves. They had stolen a number of paintings, including works by Picasso, Miró, and Goya, from a villa near Geneva. The investigation showed that the thieves had planned to obtain a load of cocaine with the proceeds of the theft.[4]

This example fits in the explanation that police officials often give for major art thefts.[5] They argue that these thefts are somehow related to the narcotics trade or other organized crimes. Stolen art is supposed to be used as collateral in large drug deals or other organized crimes, or as a means to launder the proceeds of drug deals. A number of examples can be mentioned to support the idea of a link with the narcotics trade.[6] In Italy, a painting attributed to Rafael was offered in an illegal deal to sell plutonium. The police immediately assumed that this proved stolen art was used as collateral or investment. In another case in the Netherlands, two persons were convicted for the theft of three Van Gogh paintings from the North Brabant Museum in 1990. An anonymous clue led to the recovery of one painting. Subsequently, through the intervention of the lawyer, both of the other paintings were recovered. His client, a convicted drug dealer, mediated the recovery.

Despite the popularity of the link between art theft and the narcotics trade, the incidents to support this explanation do not justify the assumption that this link can explain the majority of all art thefts, as they only comprise a small percentage of all *solved* thefts. The same goes for the use of stolen art to launder the proceeds of other crimes. However, stolen art has been used in a number of cases to obtain loans. When the loan was not repaid, the works of art ended up in the vaults of the loaning bank.[7] One of the art thefts, the booty of which was used to obtain loans, was the 1986 robbery of the Alfred Beit collection in Ireland.[8] This same robbery also showed the involvement of Irish Organized Crime figures.[9] Of this collection of cases, 50 cases under discussion here, seven are certainly connected with the drug trade and Organized Crime (14 percent of the study group).[10]

As the two main explanations for art thefts do not actually seem to cover a major part of all thefts in our study group, other explanations must be looked upon. Hereafter, the four remaining explanations will be examined: the theft of art for a "good cause," thefts by insiders, artnappings, and the "common" theft.

ART THEFT FOR A "GOOD CAUSE," OR PLAIN TERRORISM?

In 1961, Goya's *The Duke of Wellington* was stolen from the National Gallery in London. The thief demanded £150,000 to be paid to a charity that would provide free of charge radio and television licenses for the elderly and the poor in England. When this demand, as well as following demands, were not met, the thief left the painting at a train station. Four years later, he turned himself in.[11] Despite all the wild speculations, he was no professional thief, but an overweight old man who had simply entered the building via a ladder that was left there by some constructors. Interestingly enough, the stolen painting was seen hanging in Dr. No's secret hideout in the eponymous James Bond film, supposedly stolen to order by this villain—a clever inside joke on the part of the film makers, as the film was released when the Goya painting was still missing.

A good cause or higher purpose as a motive for art thefts does not seem strange at first sight. Given the high value of the objects in question, the thieves can put the owner and the government under pressure to give in to their demands. Ideological art theft is sometimes used to support terrorism, or at least attempt to do so.

Two examples can be added here. In 1974, the Vermeer painting *The Guitar Player* was stolen from Kenwood House in London. The thieves demanded the release of several IRA members who were imprisoned for several bomb attacks in London. When the demands were not met, the painting was found two months later, at a cemetery.[12] Briefly after this theft, a robbery took place in Russborough House, in Ireland, the home of the late Sir Aflred Beit, a diamond millionaire (his house was victimized by art thieves on multiple occasions). The thieves bound and gagged Beit and his wife and took 19 old masters. They then sought to exchange five paintings for the release of two IRA activists, and the other 14 paintings were ransomed for half a million pounds. Neither demand was met. The paintings were all found and the thieves jailed.[13]

From the perspective of law enforcement, the potential use of art theft by terrorists should be looked upon carefully. As the traditional terrorist groups in Europe and elsewhere are joined by new, even more aggressive groups, this provides an extra reason to fight this type of crime head on. Art theft funds terrorism.

ARTNAPPING

In December 2001, a man walked into Sweden's National Museum five minutes before closing time. He aimed a half-automatic rifle at a guard while two other men took a Renoir and a Rembrandt painting from the wall. The thieves later demanded a £4 million ransom. The museum did not give in to the demand, and the thieves were ultimately arrested.[14]

This theft is an example of the kidnap of art, so-called "artnapping." Although art theft and blackmail are nothing new to the criminal repertoire, artnapping began seriously only in the 1960s. It began in France in 1960 and 1961 with several large thefts of Impressionist and other modern paintings, for which ransoms were demanded. Soon afterward, this kind of theft spread to other countries, and a range of thefts emerged in which ransoms were demanded.[15]

The thefts came during a period in which art established itself in the public mind as a commodity with a potentially limitless value. A range of high-profile auctions, starting in London during the late 1950s, caused both the rise in prices and a change in the public perception of art.[16] A key event was the 1961 purchase of Rembrandt's *Aristotle Contemplating a Bust of Homer* for $2.3 million by the Metropolitan Museum in New York.

In most cases, the owner does not give in to a ransomer's demands. Many paintings in museums are not insured, so a deal with an insurance company is impossible. The museums themselves cannot pay the ransoms, and also refrain from doing so for tactical reasons. Giving in to the thieves will encourage future thefts, showing that crime does pay. In many countries, it is illegal to negotiate or pay a ransom, as it is assumed that it will provoke further such kidnappings. An old example of this logic is the theft from the Gallery of Modern Art in Milan, from which 28 paintings were stolen in 1975. The gallery paid a ransom, only to see another theft three months later in which 38 paintings were stolen.[17]

When the owner gives in to a ransom demand, this can make the arrest of the thieves more likely, as obtaining the ransom without exposing oneself in practice turns out to be far more difficult for criminals than the actual theft. An example is the 1994 theft of Edvard Munch's *The*

Scream. Charles Hill, an art cop from New Scotland Yard, posed as a representative of the J. Paul Getty Museum interested in buying the painting. He managed to contact the thieves, who demanded £300,000 plus expenses. Hill accepted their demand, but the thieves were arrested as they attempted to transfer the money. In another case, the thieves of a Mondriaan painting were arrested after they demanded a ransom for the return of a painting that was stolen from the Middelburg region of the Netherlands, in 1998. The thieves of three Van Gogh paintings from the Kröller-Müller Museum in the Netherlands in 1988 also failed in their attempt to extort a ransom from the museum, and were quickly arrested. It turned out that the thieves were some local men who had casually decided to rob the museum while drinking together in a pub. Before they actually stole the paintings, they drove to the museum several nights running, but did not dare go in.[18]

In a number of cases, it is unclear whether a ransom has been demanded and paid. Every now and then, stolen paintings turn up at train station lockers or other anonymous places. It is often assumed that the thieves realized the paintings they had were so "hot" that they could never safely find a buyer for them. However, one can easily doubt this argument, as it does not make sense that thieves would simply abandon the goods for which they took so much risk. In such cases, it seems more logical that a private, clandestine arrangement was organized between the thieves and the insurance company, museum, or collector.[19]

In a number of cases, police officers have posed as potential buyers and lured the desperate criminals to offer the stolen art. However, this is not without complications, as it is illegal to negotiate deals with criminals in many countries. An example of a case in which a ransom was paid is the third robbery at the hapless Russborough House, in 2001. Lengthy negotiations with underworld figures allegedly preceded the return of two paintings. The 1981 theft of 15 paintings from the French Musée des Jacobins is another example. Four years after the theft, the curator of the museum received an anonymous phone call that the paintings could be found in a locker at the airport. Finally, the October 1994 theft of seven Picassos from a Zurich gallery provides an example of a variation on the ransom theme. In February 2000, five of the paintings were returned. According to a statement by the police and prosecutors, the paintings had been recovered with the help of an unnamed intermediary, who was rewarded by being allowed to keep two of the seven paintings.[20]

INTERNAL THEFTS

In 1998, the FBI announced that they had undertaken an investigation into thefts from museums.[21] They found that 83 percent of the known thefts could be classified as "internal thefts," which meant that museum staff or others with privileged access to collections, like scientists, security officials, or restorers had been involved. Although this study was limited to the United States, it points at an important indication of what may be going on elsewhere.

During a 1991 burglary of the Van Gogh Museum in Amsterdam, thieves took 20 paintings, worth about €500 million, from the museum. The paintings were soon recovered, and it turned out the thieves had cooperated with a security official who was on duty the night of the theft. A similar case occurred in 1998.[22] The National Gallery of Modern Art in Rome was robbed by an armed group that worked together with one of the security officials on duty. During the same year, two thieves stole paintings in collaboration with the curator of the museum. A week later, the paintings were found on a boat in a nearby town, and the curator was later sentenced to 18 months in prison. Two of the stolen and recovered paintings, a Monet and a Sisley, were stolen again in 2007. This second theft has not been solved.

In the summer of 1983, Nelly Dehem, the 88-year-old daughter of the painter Herni Dehem, was hospitalized in Cannes. She had entrusted the care of her villa and her collection of Impressionist paintings to a hospital worker and his wife. During her stay in the hospital, they took 40 paintings by Monet, Gauguin, Renoir, Pisarro, Sisley, and others. With the assistance of a Parisian art dealer, the paintings had been sold in a number of countries spread all over the world.[23] Another old but telling example of internal thefts is the case of the Edvard Munch Museum in Oslo. Between 1961 and 1968, numerous paintings by the Norwegian master appeared on the English market. In many cases, certificates were later issued from the curator in the Munch Museum who was considered an expert on Munch paintings. When a painting was returned to the museum while the curator was on holiday, the deputy director recognized the painting as being part of the museum's collection. He went to the police, and Scotland Yard later traced 30 paintings that were sold by the curator in London.[24]

Finally, in August 2001, 15 paintings by Goya and Brueghel among others were stolen from the apartment of Esther Koplowitz in Madrid. The thieves first tried to extort a ransom from Koplowitz, and subsequently agreed to an offer to buy the paintings from a collector, who turned out to be an undercover agent from the FBI. When the thieves were caught, it turned out that Koplowitz's security staff had played an important role in the theft.[25]

COMMON ART THEFTS

In April 2002, five thieves burgled the Brücke Museum in Berlin, taking nine Expressionist paintings. Within a month, they were caught. It

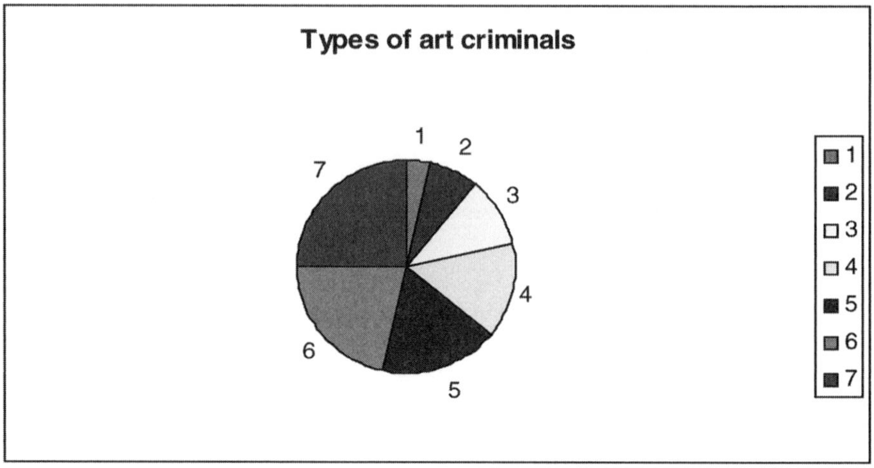

1. Dr. No (number of instances, relative to other categories of art thieves: 1)
2. Compulsive thieves (1)
3. Theft for a "good cause" (3)
4. Internal thieves (6)
5. Organized crime and drug trade (7)
6. Common theft (10)
7. Artnapping (11)

Figure 4.1 Categories of Art Thieves.
Diagram courtesy of the author.

turned out that the thieves were also involved in other art thefts and had tried to sell the paintings.[26]

This case illustrates what can be described as the "common" theft: a theft with the straightforward purpose of selling the paintings as quickly as possible. A case in 2000 illustrates how thieves are not intimidated by the difficulties of selling stolen paintings: after they robbed the York City Gallery of a range of paintings, one of the thieves hired a conference room to negotiate about the sale of the paintings. This led to his arrest and sentence of 15 years' imprisonment.[27]

Common thefts comprise the majority of fine art thefts. Usually a gang or small group of criminals is involved. But two examples of thieves working alone will be described here. At the Lefevre Gallery in London, a lone thief walked in and took a Picasso painting from the wall, while he pointed his gun at a staff member of the gallery. He fled in the same taxi in which he had arrived at the scene. It turned out later that this theft was just part of a spree of robberies to finance his wild lifestyle. A second example is the theft of an Edvard Munch painting in Oslo in 1998. Six months after the theft, the thief walked into the police headquarters. He admitted to have stolen the painting to pay off his gambling debts.

CONCLUSION

Based on the study group of solved thefts of paintings from museums described here, some conclusions may be drawn about the perpetrators of such crimes. The best-known explanations of high-profile art thefts, in fact, explain only a small percentage of the thefts in this study group. Thefts to order are rare. Thefts related to drug trafficking and/or Organized Crime do occur, but less frequently than is assumed by most police officials, at least as far as this study can determine. Cases involving the most famous artworks—those that have obvious value in barter or collateral deals—are the likeliest candidates to involve Organized Crime. The most frequent categories of fine art thefts are artnappings and common thefts. Besides these two categories, internal thefts are important, and police will first interview individuals who work at the victimized institution as potential suspects. This category is crucial because internal thefts are often repeated after an initial success, and can involve a large number of paintings. To be sure, the three categories mentioned here can often be hard to distinguish from each other and need not be mutually exclusive.

It is fascinating, though, that the two explanations with which this essay began are repeated over and over again. Obviously, the Dr. No figure has a lot more appeal to the media than the many clumsy, unromantic thieves who comprise the largest part of art thefts. Furthermore, Organized Crime functions as a more challenging and interesting opponent for police forces investigating art crimes than thieves who are indeed clumsy and less professional than expected. This study is merely a starting point. More research, most ideally in collaboration with police agencies specialized in art crimes, should shed more light on the types of criminals involved and their modus operandi. To be sure, most crimes are never solved, and therefore, a lot is still to be learned about this tragic, though fascinating, type of crime.

NOTES

1. Editor's Note: Tijhuis's chapter examines categories of art thieves. His contribution is particularly interesting, and useful to the dialogue among educated scholars, because his analysis differs in some ways from the opinions of other art crime experts, particularly with regard to the level of involvement of Organized Crime in art crime. He makes the excellent point that most experts are going on hearsay from police about Organized Crime and art crime, with relatively little empirical data and evidence beyond the word of police, undercover agents, and criminals. Tijhuis does not dismiss the notion that most art crime since the 1960s involves Organized Crime at some level, but rather makes the legitimate point that, while we art crime scholars have heard a lot of anecdotal evidence, we have not seen concrete data to back it up.

This key point really highlights the biggest problem with the study and analysis of art crime: lack of data to back up the hearsay. Too much anecdotal rather than empirical evidence means that, for the time being, art crime cannot really be a proper "scientific" field of study, as we must still rely too much on non-empirical evidence. Scholars may analyze based on the data available, which is necessarily a fragment of what is actually happening. We may choose to use anecdotal information to expand upon the limited empirical data, which has been the route of most scholars, for lack of a better option. Tijhuis prefers to stick with the available data sets, however limited, and analyze based only on them. The result is certainly more "scientific" in a proper sense of criminology as social science. It does result in some statements that differ from those of other scholars in this collection (the editor included).

His point is well taken, and any friendly, respectful, intelligent debate benefits the field in general. Noting the limited empirical evidence to go with the massive anecdotal evidence in the field of art crime is important to underscore—indeed, it is exactly what ARCA and this book is trying to counter. Limited progress may be made unless (1) police worldwide begin to keep good data on art crimes in their jurisdiction; and (2) police make the data available to scholars, who can then conduct better-informed, more scientific research and analysis, to (3) help police in the future.

2. Fox Butterfield, "Boston Museum Says It Was Uninsured for Theft," *New York Times*, March 20, 1990.

3. Editor's Note: The author of this essay, Dr Tijhuis, will be reviewing Breitweiser's book in the premiere issue of *The Journal of Art Crime*

4. Neil Brodie, Jenny Doole, and Peter Watson, *Stealing History: The Illicit Trade in Cultural Material* (Cambridge: McDonald Institute for Archaeological Research, 2000).

5. Editor's Note: Other notable examples appear in several different chapters, including the Introduction: Art Crime in Context, and Chapters 6 and 20.

6. Edgar Tijhuis, *Transnational Crime and the Interface between Legal and Illegal Actors: The Case of the Illicit Art and Antiquities Trade* (Nijmegen, Wolf Legal Publishers, 2006).

7. John Conklin, *Art Crime* (Westport, CT: Praeger, 1994).

8. This is the Martin Cahill case, described in the Introduction.

9. Nora Koldehoff and Stefan Koldehoff, *Aktenzeichen Kunst—Die spektakulàrsten Kunstdiebstähle der Welt* (Cologne: Du Mont, 2004).

10. It should be noted that the study group of 50 cases used here is, as defined by Dr Tijhuis, comprised of solved thefts of paintings from museums. Therefore, the study group reveals that approximately 14 percent of solved thefts of paintings from museums can be firmly attributed to organized crime.

11. Hugh McLeave, *Rogues in the Gallery—the Modern Plague of Art Thefts* (Boston: Codine, 1981).

12. Andy Roberts, "The Baroque Guitar," Darnet, April 4, 2005,http://distributedresearch.net/blog/2005/04/04/the-baroque-guitar.

13. Koldehoff et al., *Aktenzeichen Kunst.*

14. Museum Security Network report, "Stockholm art thieves jailed," July 28, 2001,http://www.museum-security.org.

15. McLeave, *Rogues in the Gallery.*

16. Simon Houpt. *Museum of the Missing: A History of Art Theft* (New York: Sterling Publishing, 2006).

17. Conklin, *Art Crime.*

18. Ton Cremers, "Schilderijendiefstal: meestal trivial, zonder romantiek en zelden beredeneerd," May 14, 2003, http://www.museumbeveiliging.com/2003/05/14/schilderijendiefstal-meestal-triviaal-zonder-romantiek-en-zelden-koel-beredeneerd.

19. Editor's Note: The most recent and prominent such example was in the case of the 2008 Bührle Collection theft, for which there exists no plausible explanation beyond a ransom having been quietly paid for the return of some of the recently stolen paintings.

20. IFAR Report, "Picasso's Recovered 5 Years after Zurich Gallery Theft," December 1994.

21. Museum Security Network, 'Art theft from within museums', Museum Security Network Report, www.museum-security.org, March 21, 2002.

22. Ton Cremers, "Schilderijendiefstal: meestal trivial, zonder romantiek en zelden beredeneerd," May 14, 2003, http://www.museumbeveiliging.com/2003/05/14/schilderijendiefstal-meestal-triviaal-zonder-romantiek-en-zelden-koel-beredeneerd.

23. IFAR Report, January–February 1985 and IFAR Report July 1985.

24. Robert Keith Middlemas, *The Double Market—Art Theft and Art Thieves* (Westmead: Saxon House, 1975).

25. Koldehoff et al., *Aktenzeichen Kunst.*

26. Ibid.

27. Museum Security Network, "14 Years for Armed Robbery of York Gallery," Museum Security Network Report, February 12, 2000, http://www.museum-security.org/00/023.html.

Chapter 5

The Affair of the Statuettes Reexamined: Picasso and Apollinaire's Role in the Famed Louvre Theft

Silvia Loreti

The "affaire des statuettes" is a landmark anecdote in the history of Picasso's early masterpiece, the 1907–9 *Demoiselles d'Avignon.* The artist's ownership of two carved Iberian heads, stolen from the Louvre in 1907, was fundamental in establishing the chronology of the painting. His illegal possession of the heads, however, has been largely downplayed by biographers as an unfortunate, if humorous, episode in which Picasso was unknowingly involved.

In most accounts, the strange and complex story of the Louvre Iberian heads has been dismissed as a theft of which Picasso became aware only after the fact, and of which his friend, Guillaume Apollinare, was unjustly accused. This oversimplification rests largely on two facts. First, despite the extensive press coverage of the affair at the time, the accounts given by Picasso and Apollinaire remain fragmentary. Secondly, by the time Picasso's name was publicly linked to the event (in 1933), a plethora of admirers had begun to celebrate him as the star of modern art. His fame wove a screen around him. Not only had no conclusive evidence been found to condemn him of the theft, but little action has been taken to reexamine the surviving documents in order to investigate his possible responsibilities. Ironically, since the Iberian statue incident, Picasso's own art has become the target of frequent theft—Picasso's art is stolen far more often than that of any other artist.

A more objective assessment of Picasso's responsibility in the Louvre thefts seems warranted for different reasons. For historians of crime, the affair is a good example of the romantic mystification surrounding art thefts. For art historians, a more active involvement of Picasso in the "affaire des statuettes" could lead to a better understanding of the artist's sudden, but profound, fascination with Iberian sculpture in 1907. Furthermore, to investigate anew the "affaire des statuettes" is an important step toward an effective alliance between art historians and criminologists, who together may reconstruct and shed new light on unsolved crimes. Adding the contemporary reports of the Louvre administration to the public and personal accounts of the affair's protagonists, the following analysis aims to highlight the possibilities of this collaboration.

THE AFFAIR

The "affaire des statuettes" broke in September 1911, as part of the much more sensational scandal regarding the disappearance of *Mona Lisa* from the Louvre in August of the same year. While the theft of *Mona Lisa* made world headlines, three highly circulated Parisian newspapers, *Paris-Journal, Le Matin,* and *L'Intransigeant,* mounted a campaign berating the Louvre for its poor security. How, they asked, had it been possible to steal such a masterpiece from the museum? Mistrusting the authorities, whom they accused of laissez-faire security and of trading with the emblems of the Republic, the press thought it safer to conduct its own investigation. To this end, *Paris-Journal* offered 50,000 francs for the restitution of the *Mona Lisa,* no questions asked.

Then the affair exploded. On August 29, 1911 *Paris-Journal* published a front-page photograph of an Iberian female bust under the title "A Thief Brings Us a Work Stolen from the Louvre." The accompanying article quoted the letter of an anonymous writer. He declared himself the perpetrator of the theft and, describing the stolen statue as Phoenician (a mistake worth noting), he claimed to have stolen the statue from the Louvre's Department of Oriental Antiquities on May 7 of the same year.[1]

The piece was immediately recognized by the curator of the Department, Edmond Pottier. In his official report to Théophile Homolle, the then-director of the Louvre, Pottier explained that an editor of *Paris-Journal* had contacted him a few days before the scandal broke. The journalist had asked the Louvre curator whether he was aware of a recent theft in his department. Pottier knew nothing about it. Upon seeing the piece, however, he was obliged to admit that it belonged "to the series of Iberian antiquities, which are for the most part exhibited in a small room between the large one of Magnesia of the Meander and the wardens' refectory."[2]

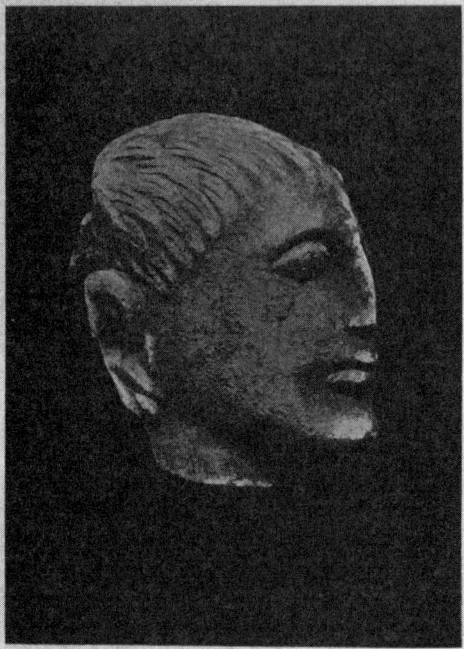
Fig. 281. — Tête du Cerro (Louvre).

Tête du Cerro (Ancienne collection Saviron), © cliché Bibliotheque due l'Institut national d'histoire d l'art, collections Jacques Doucet, France. (Our thanks to the Library of the National Institute of Art History, the collections of Jacques Doucet, and the kind release from Dominique Morelon.)

Thus began the so-called Iberian affair. The mysterious thief continued by saying that the piece later recognized by Pottier was neither the only nor the first Iberian sculpture that he had stolen from the Department of Oriental Antiquities. "It was in March 1907," he wrote, "that I first penetrated the Louvre."[3] Over the course of two days, he stole one female and one male Iberian bust, which he sold to one or more of his friends in Paris. He then fled.

The thief continued his admission, saying that, once back in France in 1911, he paid a further visit to the Louvre, stealing another bust from the same department: "I took the new head to the flat of a friend, where there were some ten writers and artists, who laughed when they knew it came from the Louvre."[4]

The thief named none of his buyers, identifying them only as "friends." Probably disconcerted by the uproar resulting from the publication of the letter, one of these friends brought the two heads that had

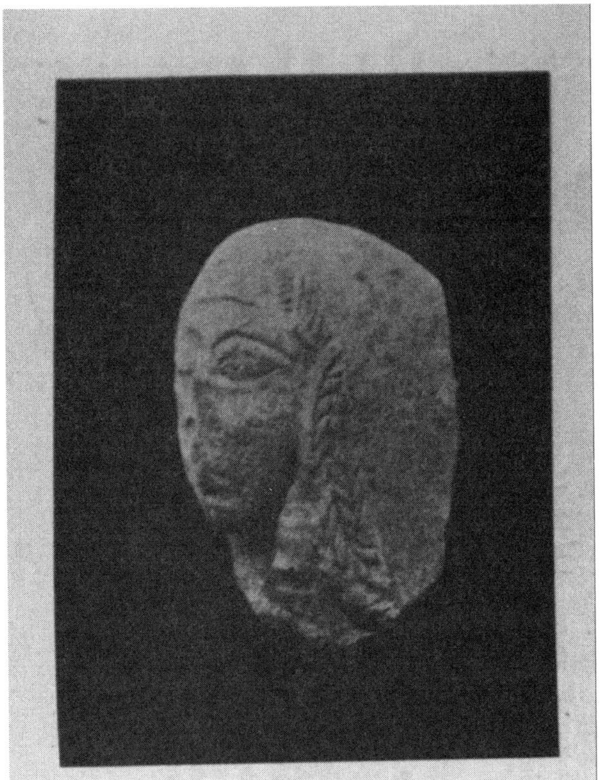

Fig. 166. — Ancienne collection Savirón.

Tête du Cerro (Ancienne collection Saviron), © cliché Bibliotheque due l'Institut national d'histoire d l'art, collections Jacques Doucet, France. (Our thanks to the Library of the National Institute of Art History, the collections of Jacques Doucet, and the kind release from Dominique Morelon.)

been stolen in 1907 to the office of *Paris-Journal.* The press thus succeeded in recovering stolen art, where the police had failed.

The article that followed stated that the man had acquired the pieces without any idea that they came from the Louvre: "One would not think that such rough specimens could have come from the Louvre and, seduced by the relatively cheap price, he acquired them."[5]

THE CULPRITS

The unfortunate individual turned out to be the avant-garde poet, art columnist, and modern-art mentor Guillaume Apollinaire. He was arrested on September 9, accused of harboring the thief of the Iberian statues and, in the absence of other leads, also charged with the theft of the *Mona Lisa.* Apollinaire declared himself innocent of the robberies, but admitted to knowing the thief, a certain Joseph-Honoré Géry Pieret of Brussels, whom he had housed at the time of both thefts. The poet had employed Pieret as his personal secretary, but, probably due to the man's criminal attitude, he was soon dismissed.[6]

A letter written by Pieret in Apollinaire's defense, and published in *Paris-Journal,* led to the poet's release from jail after a few days.[7] Nonetheless, the episode was to leave a permanent mark on Apollinaire's reputation. His suspected involvement in the theft of *Mona Lisa* led to a right-wing attack on his Polish nationality. Eventually, as pointed out by Peter Read, the "affaire des statuette" became the indirect cause of Apollinaire's death: eager to prove his loyalty toward his adopted country, Apollinaire voluntarily enrolled in the French army at the outbreak of the First World War, dying of influenza while in a hospital because of a head wound received on the battlefield.[8]

Yet, while it was true that Pieret had kept the female bust (stolen in 1911) at Apollinaire's flat, the two heads stolen in 1907 that the poet returned to *Paris-Journal* had been in the possession of someone else—his Spanish painter friend, Pablo Picasso. In her 1933 biography of Picasso, his then-lover, Fernande Olivier, was the first to publicly associate the artist's name with the affair. Olivier told of how, on September 5, 1911, she and Picasso returned to Paris from their holiday at Céret, in the south of France, and immediately met with Apollinaire. "Picasso," she wrote, "was scared to death."[9]

According to Olivier's account, the painter and Apollinaire spent that night together, discussing whether or not they should get rid of the two Iberian heads by throwing them into the Seine. They even went out of the house with the heads in a suitcase, intent on disposing of them. But, "at two in the morning they were back, worn out and still carrying the suitcase with the statues inside . . . In the end Apollinaire went to *Paris-Journal* the next morning, where he returned the unwanted statues under a pledge of secrecy."[10]

Pottier wrote in his report that the director of *Paris-Journal* had informed him that "an honourable person, who had once bought the two heads for a little sum, had been worried by the rumours made in the press about the thefts of the Iberian statuettes, and thinking that he could, without knowing it, own stolen objects, he took them to the newspaper."[11] Relying on his connections at *Paris-Journal,* Apollinaire must have felt safe enough to take it upon himself to return the stolen goods in Picasso's stead.[12]

However, in an interview that he gave to *Le Matin* upon his release from jail, Apollinaire referred to "one of my painter friends" as the unwitting recipient of the two sculptures stolen in 1907. Apollinaire said that he himself had known of the sculptures' provenance, but that, in contrast, his friend was totally unaware of it. He had to admit this, as the police had seized his correspondence, in which they found Pieret's letters relating to the thefts.[13]

Apollinaire told *Le Matin* that, despite his efforts to convince Pieret to return the sculptures immediately, the man wanted to find a buyer at any cost. Thus, according to the poet, one day Pieret heard him mentioning the name of a close artist friend, and decided to pay him a visit. Apollinaire wrote that Pieret went to see Picasso, and that "without imagining that the objects had been stolen, [the artist] bought one of the sculptures for 50 francs. Since he refused to buy the other, Géry Pieret kindly gave it to him."[14]

Although Apollinaire was obliged to give Picasso's name to the police, ending the mystery around the identity of his "artist friend," the poet never made Picasso's name public. It was only in a private letter, dated July 1915, that the poet spoke openly of the painter in association with the theft of the statuettes. This letter was addressed to an intimate friend of Apollinaire at the time, Madeleine Pàges, in response to the woman's shock in learning in the newspapers of the poet's former imprisonment. Apollinaire told his story as follows:

> In 1911, I gave hospitality to a young man, intelligent but crazy and without scruples—a stupid person, rather than a bad one. In 1907 he had stolen from the Louvre two Iberian statues that he sold to Picasso, a great artist, but also without any scruples and whose name was never associated with the affair thanks to my intervention. I tried—in 1911 and in 1907 or 1908—to persuade Picasso to return those statues to the Louvre, but his aesthetic studies urged him to keep them, and from that Cubism was born. He had told me that he had broken [the statues] to discover the mysterious principles of the ancient yet barbaric art to which they belonged. In the meantime I had found a way of liberating him from [this problem] without endangering his honour. My friend Louis Lumet, an official to the Ministry of Fine Arts to whom I had told the story, had thought to turn [the theft] to good purpose by exposing the Louvre in a journalistic coup. We would have proposed to *Le Matin* to show to the public how badly the Louvre's treasures were looked after by first stealing one statue—big deal—and then another—another big deal.[15]

Apollinaire also told Pàges of how Picasso's affection for the two statues ended abruptly in the summer of 1911, after the theft of the *Mona Lisa* and Pieret's (anonymous) appearance in the press: "I went to see Picasso and told him how stupid his behaviour had been, and the risks that he was running. I found a terror-stricken man who told me that he had lied, as the statues were intact. I told him to return them to *Paris-Journal*, which he did." To conclude, the poet recounted his unjust imprisonment, and of how he "was obliged not to say what Picasso's role [in the affair] had been, but that he had been abused and that he did not know that the antiquities that he had bought came from the Louvre."[16]

Although this letter was written long after Apollinaire had made his report to *Le Matin* (and with the clear intent on the poet's part to rehabilitate his image in his beloved's eyes), the intimate character of the document, as well as its temporal distance from the facts, add plausibility to this version of the story. At the time when he was accused of the *Mona Lisa* theft, Apollinaire ran the same risk against which he had warned Picasso: deportation from France. Much of what Apollinaire did and said in 1911 should be considered in relation to his awareness of this risk. It is in this context that the poet's intervention in the affair should be reinterpreted. As he wrote to Pàges, he wanted to help Picasso to get out of the trouble, without harming his reputation. This is why, even when obliged to make the painter's name public, the poet did not divulge Picasso's role in the affair, but defended him, going so far as to say that the painter had no idea where the statues came from.

THE SUSPECTS

In fact, as implied by Apollinaire in his 1915 letter, Picasso knew very well that the two heads came from the Louvre. As recorded by the Italian painter and critic Ardengo Soffici, who was in Paris in 1905, Picasso was a frequent visitor to the Louvre, where he especially "paced around like a hound in search of game between the rooms of Egyptian and Phoenician antiquities."[17]

By this date, Apollinaire was close to both Pieret and Picasso.[18] A postcard sent by Pieret to Picasso in April 1907, and the fact that the man repeatedly referred to the Spanish painter in his correspondence to Apollinaire, document at least a protracted acquaintance between the two men, if not a friendship.[19] From this correspondence, we know that, early in April 1907, Pieret owed the painter money for a commissioned painting. Pieret wrote to Apollinaire from Brussels to say that he "would have paid [Picasso] generously upon his return [to Paris]."[20]

Picasso, who was then living in a bohemian Montmartre squat called "Bateau Lavoir" ("The Laundry Boat"), settled permanently in Paris in 1904. In September of that year, the Louvre inaugurated a little room on its ground floor, dedicated to the museum's Spanish collection.[21] The Iberian room showed reliefs from Osuna and heads from Cerro de los Santos, two important sites in Picasso's native Andalucia. The two heads later owned by Picasso were among the exhibits and were still in the Iberian room when Pieret stole them in 1907. As we learn from Pottier, it was at the end of 1907 that "the majority of the heads" were put in storage.[22] It is in storage that Pieret went to look for the third head that he stole in 1911. Since 1897, Iberian sculpture had featured prominently on the

Louvre's first floor in the form of the famous female bust known as the *Lady of Elche.*[23] Picasso was thus acquainted with some of the best examples of this prehistoric art from the Louvre. Interestingly, at least one French archaeologist suggested that the theft of the *Mona Lisa* might have been conceived by a Spaniard to retaliate against the museum's acquisition of the *Lady of Elche.*[24]

Picasso scholar Anne Baldassari discovered a photograph in the Picasso Archives—which she identified as taken by the artist himself in his "Bateau Lavoir" studio—that shows a man posing next to a plaster cast of the *Lady of Elche.*[25] According to Picasso biographer John Richardson, there are no elements to suggest that the photograph was taken at the "Bateau Lavoir."[26] In fact, a document in the Louvre Archives tells us that a plaster copy of the *Lady of Elche* had been cast in December 1908, as a private donation to the museum to be displayed the Louvre's Iberian room.[27] If the photograph was taken in Paris between 1908 and 1909, as Baldassari believes, then the statue appearing in it is most likely to be the cast belonging to the Louvre. Whether Picasso bought the image at a later time or took it himself, this picture attests to his protracted interest in the contents of the Iberian Room.

In the letter to Pàges, Apollinaire contradicted his previous statement by clearly indicating that Picasso had purchased both statues from Pieret, rather than having been offered one of them as a gift. There are two pieces of evidence that further support this alteration of what Apollinaire had told the police and *Le Matin.* First, Pieret had described the "gift statue" as "a man's head with enormous ears—a detail that fascinated me," which is precisely how, years later, Picasso was to refer to the influence of Iberian art on *Les Demoiselles d'Avignon.* In an interview of 1960, the painter said: "Do you remember that episode in which I was involved? When Apollinaire stole some statuettes from the Louvre? They were Iberian statuettes [. . .] well, if you look at the ears of *Les Demoiselles d'Avignon,* you'll recognise the ears of those sculptures!"[28] Second, the fact that Pieret mistakenly described the statues as Phoenician indicates that someone else must have directed his attention towards the small and out-of-the-way Iberian Room—someone who had a special interest in the sculptures displayed there. This person was most likely Picasso. Alternatively, it could possibly have been Apollinaire, who perhaps commissioned Pieret to steal the sculptures, to please his painter friend.

As noted at the time, the Iberian pieces had no financial value then: they were pre-classical artefacts made of poor materials (bronze and limestone). Their interest, as Pottier wrote, was specifically archaeological in nature, relative to the little-known history of the Iberians, the pre-Roman inhabitants of today's Spain, an ethnic group only recently studied.[29] This is why an article on the first Iberian theft of 1906 suggested the possibility that the thief might have been "a possessive and discrete collector who has no interest in money, but keeps [the statues] in the most secret part of his flat, getting drunk on their beauty in solitude."[30] The identikit corresponds to that of Picasso, who, as partner Fernande Olivier wrote, "Took great care of his [1907] *gifts*, and kept them buried in a wardrobe."[31]

Around this time, Picasso had begun to collect feverishly. In 1908, he bought a large female portrait by the Douanier Rousseau, and was filling his studio with African art.[32] It has been noted that a compositional model for *Les Demoiselles d'Avignon* was a painting by El Greco, *The Opening of the Fifth Seal* or *The Vision of Saint John*, which Picasso knew in 1907 from the collection of a fellow expatriate in Paris, the Spanish painter Ignacio Zuloaga.[33]

Picasso's renowned passion for collecting verged on the pathological. He loved to surround himself with Spanish souvenirs, and must have been prompted by Zuloaga's example to own his own specimen of "Iberian art." Furthermore, the account that Picasso would later give of his first visit to the ethnographic museum of the Trocadéro, around the time he acquired the Iberian heads, reveals his taste for trespassing behind the closed doors of museums.[34] As we learn from Pottier's report to Homolle, the small, hidden Iberian room was closed more often than not.[35]

Pieret and Apollinaire tried to spin the Iberian thefts as a philanthropic act, the intention of which was to demonstrate that the Louvre was badly guarded. However, this was hardly news at the time: Pieret's thefts had not been the only thefts in the Department of Oriental Antiquities, nor had they been the first to hit the headlines. Late in 1906, several French newspapers reported the disappearance of two small bronzes, an Egyptian statuette and a small Iberian bronze representing a female figure.[36] The latter had entered the Louvre collections only a few months earlier, and was kept next to the *Lady of Elche*, on the museum's ground floor.[37]

Both objects were found two years later in the shop of a hairdresser, leading to the imprisonment of one of the Louvre's guards. After the "affaire des statuettes," however, the guard's lawyer wrote to *Le Matin* to reassert the innocence of his client, saying that, "given the [new] evidence," it was possible that Géry Pieret was the author of the 1906 theft as well.[38] Whether this was the case, we will probably never know, but the three "stealing campaigns" of Iberian objects in the Louvre certainly have a common trait: the thieves knew very well what they were after.

There are further, practical arguments suggesting that Pieret was not alone in carrying out the thefts. The heads that he admitted to having stolen weighed approximately seven kilos each. After the restitution of the first statue, the press rightly wondered how, despite the bad security conditions of the Louvre at the time, the thief had managed to carry a piece of that weight under his coat without catching people's eye. Knowing that Pieret lived at Apollinaire's home at the time of the thefts, his deed seems all the more remarkable. In his letter to *Paris-Journal,* Pieret gave an epic account of how he had slipped away from the Louvre in 1911, hiding the Iberian bust under his coat. Considering, however, that Apollinaire was then living in Auteil, in the distant 16th arrondissement, it seems unlikely that Pieret carried the bulky and heavy statues all the way there. It is even less likely that he brought the two heads stolen in March 1907 to Apollinaire's home by himself; for at that time, the poet was living even further away from the Louvre, in the village of Le Vésinet at the outside edge of Paris. It seems plausible that someone waited for the thief outside the Louvre, probably in a carriage, and helped him to carry the loot. This same person could have helped Pieret within the museum, not only carrying the statues outside, but also directing his choice while inside. This person may have been the same one who, directly or indirectly, had prompted him to steal the heads.

Was it Picasso, eager to surround himself with Iberian souvenirs with which he would have been familiar from his years in Spain, and that he wanted to liberate from the Louvre?[39] Or was it his friend Apollinaire who, combining adventure, anthropological interest, iconoclastic bias, and friendly generosity, directed Pieret's egocentrism towards Picasso's interest? Moreover, was the theft commissioned, or was the choice of Iberian statuary the random selection of Pieret, who "happened" to choose the type of statuary that interested Picasso the most at the time?

An answer could only be provided by new documentation. What seems to be certain is that Picasso was aware that the two heads that he owned had been stolen by Pieret, and that these particular statues had been chosen because Pieret expected Picasso to buy them from him, since they had no financial value. The painter had seen these heads in the Louvre and admired them. Significantly, once they were in his possession, he did not keep them on display, but inside his wardrobe. There is already enough evidence to convict Picasso of having knowingly purchased stolen art. There is substantial circumstantial evidence that either he or Apollinaire commissioned the 1907 Iberian thefts, and perhaps even helped Pieret to carry them out.

The reexamination of Picasso's involvement in the "affaire des statuettes" is interesting for other reasons as well: on the one hand, it reopens the art-historical debate on the role of Iberian art in Picasso's œuvre between 1904 and 1907, leading art historians to rethink the relationship between European prehistory and the "discovery" of non-Western art by modern artists. On the other hand, it prompts a reconsideration of the boundaries between artistic appropriation and theft. Furthermore, this still-unsolved case shows the possibilities offered by the collaboration of scholars and investigative authorities to shed light on art crimes of the past, the present, and the future.

NOTES

1. "La Joconde a disparu du Louvre!" *Paris-Journal,* Aug. 23, 1911, 1.

2. Edmond Pottier, August 29, 1911, Archives des musées nationaux, Musée du Louvre, folder A15. All translations are by the author.

3. "Un voleur nous rapporte un œuvre derobée au Louvre," *Paris-Journal,* Aug. 29, 1911, 1. The two heads stolen in 1907 were recognised by Pottier as entries AM 1140 and 1141 of the Louvre's inventory of Mediterranean Antiquities: Pottier to Homolle Aug. 31, 1911, as in n.2.

4. This bust, stolen in 1911, carried the inventory number AM 880, Ibid.

5. "Le Louvre récupère ses richesses," *Paris-Journal,* Sept. 6, 1911, 1.

6. For the surviving biographical documentation on Pieret, see Richardson, John *A Life of Picasso: 1907–1917—The Painter of Modern Life,* Pimlico: London, 1997, vol. 2, 20–21.

7. Ignace D'Ormesan (alias Géry Pieret), Letter, Sept. 9, 1911, published in *Paris-Journal,* Sept. 12, 1911, 1.

8. Peter Read, *Picasso et Apollinaire. Les métamorphoses de la mémoire 1905-1973,* Jean-Michel Place: Paris, 1995, 71.

9. Fernande Olivier, *Picasso et ses amis* (1933), Pygmalion: Paris, 2002, 184.

10. Ibid., 184–85.

11. Edmond Pottier, Sept. 6, 1911, as in n.2.

12. Apollinaire had long worked for *Paris-Journal.* Ironically, he had been among the first correspondents to comment on the *Mona Lisa* theft as the art columnist of *L'Intransigeant:* Apollinaire, Guillaume, "Le rapt de la Joconde," *L'Intransigeant,* Aug. 24, 1911, 1.

13. Christine Jacquet-Pfau and Michel Décaudin, "L'Affaire des statuettes. Suite sans fin...," *Que vlo-ve?,* 23 (July–Sept. 1987), 21–23.

14. "M. Guillaume Apollinaire raconte l'histoire de son secrétaire Géry Pieret, baron Ignace d'Ormesan, voleur au Louvre et en quelques autres lieux"; "M. Apollinaire prouve que Géry Pieret n'a pas pu voler la *Joconde,*" *Le Matin,* Sept. 13, 1911, 1.

15. Guillaume Apollinaire, Letter to Madeleine Pàges, July 30, 1915, in Apollinaire, *Lettres à Madeleine. Tendre comme le souvenir,* Gallimard: Paris, 2005, 96–98.

16. Ibid., 98.

17. Ardengo Soffici, *Ricordi di vita artistica e letteraria,* Florence, 1931, 47.

18. A caricature of Pieret by Henri Frick was drawn in Apollinaire's diary on September 30, 1904. Read as in n.8, 71.

19. Postcard addressed to Picasso from Bruxelles and signed Guillaume Apollinaire and Géry Pieret, April 13, 1907: Caizergues, Pierre and Seckel, Hélène (eds.) *Picasso Apollinaire. Corréspondances,* Gallimard: Paris, 1992, 59.

20. Letter and postcard sent by Pieret to Apollinaire from Brussels respectively on date April 4, 1907, and April 7, 1907: Stallano, Jacqueline "Une relation encombrante: Géry Pieret," in Michel Décaudin (ed.), *Amis européens d'Apollinaire,* Sorbonne nouvelle: Paris, 1995, 17.

21. *Chroniques des arts,* Nov. 24, 1904, quoted in Charles Aulanier, *Histoire du palais et du Musée du Louvre,* vol. 9, Musées nationaux: Paris, 1964, 137; Maria-Luisa Catoni, "Parigi, 1904: Picasso 'iberico' e le *Demoiselles d'Avignon,*" *Bollettino dell'arte,* nos. 62–63 (July–October 1990).

22. Pottier, as in n.2.

23. The *Lady of Elche* was on display in the Sarzec room on the first floor. See, Pottier to Homolle, Aug. 30, 1911, as in n.2.

24. Letter of the directer of the *Revue des études anciennes* to Homolle, Sept. 6, 1911, as in n.2.

25. Anne Baldassari, *Picasso Photographe, 1901–1916,* Réunion des musées nationaux: Paris, 1994, 106–7.

26. Richardson, as in n.6, 256.

27. Archives des musées nationaux, Musée du Louvre, A8.

28. Romuald Dor de la Souchère, *Picasso à Antibes,* Hazan: Paris, 1960, 15.

29. Pottier, as in n.2.

30. *Le Matin,* Nov. 10, 1906.

31. Olivier, as in n.9, 183. Emphasis added.

32. For Picasso's collection of Henri Rousseau's paintings: Frèches-Thory, Claire "From Sarcasm to Canonisation: Critical Fortune," in F. Morris and C. Green (eds.), *Henri Rousseau: Jungles in Paris,* exh. cat., Tate Modern, London, 2005, 174–76.

33. Richardson, as in n.6, 429–31.

34. André Malreaux, *La Tête d'obsidienne,* Gallimard : Paris, 1974, 18.

35. Pottier, as in n.2.

36. "On vol au Louvre", *Le Matin,* Nov. 10, 1906; "On a volé au Louvre, et on y volera demain, si des solutions serieuses ne sont prises." *L'Intransigeant,* Nov. 11, 1906, 2.

37. Gift of Horace Sandars to the Louvre (between Dec. 7, 1905, and March 3, 1906), as in n.25.

38. "Les vols du Louvre. Un défendeur s'interpose en faveur de son client", *Le Matin,* Sept. 22, 1911.

39. For Picasso's knowledge of Iberian art since his years in Barcelona, Patricia Leighten, *Re-Ordering the Universe. Picasso and Anarchism, 1897–1914,* Princeton University Press: Princeton, NJ, 1989, 79–80.

Chapter 6

Art, Terrorism, and Organized Crime

Bojan Dobovšek

Professor Dobovšek is a member of the Commission for the Prevention of Corruption (which is a prototype for preventing corruption in all EU nations) as representative of the judiciary branch of power and representative of Slovenia in GRECO. The editor, Noah Charney, asked the questions of Professor Dobovšek and it is used with permission.

What is the definition of "organized crime" or a "criminal syndicate"?

Organized crime varies between countries, but one common worldwide definition would run as follows: To qualify as organized crime, a group of at least three professionally linked individuals would need to work together over an extended period of time, in criminal enterprises that may include extortion, corruption, intimidation, smuggling, confidence tricks, or money laundering, with the goal of earning money through criminal acts. Another key is that organized crime is distinguished by favoring long-term mutual goals over short-term enrichment. A criminal syndicate is a more organized, hierarchically structured, larger organized crime group, with a command structure that sends criminals on assignments for the benefit of the syndicate—the distinction being that an organized crime group could be four partners who rob banks together, whereas a criminal syndicate would be a larger enterprise where the leaders hire lower-ranking criminals to rob banks on behalf of their syndicate.

What are methods by which crime syndicates smuggle illicit goods, such as drugs, arms, and stolen art, across borders?

Methods are traditional, dating back many decades, and in some cases centuries. The old Balkan route and Silk Road are still primary arteries for the movement of illicit goods. What began as drug smuggling routes, has now evolved into two-way arteries for all manner of illicit goods. The route used to be one-way: drugs were smuggled to Europe to be sold. Now drugs still flow into Europe, but other goods flow out to Eastern Europe, the Middle East, and Asia. For instance, stolen cars, as well as stolen art, are flowing out of Europe.

Criminals constantly invent new smuggling methods, some sophisticated, and some incredibly primitive. An example of the primitive: hiding goods in the base of a truck, which is then filled with other legitimate goods. An amusing example of the sophisticated: drugs were imbedded in the plastic hangers of men's dress suits. The suits were sold legitimately to members of a syndicate, who were interested only in the drugs inside the plastic hangers.

Is there an estimated quantity or value on the money made per year by organized crime in the drug trade, in the arms trade, and in the illicit art trade?

No number is sufficiently grounded in hard data to be certain, mostly because we are only aware of a portion of the total amount of crime that occurs. If we knew of all of it, we would be able to stop more of it! Depending on who you ask, the numbers are always different. The most popular number with reference to criminal profit from trade in illicit art and antiquities is $6 billion per year. But this is just a guess based on the incidents of which we are aware, and the real number is certainly much higher, because we are not aware of much art crime. The drug and arms trades are significantly larger than art crime, coming in at numbers one and two, respectively, on the scale of largest criminal trades worldwide. Art crime has averaged at number three on that list for decades, since the early 1960s. The largest well-informed, scholarly estimate I have heard is that the total black market (including all black market goods) could be worth as much as 50 percent of the total world's annual legal market.

Roughly how many known organized crime syndicates operate worldwide?

Each country has at least one of its own syndicates, and within those syndicates exist countless subgroups, which qualify as organized crime. There are the obvious ones, such as Cosa Nostra, the Camorra, and the N'Draghetta in Italy. But they are not exclusively national. Turkish and Serbian Mafias operate in Germany, for instance, thanks to immigration and the open borders in the EU. Likewise, it is common for Mafias from former colonies to operate within the colonial nation. For instance, in France, there are Algerian and Moroccan syndicates. Regional syndicates operate within countries (in Russia, there is a Chechnyan Mafia, for instance). Ex–secret police are commonly syndicate leaders in former Soviet bloc countries. Nowadays, Yakuza in Japan or Hong Kong Triads are most influential worldwide.

What is the organizational structure of organized crime syndicates?

There tend to be two bureaucratic patterns.

1. A pyramid structure, with one or more bosses at the top, and a strict descending hierarchy. This is the so-called Weber model (he was the criminologist who published a definition of it), and is used by state institutions like the police to reconstruct criminal syndicate structures. But the state's attempt to fill in the pyramid never looks as clean as it does in our criminology textbooks! More small groups (called *coscas* in Italy) form a bigger group, a Mafia. A group of syndicates form an even bigger group like La Cupola.
2. Cell structure, with family-based smaller groups that function independently within a given territory. This is common in Russian and Albanian organized crime, and may be most familiar to people in terms of Afghani warlords ruling over small pocket territories. These independent cells, which may consist of as few as 10 people, are the most difficult to infiltrate, because they are often formed based solely on extended family relations—to join, you would have to marry into the family. Conglomerations of such smaller territory-based groups combine to form something like the Camorra in Naples. Smaller groups have territories, which they cover under the overall umbrella of the larger group. These smaller groups often compete with each other, fighting amongst themselves, although they are all ostensibly in the same overall syndicate. Smaller groups cannot earn a lot of money without sharing it with the larger group. So while smaller groups may launch their own independent operations, the umbrella syndicate must benefit from the crime. Much art crime is on the initiative of these smaller groups.

Keep in mind that a group of individual small-time criminals who plot one or more crimes together with communal, long-term goals beyond immediate financial benefit, also qualify as organized crime.

How does the barter and collateral system between syndicates function?

More and more, we see a simple exchange of goods. This is due to the advanced technology that permits money-tracking by security or police. As policing grows more high-tech, crime retreats to more traditional, low-tech methods, which fly beneath police radar. It is now common to see virtual money deals, referred to as "Hawala Banking," where no actual money for an illicit deal is moved, but equivalent values are moved by representatives from within the same international crime syndicate.

For example, a member of an international syndicate, who is based in the Netherlands, arranges to buy a shipment of drugs from a member of another international syndicate, for €1 million. The drugs are handed over in the Netherlands. But rather than transfer the money within the Netherlands (which will arouse suspicion), a member of the purchasing syndicate—based in Albania, let's say—will give the €1 million to a member of the selling syndicate, who is also in Albania. So the €1 million is changing hands between syndicates, but the monetary transaction is remote from the exchange of goods. This removes the possibility that individual bank notes can be tracked, and lessens the likelihood of the drug transaction and the monetary transaction being linked. The other big problem is when migrants are selling money from EU countries to home countries through Hawala banking system without being noticed in legal market. They usually earn money through illegal economy so they can not transfer it through banks.

In general, crime syndicates have more money and are better technically equipped than police. Still, criminal syndicates often have found that simpler methods are more effective. They therefore combine high- and low-tech techniques.

What is the relative difficulty level of turning drugs, illicit arms, or stolen art into cash on a black market? Is there a calculation of risk and relative profit for each category?

It is harder and harder to launder money, thanks to new tracking techniques. On the other hand, the tax-free nations around the world (Luxembourg, Arab states, Cayman Islands, etc.) make it easy to hide money. Money is often used to corrupt politicians now, while trade involves money less often and rather relies on the harder-to-track barter system. Organized crime, generally speaking, has enough money, in their opinion. That may sound funny, but among the leaders of criminal syndicates, the money is of secondary importance to power. These days at the highest level, organized crime is fighting for political power, not money. So trade is in barter, but money is used to buy power—corrupting politicians, for instance.

After September 11, terrorism became infinitely more difficult. But organized crime was affected, too, because, to fight terrorism, governments cracked down on the drug trade and money laundering. So organized crime had to come up with new ways to hide money. Art crime is one of those ways. We also see more production in fake brand-name clothing. Buying art legitimately, too, is a way that criminals can launder money in a legitimate investment that will retain its value over time.[1] Buying factories, property, art—criminals on average may lose about 30 percent of their dirty money in the transaction, by overpaying or paying to cover for the fact of their money having a dirty origin. But if they end up with an artwork or property worth 70 percent of the money they began with, it is now invested in legitimate goods that retain their value; and no one can hunt down the dirty money, as it has been converted into a legitimate possession.

Who works for organized crime syndicates? Is there any general profile for leaders and administrators?

This always varies, and generalizations are not particularly helpful. We cannot say based on someone's background who is a candidate to become a criminal syndicate leader. But we can define the common goals of criminal syndicate leaders—not who they were, but who they hope to become, what they hope to achieve by their "work."

They all want to become important, rich, influential society members, appearing in magazines, entering the elite—becoming a new aristocracy. And you can see how collecting or being involved in art can achieve this goal. Syndicate leaders buy castles, yachts, and legitimate art. They seek publicity that their wealth and influence can bring, and simply gloss over the fact that their wealth and notoriety comes from criminal activities, which are hidden behind legitimate-looking front operations.

But leaders, particularly in Balkan syndicates, can become folk heroes to ordinary people, workers and the poor, because organized crime members give the people what they want in material terms, literally distributing goods to buy loyalty and support and silence. They also embody the ideal of hard work leading to success (even if it is criminal). In Eastern Europe, it's still hard to get a job, but organized crime will give you a job, that sort of thing.

People note that stolen art worth €10 million on a legitimate market might be sold on the black market for €200,000, and assume that criminals are inept or somehow losing out. How do career criminals see this equation? Are they frustrated by the economics?

For a street criminal, the equation is not the difference in earnings between €10 million and €200,000, but rather from having started with zero, paid out nothing, and ended up with €200,000 in tax-free profit. Most of the money in such transactions will be in cash, so it needs to be invested into something legitimate that will retain its value. So profit from an art theft might be invested in buying art legitimately at auction, to hide the dirty money in an "investment" that will retain its value. Ironic, isn't it?

With regard to international crime syndicates, we must switch our mind-sets. Big criminal syndicates have a lot of money. They do not know what to do with it all. Their main problem is how to hide the money that they already have. Leaders are most concerned with laundering the money they have, even if they lose much of it in the conversion to clean money. So dirty monetary value is less important than goods which can lead to clean money.

This mind-set, this long-term thinking, is a key component that separates the most successful crime syndicates from small gangs of thieves. The former are interested in turning criminal activity into legitimate wealth, social elevation, and power. The latter are interested in getting as much money as possible, as quickly as possible, to satisfy short-term goals, without regard for the money being dirty.

When and how did organized crime turn their attentions to stealing art?

There are examples throughout history going back centuries. You can look at Adam Worth's theft of Gainsborough's *Duchess of Devonshire* in 1876 as one early example—he ran his own international crime syndicate. But the big date is 1960–61, when the Union Corse, which is the Corsican Mafia based in Marseilles, began stealing Cézanne and Picasso paintings from the Riviera. From that point on, other syndicates started to notice that art was high-value, was easy to transport and smuggle, and was not particularly well guarded.

Art crime, particularly antiquities looting, has been linked as a significant funding source for terrorist groups. How does this function? Why particularly antiquities?

Areas where terrorist groups are based tend to be full of antiquities still buried in unexcavated archaeological sites. Antiquities are cheap and may be sold at full value with only a fake provenance. Antiquities are easy to smuggle through organized crime trade routes, passing them off as modern fakes, like tourist souvenirs. Antiquities can even be sold on eBay.

It is also useful in terms of getting money to terrorist cells in target countries, such as Europe or the United States. Money received from the purchase of antiquities remains in the country of purchase, for instance the United States. The money does not get wired back to the country of origin of the terrorist group and the looted antiquity. This therefore saves the trouble of getting the money from the origin country to the target country. Police focus on following the money trail, which they hope will lead back to leaders of terrorist groups. But gathering valuable goods from the earth, which are registered nowhere and do not "exist" to the modern world until the moment they are illegally excavated, then selling them in Europe or the United States, allows the money to remain in the target country, preventing the tracing of the source of the money.

Which organized crime groups are active in the Balkans? How much art crime happens in the Balkans?

In the Balkans, there are groups by nationalities within states. The main operators are Albanian, Turkish, Serbian, and Montenegrin. Most art trade from the Balkans is in icons, traditional paintings, or statues by unknown artists, which are sold for low thousands of euros—well below what most authorities would pay attention to, but national heritage nonetheless. These works are often stolen from churches, which tend to be uninsured and without security. The traditional Balkan black market is in goods that are less important, less valuable, and that do not attract attention, but accumulate in value by quantity rather than quality.

A notable example of a Serbian organized crime group was run by Arkan. Arkan was leader of a Serbian paramilitary group, who used the Balkan War situation to loot for private use, pillaging territories that his small army had secured. They mostly took TVs, DVDs, and such. But they also seized castles, museums, and libraries. After the war, the goods within these buildings were gone, but no one knew at which point they were taken. Of course, in the heat of war, people were busier trying not to get killed, and were not paying attention to what was happening to cultural goods.

Arkan's small army was liberating territories and helping poor families —at the same time they were looting. The popular local mythology made him out to be something of a hero to the locals he helped. The goods he seized would be dismissed as a means of paying for the army's upkeep. He was long suspected to have been involved in the theft of Turner paintings, on loan from the Tate Britain, from an exhibition in Germany.

How has the end of Yugoslavia affected organized crime in the Balkans?

Now smuggling requires more border crossings, making it more difficult. Emerging states need to fulfill standards of EU security, raising the standards. On the other hand, state institutions were reestablished in a new format, so there are still not enough well-trained and educated people in the new EU states to fight organized crime. The most experienced officers retired from public duty and formed their own private security or detective companies when Yugoslavia ended. New EU countries entered so-called "turbo capitalism," in which former Socialists want to take advantage of the new situation to earn as much money as possible, as quickly as possible. Normal employment is still hard to find in Eastern Europe, and does not pay well. Organized crime pays well and quickly.

We joke that the new national sport is how to avoid paying taxes. Tax institutions in new states tend not to be well equipped, trained, and manned to catch tax evaders. So the biggest problem in organized crime in the former Yugoslavia is the gray economy, questionable but not overtly criminal transactions, which are the most difficult to police. And people like organized crime because they supply what states prohibit or is too expensive.

Are there characteristics of art thefts that suggest that organized crime is behind it, rather than an individual thief of thieves?

There are a few.

1. If the crime is committed as one of several crimes in the same pattern.

2. If important works are stolen (because of caché, which organized crime seeks).
3. If there was an extortion attempt involved in the theft or leading up to the theft.
4. If an insider was paid off in advance of the theft.
5. If the theft was well coordinated and speed-oriented.
6. If there was a threat of violence that was not acted upon.

Organized crime usual tries first to achieve their ends through corruption, rather than violence. Speed is preferable to violence, though the implied or explicit threat of violence (rarely followed up) is common. Organized crime is usually less violent than nonsyndicate criminals. Violence is only used in extortion or collecting money, or in targeted assassinations of prominent figures. Threat of violence always precedes actual violence—violence is the last resort, only if all else fails. Actual violence in the course of theft is the realm of less able criminals.

Why has art crime gone overlooked as a field of academic study? What needs to happen in order to advance the academic study of art crime?

Criminologists are not knowledgeable about the art trade and its history, and art historians are not trained in criminology. There have been few conferences and no journals which can provoke academics to turn their attentions to the new subject, so there was no unifying factor. Conferences and peer-reviewed journals are the best ways to lure academics into a new field. This is one of the best things ARCA is doing to encourage more scholars to turn their attentions to art crime.

Educating young students, especially undergraduates, on the true nature of art crime and its severity is the best way to help the future study of art crime. Develop it as a respected field of study, and take advantage of its native appeal and intrigue.

These days, if you do not appear in the media, you are not present at all beyond your small circle of friends. Therefore we should work with the media, stepping out as spokespeople in defense of art. Working with the media is the best way to get people to focus on this field and to help curb art crime.

NOTE

1. Editor's Note: This point is developed further by Nelson in Chapter 19.

Chapter 7

Fakes and Deception: Examining Fraud in the Art Market

Kenneth Polk
Duncan Chappell

Art fraud, especially the issue of fake works, is a recurring problem for the international art market. Despite the widespread international concern we have observed in our interviews with major market figures, and despite frequent attention to this problem by the mass media, in fact, cases of such fraud rarely work their way through the criminal justice system. In Australia over the past three decades, we have been able to identify only three cases of art fraud that have been successfully prosecuted.[1] We know from our fieldwork that the problem is much greater than this record of prosecution would suggest. Understanding why there is so little attention paid to art fraud by the criminal justice system is one of the major purposes of this discussion.

ART FRAUD AND THE LAW[2]

A starting point is to examine the complicated requirements of legal steps to combat fraud, and how difficult it is to fit these onto the workings of the art market. For one, the contemporary art market is inherently international in its reach, whereas the criminal laws defining fraud vary by country and, within countries such as Australia and the United States, by state or territory. As would be expected, given the complexities of international business and capital, fraud laws are extraordinarily complicated in their makeup, structure, and workings. Nonetheless, at least in the Common Law countries such as Australia, there are likely to be a number of common evidentiary issues and elements that will need to be present before any fraud investigation or prosecution can proceed: (1) there must be some form of deception by a defendant, and (2) this deception must have produced some form of harm to (3) a victim, who was in fact deceived, and (4) there was some level of knowledge, intent, or dishonesty on the part of the defendant.[3] The precise charge(s) that may flow from any fraud investigation will depend upon the particular evidentiary mix surrounding these four elements and the peculiarities of the fraud law in any given jurisdiction.

PROCEEDING WITH A CASE OF ART FRAUD: THE MATERIAL ELEMENTS EXAMINED

Accounting for the scarcity of prosecutions in art fraud requires a consideration of the workings of these four elements. The first of these, deception, gives the unique and distinctive stamp to cases of art fraud involving suspected fake works of art, while the fourth (proving intent or dishonesty) can provide major stumbling blocks for a prosecution. Therefore, it is these to which we must devote most of our attention. While it can be involved, the harm element (the second on the list) reduces itself most commonly to a demonstration of some financial loss to a victim. The third element, calling for demonstration that the victim was deceived, can be straightforward in most cases involving art fraud.

The issue may arise in this context, however, as in the case of a group of individuals uncovered in our fieldwork who were responsible for protecting the reputation of a living but elderly Australian artist. The group had discovered that fakes of that artist were being floated onto the market through a particular dealer. Frustrated by their inability to obtain police cooperation, one of the group took the step of actually purchasing one of these fakes. This was then taken to the police to demonstrate that the frauds were taking place, but the group was then informed that no prosecution could proceed because they knew all along that the work was not authentic. That is, they had not been deceived, as is required by this element, although it may still have been possible to proceed on the basis that an attempted fraud had occurred.

PROVING DECEPTION

In common with other patterns of fraud, art fraud can take a number of forms, including involvement in insurance scams, tax violations, or misappropriation of the property of a victim. Most of the cases, and discussions, of art fraud, however, take place around the issue of authenticity, and most of these are concerned with the introduction of fakes onto the market. In these cases, the issue of deception will hinge on what can be demonstrated about a work, or body of work, in terms of whether these are what they purport to be—that is, are they "authentic?" Put in everyday language, in a typical case, what will be at issue is whether a given object can be demonstrated to be a fake.

It is highly unlikely that agents of the law or criminal justice system will possess the expertise to assess the authenticity of a work of art, so inevitably the courts must turn to art experts for assistance. In approaching this task, such experts are likely to draw upon three different lines of activity.[4]

First, they examine the *provenance* of the work—that is, what is known about its ownership history. While in some instances, especially in the case of famous works of well-known artists (particularly if they have been in public collections for an extended period of time), this may be a relatively direct matter to assess, in many other cases, the ownership history will be clouded by such problems as poor records, movement through hands of different relatives, or prior sales by firms no longer in existence (among other matters). For a famous example, while it is known that *St. George and the Dragon* (now in the National Gallery of Art in Washington, DC) was painted in 1506, and while its ownership history from about 1627 is reasonably well documented (including its accession by Catherine the Great, and then the intriguing story of the sale of the work by the Hermitage Museum in the early twentieth century), little can be established about its whereabouts for its first 120 years.[5] It also needs to be pointed out that serious fakers know that provenance is an issue, and their faking skills will be brought to bear on the issue of demonstrating provenance as well as creating the work.

Second, the expert witnesses might carry out various forms of *scientific analysis* on the work in question. Such probing might involve chemical analysis of the pigments of a painting (to establish whether the materials used are consistent with those employed by the artist or in the time of the artist), examination of the makeup of the canvas employed, various forms of photographic analyses of the underpainting of the work, and so on. Historically, science has proven most useful where it can be definitively established that the work could *not* have been done by the artist or in the artist's time—for example, as where a pigment has been used that was not in existence at the time the work was supposed to have been done. Flescher puts the matter this way: "Contrary to the layperson's perception, we have found sophisticated scientific tests to be far more effective in ruling out than ruling in."[6] While a pigment test may show that a work could not have been done at the time claimed for an artist (ruling out), a different finding that the pigment was consistent with that in use at the time only supports a claim of "consistency" of materials, not the conclusion that this material was used by the particular artist for this specific painting (inability to rule in).

The third line of assessment of experts will be to carry out a *stylistic analysis* of the work to establish if the elements of the work are consistent with the known style of the artist. In using this approach, the expert will be drawing upon a wealth of experience regarding the artist in question, and will range over issues concerned with technique, the motifs being explored at the particular time in the life of the artist, the way the subjects are treated within the work, and similar issues. While the assessment may be influenced to some degree by scientific analysis, often the ultimate result is an opinion that may seem highly qualitative and subjective in nature.[7]

CASES WHERE FRAUD IS NOT AN ISSUE

When the art experts examine the art material in question, their findings can go in a number of directions. In at least two of these, any attempt to prosecute will founder.

One kind of finding, of course, is that the works are actually not fakes; that is, they are authentic. Such findings are obviously to be anticipated, since one has to assume that a majority of art sales involve art that would pass authentication muster. To be sure, at times, peculiar twists and bends might be encountered. Quite often, for example, known artists have painted many different versions of the same scene. Therefore, what might at first appear to be an unauthentic copy of a known work of a master in fact is done by the hand of that master. This was illustrated recently when a painting previously thought to be a copy by another artist (because of another rendition of the same subject, which is part of the collection of the Musées Royaux des Beaux-Arts in Brussels) was determined to be an authentic work by Frans Hals, and was then placed on the market at auction by Sotheby's London.[8] Occasionally in the history of a painting, spurious additions have been made that might cloud the authenticity question. Sometime, probably in the eighteenth or early nineteenth century, an individual, apparently attempting to increase the sale price of what was considered to be a not particularly distinguished Dutch painting, falsely attached to the work the signature of the then-popular Pieter de Hooch. Some might consider the work from that point on to be a "fake," since it is certainly not a de Hooch, except that the real artist, indisputably, was the far more valuable Johannes Vermeer.[9]

A second kind of finding that will make a prosecution difficult is one in which art experts are unable to agree on the status of a work, and therefore it would prove difficult to argue for a fraud conviction that meets the standard of being "beyond reasonable doubt." One illustration of such disagreement is found in a symposium convened by the Metropolitan Museum in New York, where a large panel of experts debated the authenticity of the Chinese work *Riverbank*.[10] Some argued that the work was the creation of the modern painter/fraudster Zhang Daqian (1899–1983), while others held that it was the work of the tenth-century master Dong Yuan (active in the 1930s to the 1960s), with no clear agreement emerging from the gathering.

Probably the best-known circumstances in which there is expert disagreement concern the works of Rembrandt. In the early 1900s, it was claimed that a total of 9,428 works by this painter had been imported into the United States alone,[11] a figure that is made quite improbable by the more recent scientific and stylistic analyses carried out by the Rembrandt Research Project.[12] The work of that prestigious group has been challenged, including by the Frick Museum in New York, which rejected the suggestion that their *Polish Rider* was not by Rembrandt, and continued to display the work as by the artist despite the Project's contrary findings.[13] To show the bends and twists that can occur in the art world, the Rembrandt Research Project subsequently changed its mind regarding the *Polish Rider,* and has now concluded that the work is a genuine Rembrandt, but added that others might have had a role in its creation.

CASES WHERE AUTHENTICITY IS AN ISSUE

With these two directions out of the way, attention may be turned to those situations where, according to the expert witnesses, there is convincing evidence that the work or works in question are fraudulent. There are two major forms that such frauds can take. One is for the faker in question to copy a known work; that is, to attempt to duplicate in an exact way an existing work. The second is to create a "pastiche" or "imagined reproduction," where the faker produces a work that duplicates the style of a particular artist, but does not attempt to recreate a specific work.

The Problem of Copies

When the expert examines a particular work of art, that person may come to realize quickly, based on knowledge of the field of art, that the work is a copy of a known work of an artist with an established reputation.

Immediately, it must be pointed out that there will be many situations in which the copy has been created with no fraudulent intent. On a visit to any major collection around the globe, one is likely to find persons in front of an easel engaged in the perfectly legitimate practice of copying the work of a known master. This is a well-established tradition for the teaching and learning of art technique. Further, extending back into history, this was a way of creating more art that was more accessible than was possible with one, often extremely expensive, copy found in a public collection, or perhaps hidden away in a private collection. Today, a number of outlets offer "genuine reproductions" such as communities of artists that have emerged in China as a response to a demand for "quality" paintings that are copies of famous originals.[14] Finally, it is possible that a work was originally created as a copy, but its origins have become blurred with the passage of time, so much so that its identity as a copy becomes lost, and it comes to be identified as an original work.

There is nothing illegal in these aforementioned situations because, as described, the creation of these works does not involve dishonest deception. Where this process crosses the line into illegality is when the individual selling the art: (1) is aware of the fact that the object is not authentic; and (2) knowingly attempts to deceive a victim into purchasing that object as an authentic work rather than a copy.

This is best exemplified when the works are created with deception and fraud in mind. As an example of what would appear to be an excessive case, Kurz claims that Rohrich (1782–1834) created not just one spurious Cranach, "pretending" to represent the Duchess Sophie of Saxony, but then went on to produce "about thirty identical versions."[15] A modern variation of this scenario was uncovered in New York in 2004, when the dealer Ely Sakhai was found to have purchased 25 separate original, authentic paintings with their proper provenance documents. Sakhai had the works expertly copied, and he then sold, first, the false, copied paintings with the genuine provenance documents; then at a later date, he also sold the authentic original works.[16] Another form that such fraudulent copying can take is where inexpensive photographically produced copies of works are claimed to be created as limited-edition prints, as occurred in the 1980s with the sale of fraudulent copies of works claimed to be originals done by Dali.[17]

"Imagined Reproduction" or "Pastiche"

The most common form of work done by serious, and serial, art fraudsters—what amounts to the master fakers—consists of creating a "pastiche." In this case, rather than simply making a copy of a particular existing work, a new object instead is "made in the manner of an artist."[18] The Chinese over the centuries have been masters of such techniques, and Yang Ren-Kai suggests the term "imagined reproductions" for these false works:

> The reproductions were liable to give us a false illusion because reproducers were so familiar with the stroke styles and the regulations of the painter . . . that the reproductions were almost identical to the genuine ones, but in fact there are still distinction [*sic*] between the two in art level and spirit. . . . The reasons of reproduction are complex, the most common one is for deceptive purposes.[19]

Norman, in her discussion of the use of pastiche by master English faker Tom Keating, makes the point that all artists draw upon the achievements and experience of others, and there are many legitimate instances in which it is difficult to tell the works of one artist from another, even when there has been no conscious attempt to copy or deceive.[20] But further, to be a successful producer of fraudulent art, at the level of the likes of Keating, Elmyr de Hory, or, perhaps more recently, John Myatt:

> [Y]ou must have a technical facility which equals or nearly equals that of the artist you are copying; moreover, you must have the spiritual sensitivity to assimilate, and to some extent share, his inspiration, in other words, you must be an artist.[21]

This process of "getting inside" the work of a master can take several forms. Thomas Keating stated that there were times when he felt "spirits actually guiding my hands."[22] Another successful art fraudster, de Hory, according to his biographer Clifford Irving (who himself later became involved in the infamous Howard Hughes fraud), firmly rejected such a view, stating: "I personally think that's all the worst sort of nonsense What I did was to study—very, very carefully—the man's work. That's all there is to it."[23]

However they accomplish the task, it is the serial, pastiche fakers who create the greatest volume of mischief in the form of fakes in the contemporary art market. Will Blundell in Australia, for example, who consistently referred to his works as "innuendos" and was never charged with any crime over his pastiches, created hundreds of works in his career, and many of these can be presumed to be floating still in the Australian art market.[24] Similarly, fakers such as de Hory, Keating, or Myatt created hundreds, if not thousands of works, an unknown quantity of which have still not been unmasked as false works.

The Problem of Alterations

A further problem of causing possible confusion occurs when original legitimate works are altered, perhaps to the point where their authenticity must be questioned. Probably the most ubiquitous form of such alterations occurs in the process of "restoration." While today this is a highly refined process, over the years some of the restorations are so extensive that there will inevitably be questions about how much of the work was done by the original artist, and how much is that of the restorer. Kurz, in fact, has argued that the "borderline between extensive restoration and forgery is difficult to draw."[25] Keep in mind that the current art examiner may be looking at a work that was restored in antiquity, and perhaps as well in more recent times; so that without doubt, multiple artists have been at work on the object. Since many works have been restored, the problem for the art experts, and the courts, is to determine if the restoration work has been so extensive that the work may no longer be viewed, properly, as "authentic." This is illustrated in a recent civil case involving work done on a painting by Egon Schiele, in which the judge decided that the restoration was significant enough so that the work could not be considered as authentic, although a major factor in the decision was that the restorer had altered the signature.[26]

There are also instances in which unfinished or abandoned works of one artist have been finished by another. When they died, both Tintoretto and El Greco left many unfinished canvases, which, according to Hoving, were then completed by others in the artists' studios.[27]

The examiner's task can be complicated further when the painting is altered by a later artist so that elements are either added or taken away. There are numerous instances in which a later artist will add clothing to naked figures or, for other reasons of taste, figures may either be added or removed from the painting by later artists.[28] In all such cases, the work of the later artist is overlaid onto the original object, and can create significant problems in the assessment of its worth and authenticity.

Proving Intent or Dishonesty

Like most forms of serious criminality, a successful prosecution of art fraud will hinge upon the ability to prove a mix of physical and mental elements. Establishing that a work claimed to be by a famous artist is a fake satisfies the need for addressing the physical element of the crime of fraud (deception). Attention must then turn to the question of the intent of the person who sold the work; that is, the mental element. How the prosecution approaches this task obviously will depend upon tactics adopted by the accused (assuming a plea of not guilty).

A common line that can be expected is for the accused to claim that they had no knowledge that the art had been faked; that is, they assumed that the work was genuine when they presented it for sale. What has happened in some cases in which this has been attempted is for the prosecution to present evidence of the involvement of the accused in the creation of the works. In the cases of Drewe in England,[29] and the Libertos in Australia,[30] their claims of innocence were compromised by the finding of either partially created works (and the necessary equipment for their creation) or items necessary for the fraud in the residence of the accused.

For a variety of reasons, in dealing with serious fraudsters in many cases, it is not necessary to prove this potentially contentious element. In some instances (for example, the much-publicized case of Elmyr de Hory), there is such a huge body of faked work that is available, and the methods of distribution and sale are so clearly demonstrable, that any claim of innocent intent is unthinkable.

It is not uncommon that there is a certain sense of both relief and satisfaction when the identity of the artist who produces the faked works becomes known. Thomas Keating, for example, basked in considerable limelight (especially in terms of television appearances), after his frauds were unmasked. Elmyr de Hory was the subject of an Orson Welles film, *F is for Fake,* and an internationally best-selling biography. Probably the most bizarre case is that of Hans van Meegeren, who, after a successful career of faking that involved the production, among others, of multiple fakes of Vermeer, found himself in a position where he had to prove his skills as a faker, that is essentially to confess to art fraud, in order to escape a more serious charge that involved allegations of collaboration with the Nazis (by selling valuable Dutch old masters to the Nazis) during the occupation of Holland in World War II, the punishment for which was execution.[31]

These examples aside, police and prosecutors can anticipate that significant obstacles to a successful prosecution may be created by the mental element of intent. This can become exceptionally complicated in cases involving Australian Aboriginal art, as it did in the O'Loughlin case in New South Wales in the early 2000s.[32] The problem may arise because of cultural differences in the idea of "ownership" involved in the creation of a work. There will be situations involving Aboriginal communities where what is central is the notion of ownership and the custodial responsibility assumed by a particular family group within a clan over the themes portrayed in the object. Particular ideas expressed in a painting, for example, might be viewed as "owned" by persons not involved in the creation of the work, and within the Aboriginal community, it could be viewed as "proper" that their names be signed to a work as the legitimate owners of these themes. This can produce a variety of lines of defense for alleged offenders if they can argue either that they have "ownership" or if by some process "ownership" has been conveyed to them. While O'Louglin ultimately pleaded guilty (to a lesser charge of fraud), during the trial, one of the claims of the defendant was that he had undergone a particular bonding ceremony with the named artist, and as a result he believed he was entitled to engage in some amount of creative work involving art.

SOME ISSUE WITH WORDS

Those engaging in professional work addressing cases of art fraud will have to negotiate a discursive terrain that is cluttered with meanings that may cause occasional confusion. There are many popular words used, especially in contemporary media, with a looseness that is not helpful, two of these being "forgery" and "fakery."

The problem with the term "forgery" is that, because of an English legal precedent, technically it is inappropriate to use this term to apply to art. An early case, Closs (1857), found specifically (and perhaps peculiarly) that the term "forgery" does not apply to works of art, but only to the forging of documents or writing. In the 1857 case, the defendant sold a painting on which appeared to be the signature of the artist, one John Linnell. The signature was, in fact, false. Even so, the court held that the case was not one of forgery, Chief Justice Cockburn asking rhetorically, "can a sculpture be the subject of a forgery?" The Court stated that:

> A forgery must be of some document or writing, and this was merely in the nature of a mark put upon the painting with a view of identifying it and was no more than if the painter put any other mark as a recognition of the picture being his.[33]

Commentators in the art world, of course, pay little attention to this. Thomas Hoving, who has written one of the most knowledgeable books on art fraud (1996), uses the term "forgery" interchangeably with others used to describe fakes and frauds. One of the better-known perpetrators of art fraud, Eric Hebborn, used the term as a title for one of his books, *The Art Forger's Handbook* (1997). Until the matter is clarified by later legal findings, those in the criminal justice system might have to be aware that the finding in Closs, though 150 years old, does close certain options for prosecution in terms of claims being made about a work of art. At the same time, as in the Drewe case, when art fraudsters manufacture false documents as part of the supporting material in an art fraud (for example, in order to generate false provenance), that may open a possible line for successful prosecution.[34]

The problems posed by the word "fake" and "faker" are somewhat different. In their common use (and as used in numerous examples in our own present discussion), these words are likely to convey both the physical element of a deceptive work and a mental element of intended fraud. When used to describe the actions of the likes of de Hory, Keating, or van Meegeren, the conflation of these two elements is accurate.

There are numerous other examples, however, where there is a tendency to apply the term "fake" when there is no demonstrable intention to defraud. Recently, the National Gallery of Victoria (NGV) was embarrassed to find that a work that had been claimed by the gallery for many years as being produced by Vincent Van Gogh was found by expert examination to be, in fact, the work of another, as yet unidentified, artist. It was the position of the gallery that while the earlier description was not correct, neither is it accurate to treat the work as a fake or forgery, since in their view it is a legitimate art object than can stand on its own merits.[35] The news reports of such reclassification, however, consistently refer to the downgraded work as a fake. But the NGV position is quite understandable, and in terms of the present discussion, there is no suggestion in the tale that there has been intention to defraud. To further complicate the problem, the same museum had the novel experience recently of having two works by well-known masters "upgraded" since previously there had been doubt cast on the authorship of works by Tintoretto and by Titian, which have now been identified as works of these masters.[36]

What this underscores is the difference between the art experts, with their concern for "authenticity," and the criminal justice system, with its focus on fraud. Strictly speaking, the art expert is concerned with the assessment of the physical element (authenticity). It will be the task of the criminal justice system to gather the necessary information to establish the mental element involving intent and/or dishonesty. There are numerous circumstances in which a work can be established indisputably to be not authentic, but where there is no hint of dishonesty or criminal intent, at least in the presenting circumstances.

A given work, to show the complications, might begin its life as a part of a complex fraud such as that perpetrated by the dealer/forger team of Drewe and Myatt—that is, it starts out as an obvious "fake." When an unsuspecting purchaser, thinking that the work is by a master, reenters the market to sell the painting, the intent element necessary for fraud would not be present. If the next purchaser somehow discovered the origins of the object, and then attempted to resell it as the work of the master, the mental element of dishonesty would recur. Thus the painting might go in and out of the market several times. At no point is the work authentic, but only at those points where fraudulent intent can be established would a crime have been committed. For the art expert, the use of a loaded term like "fake" can only confuse the picture of what transpires over the life course of such a work.

CONCLUSION

For the criminologist, what the foregoing makes clear is that much of art fraud belongs in the "dark figure" of crime. That is, while we have numerous examples from our interviews and observations of fraudulent practices taking place in the art market, only rarely are these grounds for action by the criminal justice system. To give an alternative view, Hoving argues that in his experience of examining many thousands of art works, as much as 40 percent could be misattributed; while in the Australian art market, Slogett has estimated that 10 percent of such works could be cases of "mistaken identity" (although it is unclear from such discussions what the size might be of the presumably large fraud component in these figures).[37]

It should also be kept in mind that our examination here barely opens the door on fraud in the art market. Not only has art been a part of corporate and tax frauds we have not discussed, new forms of fraud are always evolving as well, such as that recently illustrated by the role of the Internet in fraudulent practices involving art.[38]

Should more be done about these problems? Many in the art world think that serious attention ought to be paid to the issue of inauthentic art, since it tends to erode public confidence in the art market generally, and it can have a devastating effect on the sales of works of a particular artist if word spreads of fakery of works attributed to that artist (the innumerable fake works "by" Dali are perhaps the most prominent example).

Fortunately, two factors make more effective action possible. First, serious, serial fakers such as de Hory, Keating, or Drewe/Myatt tend to believe they have found a way to reenter the art market persistently and to successfully sell their fraudulent works. However, their repeated entry into the market exposes such offenders to an ever-increasing probability of disclosure because of issues such as: (1) a sudden increase in the supply of works by particular artists may well raise questions regarding how so many previously unknown works would suddenly appear; (2) a repeated use of a particular provenance by itself becomes suspicious (how many works can Granny have in her attic?); (3) experts in the art world are likely to begin to identify the distinctive hand of the faking artist; and (4) technical slipups become more likely with repetition, among other matters.

Second, the art market in any particular place (even the large commercial centers) is actually a relatively small and closed community. Rumors quickly begin to spread when suspicious works begin to circulate, and it is not uncommon for insiders to be able to identify both the dealer and the artist producing the problematic works long before matters reach the point at which criminal justice intervention might occur. Increased cooperation between the criminal justice system and the art market might therefore result in the creation of serious barriers for any potential serial faker to overcome.

NOTES

1. Two of these are cited in our cases below, the other is referred to by Baker 1999.
2. Cases referred to in this essay include: R v Closs [1858] 169 ER 1082, R v Ivan Liberto and Pamela Yvonne Liberto [2008] VCC 1372, R v John Douglas O' Loughlin [2002] NSWDC Unreported. Transcript 23 February 2002.
3. See in general Lanham et al. 1987.
4. For a discussion of these, see O'Connor 2004, 6; Flescher 2004, 98.
5. Pitman 2006.
6. Flescher 2004, 96.
7. O'Connor 2004.
8. Vogel 2008.
9. Kurz 1967, 57.
10. Smith and Fong 1999.
11. Innes 2005, 46.

12. For an overview, see Sutton 2004, 29–38.
13. Bailey 1994.
14. Editor's Note: See Bull's discussion of this issue, in Chapter 3.
15. Kurz 1967, 40.
16. Thompson 2004 and Usborne 2004.
17. See discussion of Catterall 1992.
18. Chanin 1990, 119.
19. Yang Ren-Kai 1997, 23.
20. Norman 1977, 299.
21. Ibid., 200.
22. Keating et al. 1977, 84.
23. Irving 1969, 233.
24. Hills 2002.
25. Kurz 1967, 40.
26. Spencer 2004, 189–215.
27. Hoving, 1997, 57, 58.
28. See discussion by Kurz 1967, 41.
29. See *The Guardian* newspaper, 1999.
30. *R v. Ivan Liberto and Pamela Yvonne Liberto* (2008), VCC 1372.
31. See in general Radnoti 1999, 21–23
32. Barkham 2001; and*R v. John Douglas O' Loughlin* (2002), NSWDC Unreported. transcript, February 23, 2002.
33. *R v. John Douglas O' Loughlin,* at 1084.
34. Landesmann 1999 and Baker 1999.
35. National Gallery of Victoria 2007.
36. Ibid.
37. As quoted by Porter 2006.
38. Spitzer 2001 and Walton 2006.

PART III

Crime and the Art Trade

Chapter 8

Implication of Art Theft in the Fine Art Insurance Industry

Dorit Straus

INTRODUCTION

A detail from Rembrandt's canvas *The Storm on the Sea of Galilee* (1633), depicting the tumultuous tempest that engulfed the frail ship of Christ and his disciples, graces the cover of Peter Bernstein's book *Against the Gods: The Remarkable Story of Risk.*[1] Reducing material and financial loss resulting from shipping accidents at sea served as a catalyst for the creation of maritime insurance in London during the seventeenth century.

Over the centuries, seafaring merchants devised different methods of protecting themselves from severe financial losses by sharing the losses amongst themselves. The Phoenicians of the ancient world and Chinese merchants divided their cargos among several boats. Thus if one boat was lost to sea, no one merchant was to lose all of the goods. Each one stood to lose only a portion of their goods.

In the seventeenth century, London bankers met informally to do business at a coffee house owned by Edward Lloyd by offering insurance contracts to merchants with goods traveling by sea, with a specific percentage of risk that they were willing to entertain in exchange for a payment, known as premiums. Those taking the risk were called underwriters, which eventually in 1769 became what is known today as Lloyd's of London.

Today, insurance continues to be a function of sharing of risks, with insurance as a means of minimizing the losses of the few by spreading the cost among many. Rembrandt's painting illustrates the physical risks faced by travelers at sea, which ship owners sought to mitigate through the pooling of risk.[2] This painting, however, evinces another type of risk: art theft. Ironically, the very image reproduced on the cover of a book detailing the history of risk and risk management was itself a victim of failed risk prevention. On March 18, 1990, two thieves posing as policemen robbed the Isabella Stewart Gardner Museum (ISG) in Boston, absconding with 15 precious works, among them the aforementioned Rembrandt canvas, as well as a seminal Vermeer, *The Concert,* and five works by Degas. In all, an estimated $300 million in art was stolen; the works remain missing and the crime unsolved as this volume goes to print.

Art theft poses a major risk to public and private art collections. While much art around the world is insured, a significant portion is uninsured. An insured collection is one whose risks have been evaluated and managed by an insurance underwriter, making it, hopefully, less susceptible to theft. Achieving a similar level of risk detection and prevention may not necessarily require purchasing insurance. Institutions and private collectors that are not insured can follow simple rules—be prepared, use common sense, and always consider the worst-case scenario.

While insurance proceeds can provide a cash payout for the replacement value of a stolen object and offers some consolation, it can never equal the return of the actual objects. Artworks are unique, and purchasing a "replacement" of comparable value and quality may satisfy some collectors, but objects taken *in situ* from cultural heritage sites are simply irreplaceable. It is thus in the best interest of both public and private collections to undertake the necessary precautions to evaluate their situation with an eye towards preventing theft. This essay will acquaint the reader with the underwriting process, which concentrates on preventative measures and security protocol recommended by many insurance companies to help stem art theft and other hazards to the collection.

SOME RECENT THEFTS IN THE NEWS

Several recent thefts highlight the security risks faced by both public institutions and private collections. The 2008 theft of four masterpieces from the E. G. Bührle Collection, a private museum in Zurich, Switzerland, represents a prime example of a violent intrusion from the outside. Three masked men entered the museum in broad daylight, removed at gunpoint four nineteenth-century pictures from the walls, which according to the media were valued at approximately $163 million, and escaped in a van with the paintings, two of which have since been recovered. Following the robbery, it was reported that visitors were not required to undergo backpack inspections, and the museum did not have metal detectors.[3]

Lack of security procedures enabled antiquities dealer E. Forbes Smiley III to smuggle nearly 100 rare maps, which he removed with the aid of a razor blade from eight U.S. and British institutions, including 20 from Yale's Beinecke Library. Smiley admitted to hiding the maps in his briefcase, which had not undergone inspection.[4]

Private homes are frequent targets for art theft. In 2007, thieves made off with two Picasso canvases from the home of Diana Widmaier-Picasso. According to authorities, a security system had been installed, but it failed to detect the break-in.[5]

Unstable political climates and times of warfare exacerbate the risk of theft, as witnessed in the pillaging of the Baghdad Museum in 2003. The looting that took place following the fall of Baghdad is proof enough that appropriate steps to minimize risk were not taken. Following the U.S. invasion, officials estimated that 170,000 objects had been stolen; after the dust settled, the actual number was reduced to approximately 4,000 objects—an unacceptable number and a major cultural loss.[6]

A GRIM PICTURE OF ART THEFT

When thefts do occur, the recovery process is often arduous and protracted. If the art is insured, the insurance company will do everything in its power to recover the stolen artworks and return the objects to the rightful owner. The movies paint an unrealistic picture of art theft, portraying it as a sexy and readily solvable crime, and the recovery process as straightforward and daring. For example, Rene Russo, acting the role of the art adjuster in *The Thomas Crown Affair,* sits down at her computer and immediately connects to a closed-circuit camera positioned inside the suspect's home—a complete fantasy when contrasted with what actually occurs in the art recovery process. Filmmaker Rebecca Dreyfus takes a more realistic approach in *Stolen,* a documentary about the ISG theft. Fine art adjuster Harold Smith spent years tirelessly attempting to solve the crime, developing several plausible theories, including one involving the IRA.

Insurance companies, when presented with a claim, deploy adjusters to investigate the cause of the loss and to make a payment. Within this subset, there are fine art adjusters who are familiar with the specifics of settling a fine art claim. Most fine art adjusters are independent adjusters working on behalf of the insurance industry, but are not employed by the insurance companies. On the other hand, some insurance companies also employ investigators with police backgrounds for special investigations, in all lines of business. They are called in to investigate a case when there is a suspicion of fraud on the part of the insured or someone associated with the insured. When law enforcement is involved, the insurance company will yield to them in order not to compromise the case.

The reality, as accurately portrayed in *Stolen,* is much darker. Art theft continues to plague commercial and cultural institutions—museums, galleries, auction houses, even private collectors' homes and cultural heritage sites. The Art Loss Register (ALR), a private, for-profit registry for stolen art, reports the top countries plagued by art theft: the United Kingdom occupies the top spot (49,722), followed by the United States (16,636), Germany (9,402), France (9,094), Italy (8,393), Switzerland (3,096), Netherlands (2,899), Belgium (2,889), Austria (1,996), Poland (1,363), Canada (1,269), and, in 12th place, Ireland (1,122).[7] These statistics represent only the thefts reported to the ALR—it is important to note that they do not represent all thefts within those countries. The number of thefts reported in the various countries is more an indication of familiarity with the ALR, or the fact that many insurance companies subscribe and report thefts to the ALR.

Of additional interest is the fact that a closer examination of the thefts reported to the ALR since its inception, particularly those in the United States, occurred in private residences (4,884), followed by art galleries and corporations (3,040), museums (889), in-transit (388), and warehouses (482). Again, it is important to emphasize that these are not total thefts in the United States, but only thefts reported to the ALR.[8]

ART INSURANCE: THE BASICS

Contrary to public perception, the insurance industry is not a monolith. It is comprised of many insurance companies around the globe, including multinational companies or nationally owned private or publicly traded companies. It also includes the Lloyd's marketplace, which is a collection of individually owned syndicates who together participate to varying degrees on direct insurance placements or provide secondary insurance known as reinsurance to spread the risk of other insurance companies.[9]

Fine art insurance is a subsegment of property insurance, and within that it is a further specialization of the marine insurance market. Underwriters who specialize in fine art frequently also insure risks involving transportation, inland and ocean, including air shipments, as well as insurance for armored cars, jewelry, and other business that involve items of high value. Not all art, however, is underwritten by underwriters specializing in art. For example, insurance companies that insure banks will also insure the fine art owned by the bank. The same can be said for insurance companies that insure law firms and other corporations that own art, along with other property such as their computer equipment. However, many museums, including the very popular blockbuster traveling exhibitions, private and for-profit galleries and dealers are underwritten by a handful of insurance companies that specialize in art along with various Lloyd's syndicates.

Art insurance is a profitable business, in part due to risk selection combined with loss prevention. The "Loss Ratio" metric, the product of the generated revenue in the form of premiums minus expenses and paid losses, is used to measure the profitability of an insurance company. Most losses, with the exception of those resulting from theft, are partial losses, which require the insurance company to pay out only a portion of the artwork's insured value. For example, should a painting undergo water damage and a section require relining, the insurance company will compensate the insured only for the partial damage that occurred. This will include the cost of repair and loss of value or depreciation. Thefts result in total losses. As many of the sensational thefts have been uninsured or underinsured—a prime example being the works stolen from the ISG, all of which were not insured—the insurance industry did not pay out these claims and has maintained, for the most part, their profitable loss ratios.

It is somewhat easier to settle a claim when an item is stolen or totally damaged, particularly when a policy is written with an agreed amount or scheduled valuation. That means that if the item has a specified value, the insurance company is obligated to pay that full amount. Say, for example, a Pre-Columbian mask is scheduled on a policy for $200,000 and is stolen from a private residence; the insurance policy is obligated to pay its scheduled amount of $200,000. On the other hand, if thieves were interrupted in the middle of the burglary and left the mask in its case in the residence, but had damaged it during the attempted burglary, the process would be a little more complicated.

First, the insurance company would have to determine the current market value of the item. This is accomplished by getting an updated appraisal or valuation by an expert. Then an objects conservator would attempt to restore the work to its former condition. When the conservation is complete, the appraiser will again examine the mask to determine if there is loss of value or depreciation due to the repair, and to what extent. The insurance policy will pay for the loss in value from its current market value as well as the costs of conservation. If the market value of the mask at the time of loss is determined to be $300,000 rather than the scheduled $200,000 and the loss of value is deemed to be 25 percent, then the insurance company will be expected to pay 25 percent of $300,000, or $75,000.

Each insurance company reports data differently, and not all reported data enters the public domain. Therefore, extracting data pertaining to fine arts is difficult, although a sampling is available. The Insurance Services Organization (ISO), a provider of insurance industry information, issued a 2005 report in which it documented the loss ratios for participating insurance companies that insure museums, galleries, and cultural institutions in the United States. In 2005, these premiums totaled $78,233,095, with $25,869,154 in paid losses due to all perils, not only theft, generating a 33.1 percent pure loss ratio—the second highest for the past 12 years.[10] After adding costs for expenses, the combined loss ratio is still under 100 percent, reflecting underwriting profitability for this sector of the insurance industry.

The U.S. government has taken steps to protect museum collections and temporary exhibitions through its indemnity program.[11] Congress created the National Endowment for the Arts' Arts Indemnity Program in 1975 to offset the costs for insuring traveling exhibitions coming from overseas to the United States, and to encourage cultural exchange. Since its inception, the program has insured nearly 900 exhibitions, saving organizers more than $230 million in insurance premiums.[12] Recently funded exhibitions, each exhibiting hundreds of millions of dollars worth of art, include *Jasper Johns, Gray,* The Metropolitan Museum of Art, New York; *El Greco to Velázquez: Art During the Reign of Philip III,* Museum of Fine Arts, Boston; and *Inspiring Impressionism,* Seattle Museum of Art.[13] The government stipulates strict requirements and indemnity limits, which contributed to a nearly flawless track record since 1975—a single loss occurred in the late 1970s, and no claims have been paid since. How was this accomplished? A meticulous review of the applicant's facilities, policies, and procedures are reviewed before the government assumes the risk associated with a particular exhibition, exceeding even the private sector's insurance industry review and diligence in risk assessment.

As the art market continues to boom with prices that skyrocketed to astronomical levels—Francis Bacon's *Triptych* (1976) sold in May 2008 for over $85 million—insurance rates have remained reasonable, while premiums did rise due to higher limits purchased to accommodate the new values. As long as paid losses do not exceeded premiums received, and competition between insurance companies for this very desirable class of business continues, it is anticipated that the current market conditions for fine art insurance will remain as they are.

WHAT KEEPS UNDERWRITERS UP AT NIGHT: RISK ASSESSMENT AND MANAGEMENT

Theft accounts for only one of the risks evaluated by the insurance underwriter. Underwriters must consider physical perils such as fire, hurricanes, floods, and vandalism, among others. Most fine art insurance policies provide worldwide coverage, insuring against all perils except those that are specifically excluded.

Artworks reside in many different locations, each posing unique risks to its safety. Risk assessment comprises the first step in risk prevention.

Let me take you through the steps that I take as an insurance underwriter to scrutinize various risks prior to making an underwriting decision. These concerns extend across institutions and private collections, encompassing the buildings housing the collections, off-site storage facilities and periods of transit, for all perils including theft.

The first step is to review the "integrity of the envelope" (i.e., the external structure housing the art, examining the construction and integrity of the building to withstand fires, hurricanes, and other natural disasters, all of which could destabilize the building and grant access to thieves). This includes an examination of the stability and combustibility of the materials used to construct the building and the number and location of entrances and exits, the number of floors, the configuration of the gallery and display spaces and their proximity to building entrances and exists. Artworks located close to entrances and exits are often more susceptible to theft.

The next step is to take into account the surrounding area: Is the building located in a neighborhood with high crime? Are potentially harmful businesses or centers such as welding companies in close proximity? Does the collection occupy a free-standing structure, a unit within a larger structure, or a structure connected to an adjacent structure?

The building's interior integrity is then inspected for fire detection and sprinkler systems, when the systems were installed, and if they are inspected regularly. Exposures to manage smoke and water damage and evacuation procedures are also reviewed.

Specific to the theft assessment is the evaluation of the security measures taken to protect the building and its surroundings: the electronic alarm system, security cameras, and closed-circuit televisions linked to a monitored central command center, as well as exterior perimeter protection and outdoor lighting.

Security personnel complement electronic monitoring in many institutions and in some significant private collections. The number of security guards, their roles and responsibilities, posting locations, and background checks prior to hiring will differentiate an ordinary risk from a superior risk. Employees with access to the collection, even domestic workers in private collectors' homes and individuals transporting the art from one location to another, need to undergo background checks. Security personnel are responsible for monitoring visitor flow in lobbies and galleries, inspecting bags and detecting and reporting suspicious activity. Competent, attentive individuals are required to carry out these tasks effectively. Proper coat and bag check procedures can deter theft.

Insuring a private collection in a private residence or an apartment building will require a different evaluation from a public institution, including the private security in the residence as well as the building as a whole. This will include an evaluation of external security and identification of all accessible entrances including the building's main entrance, garage, and roof access. A doorman in a multiple-occupancy building serves as the first line of defense. The doorman's and other staff's responsibilities may include signing in visitors and escorting them to their destinations, manning elevators, and supervising deliverymen and other contracted workers entering and exiting the building.

The display of artworks can increase or reduce the potential for theft. How objects are affixed to walls and floors, whether frames hang freely on hooks or are anchored to the wall with screws, and if sculpture bases firmly secured to the floors? The integrity of display cases and locking mechanisms need to be examined. The proximity of artwork, especially easily removable artwork, to entrances and exits is noted. Should a theft occur, proper documentation of an object will ease the search and recovery process. A collection management system with each object is assigned a unique collection ID number, and a regularly updated collection management system is regarded as a better risk from one that has not put in the effort and resources to document the collection.[14]

Following the risk assessment and identification of deficiencies, underwriters suggest ways in which to reduce obvious exposures. Some suggestions may include: strengthening electronic security systems with additional cameras and motion sensors; installing outdoor lighting; hiring additional security personal and stationing them in key areas; removing small items from proximity to exists; installing cases for small objects with security screws and other new technology; developing emergency contingency plans; and even hiring a security consultant to address general security concerns.

Many collections are stored at off-site facilities. Museums display on average only 5 percent of their permanent collections, with the remaining 95 percent is housed in on-site and off-site storage facilities. Off-site warehouse storage poses additional theft-related risks. Knowing the correct questions to ask of storage and transport companies can mitigate these risks. When evaluating the potential for theft from an off-site storage facility, underwriters start with the same process of analyzing the construction and location of the warehouse; burglary protection; alarm maintenance and security continuity; storage conditions; and warehouse management. Of particular concern to underwriters is inventory control. Many warehouses provide open storage, allowing multiple artworks from a single collection to be dispersed throughout the warehouse. Without proper documentation and tracking, these artworks are more susceptible to disappearance, theft, or delivery to the wrong recipient.

Potential for theft or damage increases when artworks are in transit. Whether transporting locally or shipping a museum exhibition overseas, adopting standard written procedures for sending and receiving is necessary. The procedures should include vetting the transport company and approving the route and checkpoints. Copies of the inventory list should be provided to the shipper and receiver, and the shipper should furnish a receipt upon delivery. Some high-value shipments require follow cars and couriers and, most of all, should never be left unattended.[15]

The recent theft of a Goya canvas, insured for $1 million, from a truck transporting the artwork from Ohio to New York underscores the perils faced in transit.[16] The two drivers left their truck containing the painting unattended in a motel parking lot after retiring for the evening; the next morning, they awoke to find broken locks and the Goya missing from the truck.

A CASE STUDY

To better understand the process, a sample case study may be of use.

Mr. Smith is a well-known collector who amassed a collection of art during the past 25 years. He purchased mostly from galleries, but also from auction houses. Mr. Smith was approached by a museum in Florida to lend his Rothko for an exhibition about Rothko and his times. The museum had Rothkos in their own collection that they were going to exhibit and was borrowing another 10 works from other private collectors. Mr. Smith agreed to lend his Rothko and the museum was providing the insurance under their own museum policy of "all risk" wall-to-wall insurance. The loan agreement also stated that the value of Mr. Smith's Rothko was valued at $10 million, which was what Mr. Smith purchased the painting for 10 years earlier.

The exhibition lasted for three months. During the first week of the exhibition, a visitor to the museum managed to deface one of the Rothkos that was owned by the museum by spraying it with a spray paint can. The museum immediately instituted a search policy of all backpacks and personal objects brought into the museum. Mr. Smith read about the incident in the newspaper and was very upset, and requested that his painting be returned to him at his residence in New York.

The museum packed the painting and sent the painting to Mr. Smith via a fine art transit company that they have always used for shipments between Florida and New York. They also included in the shipment the Rothko painting that was defaced so that it could be examined and conserved by a conservator in New York that is known for expertise with Rothko. The transit company consolidated the museum shipment along with other paintings from a gallery in Florida that also needed to ship the works to New York.

The truckers stopped at a motel so that they can sleep over and left the truck in the motel parking lot. During the night, the truck was broken into and the two Rothkos were stolen. When the claim was submitted to the insurance company, and it was determined that the claim was legitimate and should be paid, Mr. Smith received $10 million. When Mr. Smith told the dealer where he originally purchased the Rothko that he got an insurance settlement of $10 million, his dealer told him that the value today of the Rothko was more in the range of $45 million — so he was out of pocket $35 million.

In the meantime, the Rothko that was owned by the museum was recovered, because during the investigation of the theft, the police received a confession from one of the truckers that he had planned the theft with an old buddy that he spent some jail time with 10 years earlier.

The painting was sent to be conserved, and following the restoration it was deemed to have lost 50 percent of its value. It was established that the market value before the loss was $50 million, so with a 50 percent depreciation, the museum could have received $25 million in an insurance settlement.

Underwriting this risk for Mr. Smith may have improved the outcome of this unfortunate situation:

1. Underwriters would have asked that Mr. Smith get an updated appraisal to reflect current market values and not the purchase price.
2. The museum should have questioned the value and asked Mr. Smith for an updated valuation.
3. Mr. Smith should have been informed that the loan agreement is the contract between him and the museum, and that the value stated on the loan agreement is the maximum amount for which he will be indemnified.
4. The valuation clause on most policies for works owned by the museum is current market value, which is why the museum would get a higher insurance settlement than Mr. Smith.
5. Underwriters would have reviewed the procedures and policies for visitor's entrance to the museum, as well as the number of guards and visitor flow. A review of the facility report may have shown deficiencies, but an inspection by the museum's insurance carrier would have provided an assessment and recommendations for improvements.
6. Underwriters would have requested that a high-valued shipment be transported by exclusive-use vehicle (not consolidated with other shipments), no overnight stops, a minimum of two drivers at all times, and possibly a follow car.
7. Closer evaluation of the museum policies could have also involved practices of outside vendors as well as museum staff for background checks.
8. The museum's policies regarding notification on losses should be examined and addressed by the board.

INSIDER THEFT

While external theft grabs the public's attention, insider theft is too often ignored by the insured and uninsured. It is an insidious problem affecting public and private institutions as well as and private collections. Security procedures often do not take into consideration that employees and domestic workers can and do pilfer objects. Insider theft is especially challenging, is difficult to prevent, and may take years to detect. A countless number of insider thefts occur in cultural institutions, yet few are reported to the authorities or in the media.

The Inland Marine Underwriters Association drafted a report in 2007 to bring attention to the problem of insider theft in cultural institutions. The genesis of this report stemmed from an American Association of Museums conference, when a representative from the FBI Art Crime Team asked participants to raise their hands if insider thefts had occurred at their respective institutions; a majority of hands went up in the air. The representative followed by asking how many individuals actually reported the incidents, generating a significantly smaller response.[17]

The writers of the report titled "Insider Theft and Employee Dishonesty within Cultural Institutions" report that insider theft is more difficult to quantify and mitigate because it involves human activities and not fixed characteristics of building. Insider theft results in both tangible losses—the disappearance of precious elements from a collection—and intangible losses—the tarnishing of an institution's reputation as a sanctuary for works of art and cultural objects.

Deception and the intent to deceive lie at the heart of all insider thefts. While curbing such deception is nearly impossible, the implementation of loss control measures may reduce insider theft. Maintaining inventory control procedures is paramount. When assessing the risks posed by insider theft, the first steps involve evaluating the inventory control procedures; establishing if all items in the collection are tagged with a unique identity number/code and are easily tacked; and assessing how often inventory is taken.

Staff evaluation should include review of hiring and management protocols, including background checks, for staff and administration; performance reviews; dissemination of procedures and protocols, and repercussions for violations; a clear hierarchy of access to the collection, stressing dual accountability; installation, maintenance, and rigorous testing of access control policies and systems; and registration policies for and monitoring of visitors and scholars accessing the collection.[18] A management culture of accountability and prosecution of criminal activities will also deter staff from even thinking about stealing from the public, realizing it is not worth the risk.

RECOVERY AND THE INSURANCE INDUSTRY

When thefts happen, law enforcement and governmental agencies should be notified as well as private art loss registries. Rewards can encourage information leading to recovery. Museums are often hesitant to publicize losses, fearing that such disclosure evidences insufficient security and will dissuade collectors and other museums from lending objects to them. Still, recoveries are rare and limited. According to the FBI, only 10 percect of stolen art worldwide is recovered—a grim statistic for those whose collections are at risk. When recoveries do occur, there is case for celebration and media blitz, as occurred with the recovery of Edward Munch's *The Scream* and *The Madonna,* both of which were uninsured in 2004 when thieves stole them from the Munch Museum. Authorities recovered the damaged paintings in 2006.[19] Other successes include the recovery of five ivory reliefs by the sculptor David Le Marchand, lent by billionaire collector Sir Kenneth Thomson and valued at approximately $1.2 million, seized from Toronto's Art Gallery of Ontario in 2004.[20] Rewards, offered by insurance companies or the institutions or collectors themselves, have sometimes a direct effect for the return of certain objects (a $120,000 reward was offered for the return of the Tompson Ivories; they appeared at a law office a week after the museum publicized the reward), but often they do not suffice in enticing those with knowledge of theft to come forward.[21] Following the theft from the Isabella Stewart Gardner, the museum issued a $5,000,000 reward for information leading to the return of the stolen paintings; they have yet to pay out the reward.

CONCLUSION: THE UNINSURED

Theft is much more prevalent in noninsured institutions and collections. Many institutions and private collections, in the United States and abroad, remain uninsured for a variety of reasons. Some risks are particularly vulnerable to loss resulting from theft, and would probably not be insurable in the private sector. These include: institutions that do not have the resources to invest in risk management and protection; archeological and cultural properties, which, due to their sheer size and remote location, are unable to achieve minimum standards of risk management regardless of resources—particularly during time of war (e.g., Iraq); and religious institutions possessing important works that are unable to control access to their collection and are unaware of its value (e.g., the myriad churches in Italy). Private collectors, whose collections may very well be insurable, may chose to remain uninsured fearing unwarranted tax consequences and public exposure.

Nevertheless, anyone in charge of collections regardless of insurance can go through the exercise of evaluating their premises and staff, and can take steps within their means to eliminate obvious gaps in their security procedures.

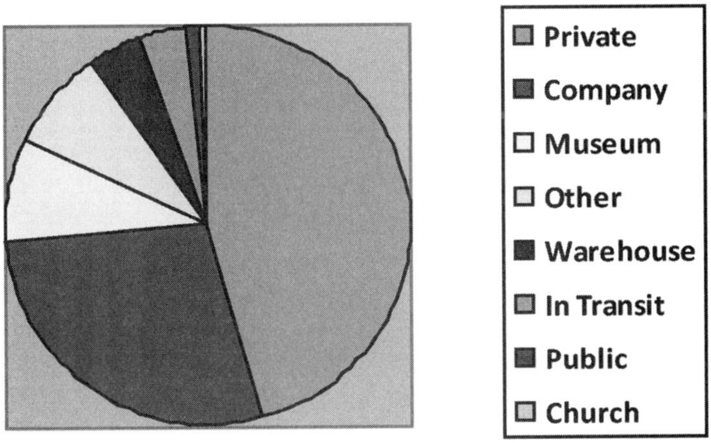

Figure 8.1 Registered Thefts in the United States, 2008, by Location.
Chart courtesy of The Art Loss Register.

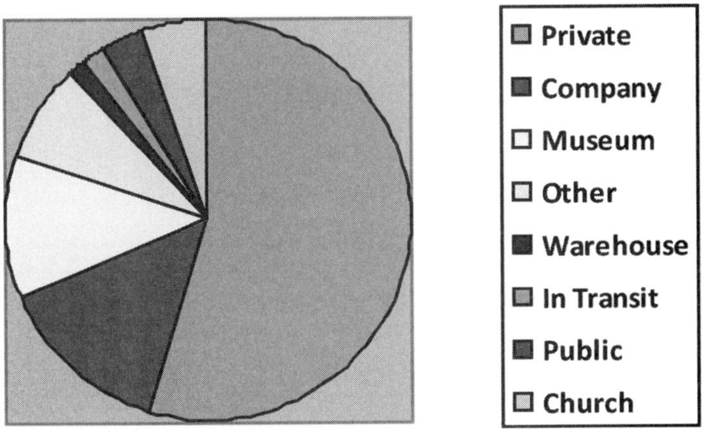

Figure 8.2 Registered Thefts by Location Worldwide
Chart courtesy of The Art Loss Register.

Figure 8.3
Registered Thefts by Reporting Countries

1	UK	49,722
2	USA	16,636
3	Germany	9,402
4	France	9,094
5	Italy	8,393
6	Switzerland	3,096
7	Netherlands	2,899
8	Belgium	2,889
9	Austria	1,995
10	Poland	1,363
11	Canada	1,269
12	Ireland	1,122

Chart courtesy of The Art Loss Register.

Figure 8.4
Items Stolen in U.S. Registered Thefts

Reported in 2007	1,098
Reported in 2006	675

Chart courtesy of The Art Loss Register.

Figure 8.5
Total Number of Theft Registries, 2007

Total registrations reported in 2007	10,273

Chart courtesy of The Art Loss Register.

Figure 8.6
Worldwide Thefts, 2008, by Crime Scene

	USA	Worldwide
Private property—residential	4,884	49,945
Company—including art galleries	3,040	12,657
Museum	889	10,780
Other/Unknown	880	7,018
Church	48	4,902
Public—including archeological sites, cemeteries, and other outdoor spaces	139	2,838
In transit	388	1,975
Warehouse	482	1,180

Chart courtesy of The Art Loss Register.

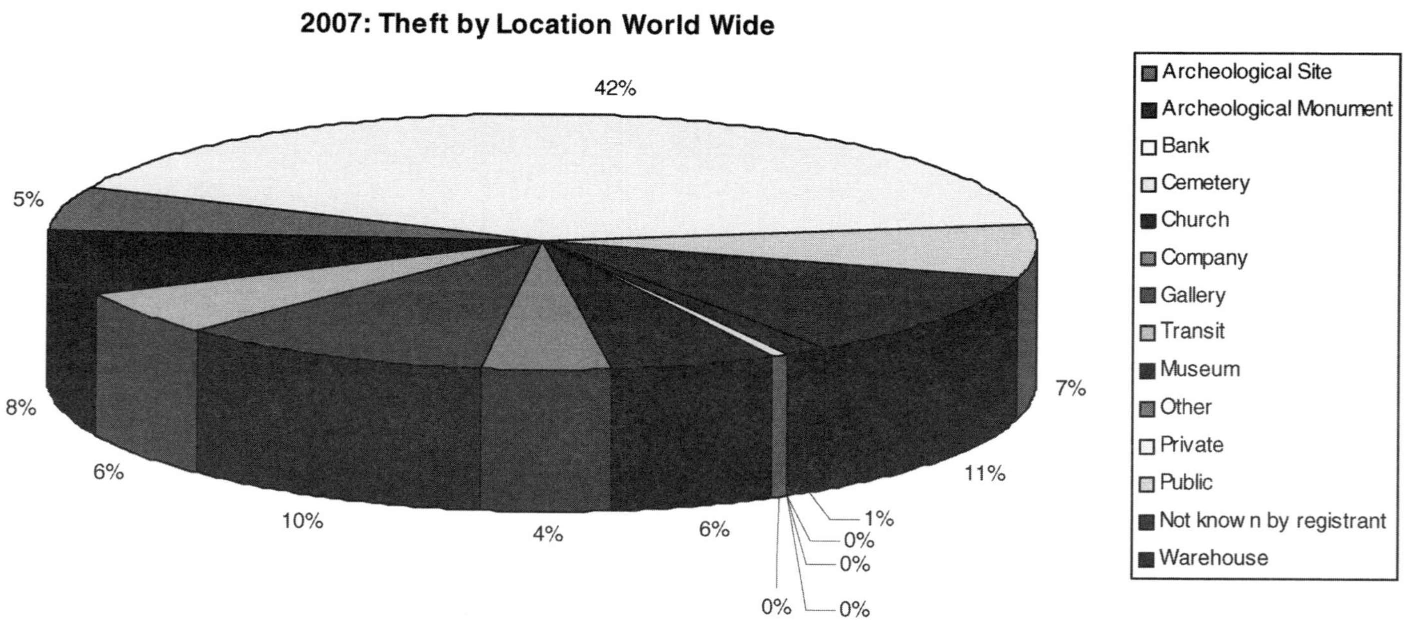

Figure 8.7 Registered Thefts with the ALR by Location Worldwide, 2007. Note that this chart (and others in Figures 8.1–8.9) represents only thefts registered with The Art Loss Register, and not the total number of thefts within any one country nor worldwide. This and other ALR charts do, however, present a good indication, upon which we can elaborate, to infer what format expanded statistics might take.

Chart courtesy of The Art Loss Register.

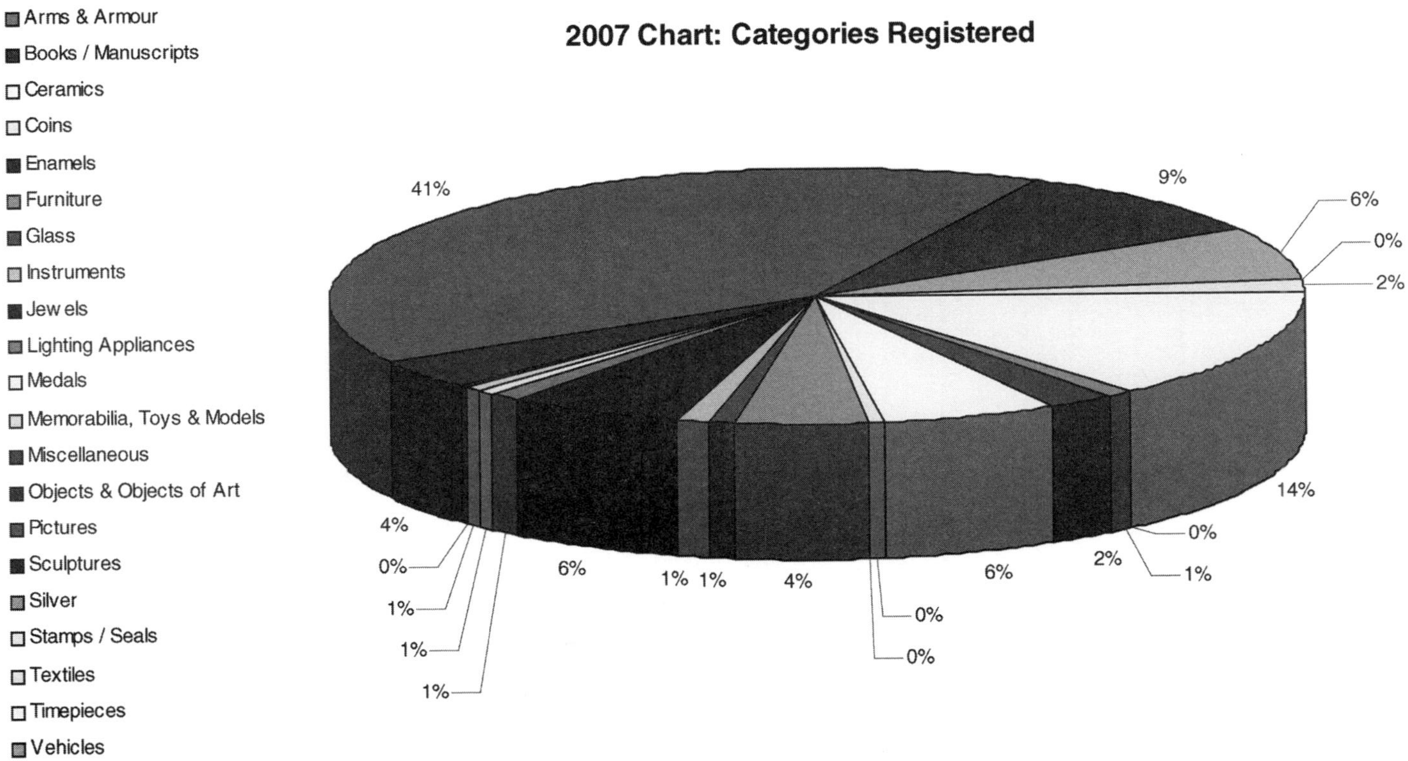

Figure 8.8 Thefts Registered with the ALR, by Category.
Chart courtesy of The Art Loss Register.

Figure 8.9
Stolen Paintings and Drawings by Artist, Registered by January 2008.

Artist Name	Total No. of Works Registered	No. of Works Registered as Missing or Stolen
Picasso, Pablo (Spanish, 1881–1973)	693	572
Miró, Joan (Spanish, 1893–1983)	388	364
Chagall, Marc (Russian, 1887–1985)	366	317
Dali, Salvador (Spanish, 1904–89)	300	275
Renoir, Pierre-Auguste (French, 1841–1919)	238	169
Dürer, Albrecht (German, 1471–1528)	226	215
Rembrandt van Rijn (Dutch, 1606–69)	209	173
Warhol, Andy (American, 1928?–87)	186	171
Rubens, Peter Paul (Flemish, 1577–1640)	138	122
Matisse, Henri (French, 1869–1954)	125	103
Dyck, Sir Antony van (Flemish, 1599–1641)	108	92
Moore, Henry (1898–1986)	96	89
Rodin, Auguste (1840–1917)	88	76
Dufy, Raoul (French, 1877–1953)	84	54
Degas, Edgar (French, 1834–1917)	84	78
Teniers, David (Flemish, 1610–90; The Younger)	82	60
Toulouse-Lautrec, Henri de (French, 1864–1901)	82	73
Pechstein, Max (German, 1881–1955)	75	62
Gainsborough, Thomas (British, 1727–88)	73	23
Hockney, David (British, 1937–)	67	66
Goya, Francisco de (Spanish, 1746–1828)	67	54
Guardi, Francesco (Venetian, 1712–93)	65	60
Klimt, Gustav (Austrian, 1862–1918)	64	59
Modigliani, Amedeo (Italian, 1884–1920)	62	56
Cézanne, Paul (French, 1839–1906)	61	51

Artist Name	Total No. of Works Registered	No. of Works Registered as Missing or Stolen
Vuillard, Edouard (French, 1868–1940)	59	48
Delacroix, Eugène (French, 1798–1863)	56	49
Ernst, Max (German, 1891–1976)	56	44
Monet, Claude (French, 1840–1926)	56	39
Boucher, François (French, 1703–70)	52	45

Diagram courtesy of The Art Loss Register.

NOTES

1. Peter Bernstein, *Against the Gods* (New York: John Wiley & Sons, Inc., 1998).
2. Ibid., 89.
3. Uta Harnischfeger and Nicholas Kulish, "At Zurich Museu, a Theft of 4 Masterworks," *New York Times*, February 12, 2008, http://www.nytimes.com/2008/02/12/world/europe/12swiss.html?ref=europe (accessed June 20, 2008).
4. Alison Leigh Cowan, "Dealer Pleads Guilty to Map Theft from Yale Library," *New York Times*, June 22, 2006, http://www.nytimes.com/2006/06/22/nyregion/22cnd-maps.html?_r=1&oref=slogin (accessed June 20, 2008).
5. "Mystery surrounds £33m Picasso theft," *Teligraph.co.uk*, January 3, 2007, http://www.telegraph.co.uk/news/uknews/1544077/Mystery-surrounds-andpound33m-Picasso-theft.html (accessed June 20, 2008).
6. Matthew Bogdanos, "Iraq Museum Investigation: 22APR-8SEP03," *U.S. Department of Defense Press Releases*, http://www.defenselink.mil/news/Sep2003/d20030922fr.pdf (accessed June 20, 2008).
7. *The Art Loss Register*, "2008 Statistics." It must be noted that ALR statistics are based only on thefts reported to and registered with the ALR, and do not reflect definitive worldwide statistics. The position of the UK as having the most registered thefts is due to the fact that the ALR is based in London, and UK clients make up the vast majority of the ALR's clients. In worldwide statistics, provided by Interpol and police departments, Italy has more than 10 times more reported art thefts than any other countries, and the UK is about average with most European countries.
8. Ibid.
9. Direct insurance placement is the agreement of the insurer to indemnify the insured in exchange for a payment (premium), their losses resulting from perils that are specified in the insurance contract. Reinsurance is the assumption by one insurance company of part of the risk that is undertaken by another insurance company

10. Most policies issued for fine art are all risk policies, which means that only what is not intended to be insured is listed as exclusions. Named perils lists the actual perils that the policy insures for such as fire, smoke, explosion, vandalism etc. Insurance Services Organization Report, "Fine Arts—Museums, Galleries Institutions," 2005.

11. The British Indemnity Program covers all public museums in Britain because those institutions do not participate in the private insurance industry. The U.S. Art and Indemnity program is indeed a program that could be used as a role model for countries, particularly when there is an open economy with a healthy private insurance industry to work in tandem with the public sector.

12. "Arts and Artifacts Indemnity Program," *National Endowment for the Arts,* http://www.nea.gov/grants/APPLY/Indemnity/index.html (accessed June 20, 2008).

13. "Recent Exhibitions—Arts and Artifacts Indemnity Program," *National Endowment for the Arts,* http://www.nea.gov/grants/APPLY/Indemnity/exhibitions.html (accessed June 20, 2008).

14. A system to catalog the items in the collection in great detail, including the description of the object, its maker, distinguishing marks, size, etc., as well as scanning pictures of the object. The system can record all the information relating to the objects, from ownership history to conditions reports to consignment at auction.

15. Usually an unmarked car with security personnel who the vehicle that is carrying the high-valued item in transit. Both vehicles should be equipped with GPS systems.

16. David Johnston, "Goya Theft Is Attributed to Inside Knowledge," *New York Times,* November 18, 2006. http://www.nytimes.com/2006/11/18/arts/design/18goya.html. Accessed June 18, 2008.

17. "Insider Theft & Employee Dishonesty Within Cultural Institutions," *Inland Marine Underwriters Association,* prepared by IMUA's Arts and Records Committee (2007; hereafter IMUA Report), 4–5.

18. Exit interviews are also important, and can reveal if there are disgruntled employees or situation that can result in theft of the collection. Adapted from recommendations made in IMUA Report, 11–15.

19. Lawrence Van Gelder, "Return of the Scream," *New York Times,* May 22, 2008, http://www.nytimes.com/2008/05/22/arts/22arts-RETURNOFTHES_BRF.html (accessed June 20, 2008).

20. Simon Houpt, *Museum of the Missing: A History of Art Theft* (New York: Sterling, 2006), 115.

21. The general rule of thumb is of a 10 percent recovery rate for stolen art. Included in that statistic are objects that are easily recognizable, as well those that are not. My general premise is that insurance rates are not affected by theft as much as by other perils.

Chapter 9

Four Art Crimes and Their Effect on the Art Trade[1]

Noah Charney

For centuries art crime was relatively innocuous, from the perspective of the global economy and international crime. Forgers fooled the occasional buyer, tomb raiders dug up what archaeologists hadn't time to reach, and the occasional nonviolent thief would steal for reasons more ideological than fiscal. Even vandalism was dismissed as part-and-parcel of the ravages of war.

But since the Second World War, art crime has evolved into the third highest-grossing annual criminal trade worldwide, behind only the drug and arms trades. Most art crime is now perpetrated either by, or on behalf of, organized crime syndicates, who have brought violence into art theft, and turned what was once a crime of passion (think of Vincenzo Peruggia stealing the *Mona Lisa* in order to repatriate it to Italy, or Kempton Bunton stealing Goya's *Portrait of the Duke of Wellington* as a protest against taxes on television sets) into a cold business. Art crime now funds, and is funded by, organized crime's other enterprises, from the drug and arms trades to terrorism. It is no longer merely the art that is at stake, and it is no longer a crime to be admired for its elegance.

The largest victim of art crime is the art trade. This multi-billion dollar legitimate industry is victimized to the tune of a conservatively estimated $6 billion per year, most of which goes into the pockets of organized crime. Here is a brief analysis of how the four main categories of art crime influence the art market. These encompass a myriad of sub-categories, but are unified in being premeditated criminal activities, undertaken for financial and/or ideological reasons, which profit from, or reduce the value of, art, and therefore affect the art market.

VANDALISM

Whether the willful damage to art and architecture is ideological, or simply spiteful, damaged art loses its value, while destroying an artwork turns a potential fortune into a pile of dust. However, for certain famous works, the caché of having endured vandalism (or theft) actually increases value. It certainly adds to popular interest, as witnessed by the tour guides in Florence and London who love to recount the survival tales of Michelangelo's *David* and *Pieta,* or Velazquez's *Rokeby Venus.* The destruction of art can also raise the values ofrelated works that survive — imagine a fire that consumes every Vermeer but one.

FORGERY/DECEPTION

This category encompasses a range of confidence tricks that involve the premeditated misattribution of art for profit. This includes a number of different methods, all of which take advantage of a degree of enthusiasm and wishful thinking on the part of the art trade. Everyone benefits if an artwork that comes on the market is legitimate: the owner makes money, the dealer receives a high commission, the buyer gets a new trophy, and academics get a new object to study. Because of this, there is a subconscious desire on the part of the art trade forpotentially questionable objects to be legitimate. This is where clever criminals can take advantage. The most common types of deception crimes are:

1. *Wholesale Forgery:* a new artwork is passed off as a piece that is either older than it really is or by a more valuable artist than the individual who actually created it.
2. *Alteration Forgery:* a legitimate work is altered in some way, for instance adding a signature that raises its value. This is much more difficult to detect, as scientific tests are designed to determine age, rather than attribution.
3. *Provenance Forgery:* the documented history of an artwork, as opposed to the work itself, is altered or falsified. Provenance is much easier to forge than the work itself. This technique is most often used to provide looted antiquities with a false history, suggesting that they were excavated before art exportation laws were put in place.
4. *Willful Misattribution:* the knowing and willful mis-estimation of the value of an artwork, in order to profit personally. This is a question of connoisseurship, and the most frequent perpetrators are the very experts that the art trade relies on to declare the value of artworks, whose value is not intrinsic. An artwork's value depends on a combination of its perceived authenticity and perceived rarity, and millions hang upon the word of experts as to a work's authorship. One need only recall Bernard Berenson's questionable, and profitable, attributions: especially if an expert is paid on commission, there is the temptation to attribute a higher value. This is the easiest

type of forgery to get away with, as an expert can always claim to have "made a mistake."

Crimes of deceit and forgery affect the art market in a generally beneficial way. The members of the art trade, galleries, auction houses, dealers, middle men, and sellers all benefit, earning money even if the item they are handling is not what they claim it to be. Only the buyers suffer, perhaps over-paying for a fake or mis-represented work of art. However, the buyer only loses out if the work is proven to be false. If the buyer and world at large remain in blissful ignorance, then the perceived value of the work remains consistent. In this way, it is in the best interest of all involved to believe that the art in question is exactly what they hope it to be.

ART THEFT

Art theft affects the art trade less than other categories of art crime, to a large extent because stolen art is rarely offered on the art market. In this Internet age, police and dealers worldwide can be notified of stolen goods in minutes, making it difficult for criminals to "shop" stolen art. Rather, criminals profit from art theft in a variety of ways that tend not to involve resale. For famous works, there is basically no market, black or otherwise. Famous art is either offered for ransom (such the Munch paintings stolen in 2004) or traded on a closed black-market system among organized criminals for an equivalent value of another illicit good, such as drugs or arms. Its value is marked at 7–10% of its legitimate auction value—the amount that criminals could sell it for, were they willing to run the risk of seeking a buyer. There is always someone who will buy a beautiful, valuable object, legitimate or not. Experts know of this estimated price because this is the value for which undercover police posing as criminal buyers were offered stolen art. Less recognizable art, and antiquities, are often altered in some way, provided false provenance, and then sold on an open market in which the actual owner is never revealed, or a gray market (this would include objects that "fell off a truck" or are stored in the basement of a legitimate dealer's shop). For such works, the art trade can actually benefit from criminal activity. With more objects to sell, the art trade will make more money, provided the illicit origins of the artworks can be disguised. The final, and most alarming method of profit, is from raw material sale. Since 2005 there has been an international rash of thefts of bronze and copper artworks and objects, linked to the astronomical rise in the price of these raw materials. Masterpieces such as Henry Moore's *Reclining Nude,* stolen from the Henry Moore Foundation in December 2005, weighing two tons, and insured for £2 million, was almost certainly chopped into pieces and sold for scrap, perhaps for as little as £3000.

ANTIQUITIES LOOTING

Perhaps comprising as much as 75% of all art crime, antiquities looting is the most difficult crime to catch. Objects taken directly out of the earth or the sea will not appear on stolen art registries because the objects never existed, at least not to the knowledge of contemporary society, before their illicit excavation. Looted antiquities can often be sold on an open market, for full value, even without a false provenance that suggests their legitimate excavation and exportation. Since the legitimate antiquities trade is laced with questionable characters and objects with incomplete provenance, the nature of this market provides shadows in which criminals can hide. Although buying a looted antiquity might seem relatively harmless, trade in illicit antiquities has been identified as a major funding source for terrorist groups. As with art theft, the art trade can actually benefit from antiquities looting. New exciting antiquities on the market benefits the trade—even if money from the transactions is going into the pockets of criminals.

Art crime is a subtle and fascinating world, one in which even the best-intentioned dealer or collector could be supporting Organized Crime through their purchases. Buyer beware.

NOTE

1. First published as Noah Charney, "Buyer Beware, Art Market Features," *ArtInfo*, August 11, 2008, https://www.artinfo.com/news/story/28263/buyer-beware/. Reprinted with permission.

Chapter 10

Trepidations of a Private Art Collector

Judah Best

I am a collector of American art. I collect oil paintings, watercolors, drawings, pastels, sketches, sculptures—anything. In short, I am hooked. The art is primarily in my home or office, although some is on loan at the Smithsonian American Art Museum (SAAM), where I am a member of the Board of Commissioners.

How do I protect my collection? That seems more complicated than I ever figured. First of all, it involves caring for the collection by buying legitimate art with established provenance, protecting and insuring this art while in my possession, and lending art in an orderly fashion that ensures its safe return. That is more easily said than done, though.

Every so often, there is news of sales of counterfeit works of art. The FBI's Art Crime Team recently announced it had broken a ring of counterfeiters and dealers engaged in the internet sale of thousands of prints by Calder, Dali, Warhol, Miró, Lichtenstein, and other noted artists, "often signed and numbered, complete with certificates of authenticity."[1] The Art Crime Team, launched in 2004, includes a curator, 13 FBI agents, and three Department of Justice attorneys assigned to prosecute cases of forged and stolen art. I served as an Assistant United States Attorney a long time ago and presently specialize in the defense of white-collar criminal matters. I am impressed with the accomplishments of the Art Crime Team. The FBI provides some sound advice as to the diligence that should be performed in the course of buying valuable works of art:

- Get a complete provenance or chain of custody on each piece to find out where the art came from originally. Was it obtained directly from an estate, for example? This information provides a way to double-check the piece's history instead of just relying on the certificate of authenticity.
- Research the dealer carefully. Check the Better Business Bureau for possible complaints. Find out if they sell only online or if they have a gallery.
- For pieces of art you already own, you can go back to the gallery and ask for provenance on your print. You can also contact artists' foundations which will do side-by-side comparisons with originals for a fee.
- And remember, when you're trying to find that one treasure from someone's garage, that's when you're more likely to let your guard down.[2]

I am mindful of the fact that even the most careful collectors can end up with stolen art and possibly jeopardize their investment and their art. Film director Steven Spielberg, a longtime collector of the work of Norman Rockwell, purchased the Rockwell painting *Russian Schoolroom* in 1989 from a legitimate dealer in Rhode Island, only to learn in March 2007 that it had been stolen from a gallery in a St. Louis suburb more than three decades ago. This painting is now valued at $700,000. In May 2007, Spielberg transferred title of *Russian Schoolroom* back to his dealer in exchange for another Rockwell piece. In the meantime the owner of the Missouri gallery sued both Spielberg and the FBI for return of the piece, and the Rhode Island dealer has sued the Missouri dealer and the Art Loss Register.[3] Oh, well.

TIPS FOR COLLECTORS UPON ACQUISITION

Meantime, I go through the necessary, if pedestrian, business of making sure that works of art I acquire meet standards of provenance and condition, and come from a legitimate source complete with written confirmation of authenticity and legitimate ownership. When I insist that dealers do research to confirm that paintings are not stolen, they moan about the cost of research and the widespread problem of stolen art. I have become impervious to their claims of pain and inconvenience, however, as I am sure the research costs are already hidden in the price for the work.

When I finally acquire the work and carefully hang it in my home, I try to take elemental precautions, such as ensuring that the alarm system is left on if I leave the house: all too often, homes and galleries are ransacked because the owners neglect to take such an obvious precaution. I have not yet addressed the prospect of installing an artwork security system designed to protect, track, and manage works of art, but I suspect that this is just a short time away.

For insurance purposes, I put together a catalog containing good photos of all the art. Since ransom is one of the primary motives for art theft, insurance is obviously indispensable, and the insurance companies have become adroit at repatriating art at a fraction of insurance value through their contacts in the low end of the art world.

A specialist art insurance company can provide valuable insights as to how best to protect your collection. Listen closely to their advice. If your collection is very large, the process of establishing prices for all works of art (rather than purchase price, which may not be adequate if you have purchased a "hidden treasure" at a price far below market) may become onerous. The process will be even more tedious if you (as I do) "trade" works and change the content and direction of the collection. I am told there are some good software programs to assist in management of the collection, and this is one more item for discussion with a qualified insurer.

The same protectiveness has to be employed in the lending of art to museums. First of all, is the work of art stable enough to withstand travel? You should ask the museum conservator to provide a fully detailed condition report before the work has begun its journey. Does the museum intend to travel the exhibition? If so, you may want to know the security arrangements, not only at the museum's home location, but everywhere the work will be exhibited. You will also want to obtain specific information about the museum's insurance policy. This is especially important overseas, where not every state-owned museum has a theft insurance policy. Along the way, you should check to see that your museum has an adequate number of guards.

THE DENNEY PHENOMENON

You should know that museums are typically close-mouthed about their art losses. For example, the Andy Warhol Foundation sent 45 drawings for examination to the Museum of Modern Art as the museum prepared for its 1989 Warhol retrospective. Within weeks, the drawings were missing, but rather than file a report with the police, the matter was hushed up and the museum's insurance adjuster covered the claim with a check.[4] Whether museums can continue to be so reluctant to discuss their failures in this age of e-mail and instant communication remains to be seen. Expect the worst, and you will not be surprised. The other concern with lending to museums may be characterized as the "Denney Phenomenon."

Let me explain. Anthony Denney built up a large collection of modern art during the 1950s and 1960s. A significant portion of the collection, worth millions of dollars, was lent to the Dallas Museum of Art in 1970. Following Denney's sudden death in Spain in 1990, 23 pictures were moved from the museum in Dallas to France by the fragile authority of letters signed "Anthony Denney." Although the letters had not been notarized, the museum required no further authorization. The collection disappeared and subsequently resurfaced as a donative grant to the City of Toulouse, thereby stripping the Denney estate of most of its movable assets.[5]

The Denney case may be one of a kind, but loans made to museums after Denney call for a written understanding and protocol for return of the loaned works of art, one that protects the owner or his estate and reduces the prospect of removal from the protections of American law. Make sure to negotiate these requirements when you agree to loan your work, and that they are specified in writing in the loan agreement you receive from the museum.

I apologize if the detail in this essay has made the collecting of art appear tedious. There is much romance in a collection: when I look at my pastel drawing of a woman by Mary Cassatt, I am reminded that a prior owner insisted her husband permit her to keep the drawing when he donated the remainder of their extensive Cassatt holdings to the National Gallery of Art in Washington. When I look at William Merritt Chase's oil portrait of his daughter Helen at her fifth birthday party, I am amused to remember that Chase's six daughters and two sons were named after famous artists: Helen's full name, after all, is Helen Velasquez Chase, an impossible burden for a little girl.

And then there is my precious small painting of New York's Coney Island by Martha Walter. I showed it to a friend, a PhD physicist, who looked at the painting, held it, and exclaimed, "that's where I grew up." She then pointed out places in the painting that she had frequented as a child. After 20 minutes or so of such reminiscences, she reluctantly handed it back to me—but only after I had assured her that she could visit the painting, and her childhood, anytime she wanted. My collection is laden with memories, rich and nostalgic, vivid and evocative, which make collecting so fulfilling for me. I am grateful for the opportunity to present this private world of mine in these pages.

NOTES

1. "Fine Art Forgeries, Global Counterfeiting Scams Uncovered," http://www.fbi.gov/page2/march08/artscam_032108.html.
2. *Ibid.*
3. *See* Chad Garrison, *The River Front Times,* June 6, 2007, found at http://www.riverfronttimes.com/2007-06-06/news/ the-Rockwell-files
4. Jason Edward Kaufman, "US Museums Meet the Challenge of Theft," *The Art Newspaper,* Sept. 1997, found at http://jasonkaufman.com/articles/us_museums_meet_the_challenge_of.html.
5. *See* A. P. Aderson, "Lessons from the Denney Collection," paper presented for discussion at the Institute of Art and Law Seminar, Cortauld Institute, London, May 13, 1996, at http://www.museum-security.org/denney/index.html.

Chapter 11

Defending Art[1]

Colonel Giovanni Pastore

It is very uncommon for a Carabinieri officer to spend 13 years in the same section and on the same post. Normally the assignment changes—together with the city, at times every three or four years. The rationale behind this is that a variety of experiences will provide a more thorough education. High competence and preparation are needed to fulfil an assignment in a Selected Carabinieri Section, such as the Command of Cultural Heritage Care. A longer experience and a deeper knowledge of the subject in question are necessary to achieve professional success.

I have been fortunate enough to serve for a long time as Chief of the Twelve Divisions of the Carabinieri Cultural Heritage Protection Department scattered across Italy. Our goal has been to fight crimes against the national cultural heritage.

Among the most recurrent crimes on which I worked over the past few years in this Special Unit, we faced national and international illicit traffics of artworks, clandestine archeological excavations, criminal art collectors, the theft and falsification of artworks, and the foreign recovery of cultural goodies illicitly acquired (even by museums), not to mention the crimes in countries at war (Kosovo, Iraq, etc.) The up-to-date knowledge of the art world and the continuous evolution of the Special Unit activities proved pivotal in this long experience to battle the new and always improved forms of crime. It is therefore not difficult for me to express today a general opinion on the state of art security and evaluate the measures adopted by some countries to safeguard their cultural heritage.

Knowledge gained from experience in the investigation of crimes against world culture (especially in countries defined as "producers" of artworks, such as Italy), has been greatly augmented by the exchange of information between the international police departments. The analysis of investigative techniques resulted in a detailed map, developed over the course of many years, which has been a valuable tool in interpreting the dynamics of the phenomenon of art crime, and locating the areas at higher risk.

I have been consulted by nations, not only individuals, on how to establish effective art police. With this in mind, I think that it might be useful to other police if I single out the initiatives that we have found most effective in caring for, and recovering objects of cultural heritage.

RECOMMENDATIONS AT A NATIONAL LEVEL

Given that every country possesses its own patrimony, composed of both material and immaterial valuables (artworks as well as traditions, for example), I believe that prevention is the best first step: an elementary safeguard against organized and specialized crime, compatible with other internal priorities. Norms and penal punishments (when those exist), the creation of dedicated police units, and international cooperation (at courts and between police departments and throughout the police hierarchy) are essential. But the results clearly show that this is just one part of a safeguard policy.

Before we consider punishment, in order to reduce the occurrence of criminal acts against public and private cultural possessions, a country would need to contemplate a series of measures aimed at:

- letting the criminals perceive the real threat of a punishment (stronger penal punishment with subsequent loss of illicit gains)
- rendering the trade and circulation of artwork more transparent (nationally and internationally)

To establish the degree of risk connected to its art patrimony, and to evaluate whether the preventative measures taken have been an effective deterrent, a country might establish a working evaluation team to formulate practical proposals for improvement. Such a team should evaluate the following subjects, in order of priority:

- norms and institutional rights
- definition of "cultural heritage"
- catalogue and location of all cultural objects to be protected
- provenance documentation and authenticity of cultural objects
- control of both licit and illicit commerce in cultural objects
- risk factors in the art market, locally, nationally, and internationally

- further professional education of staff and operators at all levels in the field
- security in museums
- relations with the proper international organizations
- customs and excise checks

The analysis of these themes should allow for:

- the development of a common strategy with coordinated initiatives between all parties and forces involved, wherever possible
- the unification of various parties over the common goal, which encourages the discussion of national priorities and the search for solutions
- the identification of common priorities, the definition of practical measures, the improvement of current implementations, and the expression of ideas in every sector
- representatives to meet, to discuss experiences and ideas, and to define their needs and expectations

The evaluation team should include persons or associations which will represent:

- owners of the cultural goods (privates, museums, churches)
- institutions supporting the safeguard, conservation, and transfer of the goods (Ministry of Cultural Goods and Activities, international organizations like ICOM, ICCROM and WCO, High Court, Police and Customs units)[2]
- the international organizations specialized in legal aspects of the safeguard and restitution of cultural goods (UNESCO, UNIDROIT)
- specialized insurance companies
- mediators and art trade representatives (critics, auction houses)
- private or nongovernative organizations, preferably nonprofit to avoid conflict of interest, confronting the illicit traffic of cultural goods (such as ARCA)

Preventative, evaluative actions should be taken both when a cultural good is first discovered or offered on the market (acting "on offer"), and when an individual or institution wishes to purchase the cultural good for export (acting "on demand"). Nevertheless, taking action when the good is first discovered or offered is often difficult, especially in the case of goods originating from poorer countries, with a less stringent control over their markets and exports. Difficulties arise from both the needs (and often desperation) of local procurers (tomb raiders or thieves) and local sellers, as well as the lack of intervention on the part of the national authorities, who may be focused on more urgent troubles or otherwise distracted from, and dismissive of, crimes involving cultural goods.

Acting on demand appears instead to be the more effective method, particularly in the primary export countries for looted antiquities, which tend to be poorer nations. The following measures may improve the situation, and facilitate on-demand evaluation. This can stop the illicit flow of cultural goods before the goods disappear, and before the police need to investigate. Prevention is the best cure.

- Improve the security and inventory check standards for museums, churches, art galleries, and archaeological sites.
- Promote frequent sharing amongst the representatives of these institutions, both nationally and internationally, working together and pooling resources to realize common initiatives against thefts.
- Agreements on security should eventually reach an international standard among similar institutions. This will let the potential thieves perceive a real and broad effort to safeguard cultural goods. Criminals will feel the strength of international unity working against them.
- Enforce the owners of cultural goods (private and institutional) to document and classify their collections.

The precise application of such procedures will discourage thieves, fences, and potential purchasers, introducing a real element of uncertainty in their relationships. Undermine the inherently suspicious relationship between thieves/looters, providers, and purchasers of illicit goods. The more complete and extensive the documentation on any cultural object, the higher the chance that investigators can retrieve it, should it go missing. An up-to-date documentation system will discourage those approaching the market of illicit artworks, introduce a level of uncertainty to illicit deals, and add an element of greater certainty to the lawful transactions. Further options include:

- Severe controls on the purchase activity of museums, galleries, art merchants, and private collectors, to ensure the purchase of objects whose licit provenance has been certified. Potential buyers should have to actively prove that the object they wish to acquire does not have any illicit history to it, rather than what is commonplace today—that buyers need only prove that they did not *know* about an object's illicit history. This would therefore turn the proof of due diligence and good faith from its current passive system to one that required active proof from the potential purchasers and the dealer/provider.

The acquisition policy of artworks by some institutions is at times rather laissez-faire. A systematic control is then needed by officers, who must be legally able to sanction or block transactions before they occur. In effect, nations should make the process of purchasing cultural goods more complex. This will result in less demand, particularly from the primarily unknowing consumers of looted antiquities—legitimate buyers who are unaware or oblivious to the true origins of the antiquities that they wish to collect. This action would, at first thought, increase black market activity, by making legitimate sales more difficult. But the actual black market for stolen art is already limited, due to its unique, recognizable nature, and such sanctions would not provide more options for criminals in the limited market. It would serve to limit the main market for looted antiquities, forcing potential noncriminal buyers to prove the legitimate provenance of the goods they wish to buy. The goal is to cut the links between the legal and illegal worlds, eliminating the blurry line that now separates the two in the art trade, and depriving the criminals of a good market slice—the noncriminal buyers who inadvertently buy illicit goods.

Translating these indications into real directives, national governments should force the sellers to provide a certificate of legitimate ownership. In this way, the burden of proof would fall primarily on the seller/provider/dealer. The actual owners would share this duty, to guarantee that their ownership of the object in question is in obedience with the correct provenance standards. Burden of proof would therefore fall primarily on the seller (who may or may not be the actual owner). Secondary burden of proof would fall on the actual owner, and tertiary burden of proof would fall to the buyer. This forces three checkpoints into each transaction.[3]

Finally,

- Adopt an international ethical code of behavior, signed by nationals institutions such as museums, galleries, and auction houses, regulating their activities through the codification of rules that must be followed by both individuals and institutions—a Geneva Convention for ethics in the art trade.
- Develop habits of legality and respect, among private collectors, for the artistic heritage of source nations. Despite the progress made by national and international laws against theft, burglary, and the traffic of artworks, the investment in the future depends mostly on the awareness of individual people, not only institutions. Thus, inform the general public as well as the art-savvy public of the dangers of art crime, and the benefits of preserving one's cultural heritage. Develop a culture of legality and respect for the cultural goods, especially in the richest countries, which are most responsible as consumers of goods illegally exported from source nations.

Art crime is the degenerate outcome of the concept of personal elevation through the exclusive possession of the cultural heritage of one's own nation and of foreign nations—even when consumers must resort to illicit appropriation.

The aforementioned measures by which nations may better care for and protect their cultural goods may not always represent the definitive solution, and may not be appropriate for some countries, due to the state of their internal affairs. It appears nevertheless as the simplest way to evaluate and exert some control over the insurgents that undermine the safety of the cultural patrimony. It forms a basic structure that may be adopted to fit the needs of individual nations.

The most important condition with which to begin any initiative resides in the knowledge of the heritage itself. The full cataloguing of goods, their detailed description, the photographic documentation, and regular inventory of their location are key elements for any type of control and safeguard.

In context, the need is to underscore what UNESCO has already stated, and apply their suggestions internationally. It is of critical importance that all countries safeguard their cultural patrimony. The job of a special unit, team, or force to care for cultural heritage is to constantly underline, enforce, and punish national and international cases of illicit appropriation by rich consumer countries against poorer source nations. The pillage of source nations, and the criminal activity that it funds, should trigger in us all a greater attention to the security of cultural patrimony.

To conclude, I firmly believe that the battle against the art crime will be either won or lost together.[4]

NOTES

1. Translated by Dr. Michele Armano, with additional edits by Noah Charney.

2. ICOM: Consejo Internacional de Museos; ICCROM: Centro Intern.de Estudios sobre la Consevaciò y Restauraciòn des Bienes Culturales; WCO: Organizaciòn Mundial de Aduanas.

3. Editor's Note: It should be noted that all other multibillion-dollar international markets have such standards built in already. Only the art trade has somehow managed to escape strict initiatives and maintained its centuries-old sense of gentlemen's agreements, codes of silence and anonymity, and clandestine deals. Imagine someone in the real estate market trying to sell a house without a complete ownership history, to prove that the current owners are not squatters, selling a house while the actual owners are on holiday. Pastore's excellent point should be taken up by an economist with knowledge of the art trade, to map out how an increase in requirements for legitimate deals would influence the black market. The logical response is that there would be fewer legitimate deals, with more goods flowing into the black market, to avoid the tighter controls. But the black market in art is so limited due to the ease of dissemination of information on stolen goods, most art being unique and instantly recognizable, that the illicit fine art market cannot be successfully flooded, as there is such a limited demand for obviously stolen artworks. The greater danger is in nonrecognizable, unregistered antiquities looted directly from the earth or the sea, for which the

primary market is the buyer who would never identify themselves, publicly or privately, as criminal. They buy antiquities at full value on the open market, assuming that they have a legitimate provenance, and perhaps not looking too hard to learn if they do not (or else lose the prize purchase).

4. Editor's Note: Pastore's most dramatic point, which will certainly be most controversial to the art trade, is his recommendation that all nations should require the sellers of cultural goods (fine art or antiquities) to provide a certificate of legitimate ownership that a nonpartisan, nonprofit group should evaluate and deem acceptable. Today, potential buyers need only prove that they did not *know* about an object's illicit history. Pastore suggests that owners, sellers, and potential buyers should have to actively *prove* that the object they wish to acquire does *not* have any illicit history to it. This would therefore turn the proof of due diligence and good faith from its current passive system to one that required active proof from the potential purchasers and the dealer/provider.

In this way, the burden of proof would fall primarily on the seller/dealer. The actual owners would share the duty of proof of legitimate ownership, which should date back as far as possible, to guarantee that their ownership of the object in question is in obedience with the correct provenance standards, which should be made international. Burden of proof would therefore fall primarily on the seller (who may or may not be the actual owner). Secondary burden of proof would fall on the actual owner, and tertiary burden of proof would fall to the buyer. This forces three checkpoints into each transaction.

PART IV

Security and Museums

Chapter 12

Q&A with Two Innovative Security Directors

Dennis Ahern
Anthony Amore

The editor, Noah Charney, asked the questions.

First, a bit of background. How did you come to work in museum security?

DA: As with most of us, I think, more or less by accident. I had been working with a large hotel group, which was going through a lot of changes. Tate was restructuring and planning the opening of a major new modern art museum, Tate Modern. I went along for an interview, and left as the new safety and security manger for Tate Modern.

AA: In 2005, I learned that the Isabella Stewart Gardner Museum (ISGM) was recruiting for a new security director. Having worked in Boston for nearly 15 years, I was aware of the museum, its amazing collection, and its unfortunate loss in 1990.

At the time, I was serving with the Department of Homeland Security's Transportation Security Administration at Boston's Logan International Airport as the Assistant Federal Security Director for Inspections. This position allowed me the opportunity to use the physical security and investigations experience I gained as a special agent with the Federal Aviation Administration to lead a team of 15 inspectors through major security assessments and investigations. When I learned that the ISGM was looking for a person with this very skill set, I met with the Director of Operations, the Chief Operating Officer, and ultimately Anne

Hawley, the museum's director, and discussed the Director of Security position. I was impressed with the ISGM's attitudes related to security. To a person, the leadership at the ISGM expressed a willingness and desire to dedicate whatever resources necessary to protect Mrs. Gardner's collection.

Back then, I felt that the security posture at Logan Airport was strong and robust and that my work with TSA was complete. I therefore felt comfortable making a move to the ISGM. It was not lost on me that I was moving from the airport from which the worst terrorist attack to occur on U.S. soil was launched to the museum at which the largest art theft in history took place. Challenges such as these don't come often in a security professional's career, and I consider myself honored to have had the opportunity to face them.

Many security directors are ex-military, like you, Dennis. How did your work in the armed forces help with your current position? Do you feel there is a crossover of skills and knowledge?

DA: I feel it helped a lot, others might say it is a hindrance—but the armed forces give you a sense of being at once objective and being led by results. Because of this, you tend not to let the smaller challenges detract you. And armed forces humor, certainly in the United Kingdom, is slightly on the dark side, so that can be a help in this line of work.

What changes did you make at the Tate Museums when you became security director?

DA: Initially, Tate Modern was a blank canvas, as the building was not yet open. Brian Gray, who was at that time the Head of Operations and Visitor Services (and my boss), was a very experienced operations manager. He had worked at Royal Albert Hall and other major venues, and had clear ideas about the infrastructure that would work best. So together we designed the visitor service levels, and went from there into security measures.

Were there different qualities that you sought in staff, or taught in training, related to the new, more proactive security measures at Tate?

DA: Horses for courses. Gallery assistants have high levels of knowledge and interest in the artworks, so they are employed, in the main, on the gallery floors. The security officers are government-licensed, and respond immediately if an incident occurs. A key element is our Duty Manager system. We have some excellent people who carry out this role, and they direct and manage all incident response. The gallery assistants handle general matters on the floor, and if there's an incident, the duty manager will direct the response, sending in the security officers as necessary.

Anthony, when you worked at Logan Airport, you began to implement some security measures, at the suggestion of Israeli Intelligence consultants. Could you talk about those suggestions, their impetus and goals, specifically with regard to airport security and guard management?

AA: Immediately following the attacks of September 11, 2001, Israeli security consultants offered a number of important suggestions for improving security at Logan Airport. However, I would submit that the most valuable post-9/11 security initiatives implemented at the airport were the result of a close working relationship forged between officials from the Massachusetts Port Authority (Massport, the governing body that runs Logan Airport), the Transportation Security Administration, and the Massachusetts State Police. Perhaps the best example of the collaborative effort is the implementation of the "Screening Passengers by Observations Techniques" (SPOT) program.

In December 2002, Lt. Peter DiDomenica of the Massachusetts State Police created the Behavior Assessment Screening System (BASS). Basically, this system established a racially neutral baseline to identify persons in the airport exhibiting behaviors outside of the norm. With the blessing of the leadership of the State Police and Massport, Lt. DiDomenica presented his program to TSA Federal Security Director George Naccara, his deputy, David Ishihara, and me. Because I was at the time primarily responsible for all of our nearly 1,000 security screeners, I saw great promise in deploying Lt. DiDomenica's BASS program to our workforce. Admiral Naccara, who is perhaps the most forward-thinking security professional I have ever met, Mr. Ishihara and I all saw the value in having our enormous workforce understand the behavioral baselines established by Lt. DiDomenica. Working as a team, we presented the program to TSA headquarters, where it was thoroughly vetted by professional behavioral scientists from government and academia and found not only to be a valid assessment system, but an exceptional tool for identifying possible criminal or terrorist behavior.

Today, Lt. DiDomenica's creation (now called SPOT by the TSA) is deployed at about 150 airports across the United States. I truly believe it is an essential layer of security in the airport environment, as it has been proven effective and is a great motivator for guard personnel. It really helps to break the monotony that sometimes affects security personnel performance while elevating the awareness of security personnel.

Another great example of the new paradigm in security set at Logan is the daily security meetings held at the airport. Implemented immediately following the 2001 attacks, Massport and federal officials began holding 8:30 AM meetings to which all airport and security stakeholders were invited. To this day, these meetings are still held every day—seven days a week—and offer the entire airport community the opportunity to express concerns and observations and also to ask questions of, and receive briefings from, state and federal officials. Each morning, representatives from all of the airport's air carriers, cargo operators, and other tenants meet with Massport, State Police, TSA, Customs and Border Protection, Air Marshals, and other security and law enforcement bodies to ensure that the whole community is on the same page related to security.

Did you find the new measures (suspect profiling, etc.) improved security at Logan? Were there any statistics you could share, regarding improvements related to the new security measures? Were more individuals identified who were genuinely up to no good (terrorism aside)?

AA: There are many success stories associated with behavioral profiling by airport security personnel. In fact, the TSA posts success stories in the form of statistics on their Web site each week. Without fail, there is mention of individuals who are arrested based on initial observations of suspicious behavior.

My favorite success story comes from Logan Airport. Lt. DiDomenica once identified an individual exhibiting suspicious behavior that was outside of the norm set forth by his established baselines. He approached the individual and found that it was actually a federal agent who was en route to test a security checkpoint by trying to slip a threat item by the security screeners. It makes great sense that BASS worked in this instance. As a person who performed such tests early in his career, I can attest to the fact that it can be a stressful experience. Further, the fact that he wasn't there as a typical traveler forced subtle and unconscious behaviors that were identifiable to the trained observer (in this instance, Lt. DiDomenica). I think this is a great example of the efficacy of behavioral profiling.

How did your airport staff react to the proposed changes? Did they implement what you wanted smoothly and effectively?

AA: In my experiences with the TSA, I found that change was never easy. We had an enormous workforce, consisting almost exclusively of brand new federal employees. Implementation of new programs were not always smooth, but I do believe that they were effective.

Were there different qualities that you sought in staff, or taught in training, related to the new, more proactive security measures at Logan?

AA: There was no shortage of people who were highly motivated and mission-oriented, and they quickly rose to the top at the airport. Many of our employees enlisted out of a sense of patriotism. The climate in the country today, sadly, seems to be changing, and the lessons of September 11, 2001, seem to be fading. But even today I hear from airport security personnel who are intensely proud of the successes we achieved at the airport.

We worked hard to identify those employees who showed exceptional leadership abilities. These people were quickly given responsibility for training their fellow employees. For example, two employees of the TSA in Boston, Carl Maccario and Heather Callahan, quickly showed an aptitude and dedication to the behavioral profiling system and today are widely recognized throughout the agency as experts in this burgeoning field.

How might you implement the lessons learned from your improvements at Logan Airport to museum security? Which aspects of the suspect profiling could transfer to museum security, and guard profiling of museumgoers to look for suspicious behavior?

AA: There are an enormous amount of lessons from the improvements that we implemented at Logan Airport that are transferable to museum security. Many of them are basic:

1. Always be aware of identification media display requirements
2. maintain a zero (or near-zero, depending on the number issued) key and access media unaccountability rate
3. be diligent when conducting background checks
4. ensure that training standards are up to par and are met.

Others, however, might not be so obvious.

Museums should always be engaged in risk management activities, looking for vulnerabilities. This can become a tiresome exercise, indeed. However, there are few things as valuable to the security of an institution as a comprehensive vulnerability assessment. Domain awareness is absolutely essential to the success of a security program, and I would encourage all security directors to gather and review—*on a daily basis*—all metrics related to their programs. There is simply no excuse for not knowing your institution's weaknesses at every moment. For instance, you need to know even if one single motion detector is not performing, because if it is not, you are that much more vulnerable. Information like that is priceless in deploying guards on a daily basis.

There is also great value in training museum gallery guards to use race-neutral behavioral observations and assessments. Behavioral observation training makes for a more engaged guard, and helps to eliminate the monotony that can come with being stationed in a gallery for an extended period of time. The benefits of this program are enormous, as I witnessed firsthand in the aviation security sector. Along these lines, I applaud forward thinkers such as Dennis Ahern, who have seen the value of behavioral profiling and have implemented it at their institutions.

How do you see museum security in general today (without naming any institutions)? Do you think it is generally effective?

DA: I think it is generally effective. I have many friends and colleagues in the sector, both in the United Kingdom and overseas. We talk a lot. Many of the same challenges come up. But the bottom line is that the statistics lend themselves to the fact of museum security being as effective as it can be, without seriously detracting from the ultimate objective—allowing the public to see the exhibits, whether it is art or other artifacts, in a safe and enjoyable environment. The balance must be struck between keeping the exhibits as safe as possible, while still granting public access to them. Given those two agendas, which are in many ways contradictory, museums do very well.

AA: Museum security today is, in my opinion, in a state of flux. Without a central set of regulations governing how all museums must operate their security systems, the policies and procedures in place are as varied in substance and quality as are the institutions themselves.

I have been very impressed with the security directors I have met, and to a person they seem dedicated to pushing the envelope in terms of bringing their institution up to speed in the latest technologies and procedures. However, budgetary constraints and a sense of "it can't happen here" have had a detrimental effect on many institutions.

I read recently the text of a presentation that museum security consultant Steve Keller gave at a cultural property protection seminar in 1999. Mr. Keller spoke at length about the problem presented by organizations that have not suffered a loss at their museum. Often, it takes a tragedy to open the eyes of the chief decision makers, and it is often only after a loss that security directors start to be heard.

Fortunately for me, the leadership at the Gardner Museum is as supportive as any I have ever encountered. From the museum director on down, there is a genuine interest and excitement over ideas and initiatives that come out of my department. This was an important factor in my decision to come aboard.

How would you rank the relative importance of various security measures (alarms, locks, RFID tags, human guards, surveillance) in most museums today? How do you think they should be ranked in importance, if this is different from what is commonplace?

DA: I do not think there is a rank as such. Each case should be evaluated using a risk assessment method. These risk assessments will vary dependent on the type of establishment and the resources available.

None of these methods of protection can stand alone. A holistic approach is essential and will include some, all, or perhaps none of these factors.

AA: This is an interesting question, and it allows me to speak to my own philosophy of security measures. First, I would say that it is not a useful exercise to try to rank the relative importance of security systems. Each institution has such varied requirements that I'd venture to say that there would probably be five to ten different rankings that would be equally valid. Second, I would posit that a layered approach to security, with multiple redundancies and transparent yet robust measures in place is the most effective approach to security.

It has become almost cliché to say that "security is everyone's business," but, like it or not, it is true. In fact, it is almost a given in the museum environment.

Consider a shopping mall. Most shoppers would not care to notice another person acting suspiciously. However, because museum visitors are so often vested with a love for the art that they have paid to look at, they are very likely to speak up if they think a person means to do harm to the collection. They therefore become an unwitting security measure and a vital layer of security, lending hundreds of sets of eyes and ears to what is going on in the museum.

Rather than ranking the various security measures, I am interested in how they complement each other and work in tandem to overlap the layers of security I have set in place. There are clearly some technologies that are absolutely essential in a twenty-first-century facility. And I believe that as global positioning technology improves and tracking devices become more easily secreted, GPS holds great promise to changing the face of museum theft as we have known it over the past centuries.

What do you feel is the best protection against the new type of "blitz" thefts, involving sudden attacks by masked, armed thieves (like at The Bührle Collection?)

DA: This is becoming a real problem. As museums "target harden" (adding security against specific offenses) against burglary or sneak theft, the options for thieves are reduced. This makes the possibility of the use or threat of violence very real, as the thieves have fewer options. The incidents of this type of theft over the last couple of years are much higher than for the preceding 10 years. It seems to be the new trend.

As to the best protection, it is very difficult to answer in an interview format, and there are people out there much better qualified to do so than I. Personally, I don't advocate the use of armed security officers. Even if that is permissible, a gunfight involving even seasoned professionals, such as armed police or military, is a frighteningly random event, where bad things can happen. Add into this mix a very busy museum, determined and aggressive villains fighting less-trained or experienced individuals, and you have a recipe for disaster.

Certainly, to try and contain robbers inside your museum, preventing their escape with art, is a real risk. You then go from robbery to a potential hostage situation, if criminals feel trapped and desperate. I prefer to avoid containment security measures, and to keep security officers unarmed.

AA: The dilemma of how to prevent blitz thefts is indeed daunting. The effectiveness of such an attack is well documented, and in some respects is limited only by the willingness of the perpetrators to employ violence. There are a number of defenses against this glaring path of least resistance, however. These include:

1. Train guard staff (including staff members stationed to monitor perimeter cameras) to identify the signs of an attack from the sidewalk in to the facility, such as the stationing of a getaway vehicle and the fast, purposeful approach of a group of individuals.
2. Arm a sufficient number of guards in key areas with handheld distress devices designed specifically to alert authorities directly and immediately in the case of such an attack.
3. Secure pieces of the collection in place to make it difficult for thieves to remove them from the facility, thus giving law enforcement a chance to respond in time to catch the thieves.
4. Design exit paths that are not easily accessed once a "smash and grab" type of theft occurs. Of course, local fire codes and issues involving handicapped access have some effect on this.
5. Deploy guard staff in a manner that acts as a deterrent to those casing the building for such an attack.

Though there is no such thing as 100 percent security, layering different methods and building in redundancies brings an institution that much closer to impenetrability.

How are human guards traditionally deployed in museums, and what are the problems with this?

AA: Guards at museums are deployed in myriad ways depending on the particular needs of the institution. At the Gardner Museum, we have guards patrolling every gallery, no matter how small, because literally *everything* in each gallery is part of Mrs. Gardner's collection and legacy. The Gardner is aggressive in the number of guards we deploy. In fact, we have as many guards, or more, on the floor each day as many much larger facilities have in the whole premises.

The problem associated with a large guard force is the rare visitor who feels that they are being watched too closely while in the museum. With the right training, however, the guard staff can do its job without impeding on visitor enjoyment. This is an important part of our guard staff management.

You use the staff at the Tate, particularly docents, in interesting ways. How did your staff and curators react to the proposed changes? Did they implement what you wanted smoothly and effectively?

DA: We now have a good mix of volunteers, gallery assistants, and security officers, all working together quite seamlessly. Initially some of the existing in-house staff were reticent about working with people on contract. But they have now seen that a properly designed and managed contract service is a cost-effective and efficient way of covering a lot of man-hours. I think the key is not having a strong demarcation between the strands of the service provision, contract workers versus in-house staff. Our contract teams are, to all external viewing, part of the Tate team—they wear the same uniforms and are trained in the same subjects.

You combine high-tech with low-tech security measures, protect objects in any one gallery with different techniques, and rotate security measures to prevent hostile surveillance. Can you talk about these techniques, how you came to choose them, and how other museums might consider working along similar lines?

DA: I feel you should always start with nuts and bolts. By this I mean literally, physically anchoring works to immovable objects, such as walls or fixed plinths. Only if this cannot be applied, for whatever reason, do you move on to other methods. These may include electronic devices. You ideally want to end up with an integrated approach, combining high-tech with low-tech. I use a range of options for different artworks, tailoring security measures to the exhibits they protect. Some tricks work better with works on walls, others with traditional sculpture, and others still with modern sculpture which can take an almost infinite variety of forms. Flexibility is key, avoiding universal solutions in favor of taking the time to design the best security for each individual object.

Do you feel there is an overreliance on high-tech security?

AA: This is a complicated question. I am a believer in high-tech security and continue to be impressed by the products that we deploy. For instance, we have recently upgraded to very impressive night-vision technology for pertinent parts of our facility, and the quality of the image that we are able to get in a room in which one can barely see his hand before his face is amazing. I am also floored by the capacity and ability of our latest-generation digital recording equipment. There are many other technologies that I think important and worthy of a great deal of reliance.

On the other hand, there is a certain danger attached to overlooking the fallibility of technology. For all the great advances in technology, and the exponential improvement in usability, the simple fact of the matter is that technology sometimes fails. Confidence in the operator to be able to respond well and implement contingencies in the event of failure shows the importance human factors play in security.

For these reasons, we at the ISGM have implemented a number of strategic redundancies to ensure that no single human or technological failure leaves us vulnerable to criminal activity.

What recommendations could you give to museums or institutions like churches that have limited budgets for security? Are there lessons from your implementation of low-tech yet effective security measures that could benefit low-budget art institutions?

DA: If I were to give one simple and cheap method for protecting objects on a budget, its high-tensile steel fishing line and good screws. If you or your colleagues can easily remove something, so can a thief. It is that simple.

We work with our conservators to practice the attempted theft of works and our reaction to it, as close to real time as we can. This helps both parties understand the challenges. Conservators are least likely to damage anything in the process of our trial thefts, and participation helps different factions in the museum feel like a team and sympathize with each other's duties.

Conservators will say "we would rather it be gone than damaged." It depends on your viewpoint.

What do you train your staff to do, if they identify a museum-goer acting in a suspicious manner (perhaps sweating and looking around nervously, or apparently engaged in hostile surveillance, looking in behind paintings and such)? What is your preferred response?

DA: In today's climate, we have to consider terrorism as well as crime, so it is an added concern, particularly in a museum as dense with tourists as the Tate Modern. But a simple and cheery "Hello, can I help you? Is everything OK?" from our staff is always a good start. It lets people know they have been observed behaving strangely. Then we keep an eye on them, and see their reaction immediately after having been approached.

If you were to suggest five measures that limited-budget museums could make to improve their security, what would they be?

DA: I would say,

1. Get a clear inventory of possessions. You cannot protect it if you do not know it is there. Routinely count or revisit the list, take photos, find unusual ingrained identifiers on works (such as cracks or faults) and photograph them clearly. Such details could help with recovery.

2. Evaluate whether each object can be protected by distance from potential thieves or vandals, height from potential troublemakers, or whether robust cases are needed. Use physics to your advantage—after all, it is free of charge, and we are stuck with it anyway.
3. Cameras are great for evidence after the event. But unless they are permanently monitored, don't assume that they are the answer to your prayers. They are a tool of the trade, not a security coverall.
4. Alarms are great, if someone can respond effectively. If not, they are just noise. Make sure your staff is trained in how to respond to alarms in a useful and timely manner.
5. Put some high-visibility markers behind or beneath vulnerable moveable objects. This trick might not stop it from going anywhere, but it will bring a theft to your attention a bit sooner than might otherwise.

AA: There are a number of measures that a security director can take at little or no cost. They include:

1. Engage the entire museum community, including employees and volunteers, to take an active role in the security of the facility. Let them know how important they are to identifying problems and potential thefts or vandalism. Museum frontline staff can be invaluable in identifying or taking immediate action in the case of an incident of theft or vandalism.
2. Be vigilant in enforcing measures such as ID display and the issuance of property passes. Don't be afraid to be a "nag" to your fellow employees. Regular reminders of protocols and the importance of security procedures is essential.
3. Work with local police to express your needs in terms of response and perimeter security. Knowing the local officers who patrol your area is key.
4. Train your guards in race-neutral behavioral profiling and SPOT methods.
5. Deploy your staff based on risk rather than tradition.
6. Perform regularly-scheduled in-house training.
7. Communicate your goals for the security staff so that they feel vested in the program and understand why you are making the decisions that you have.

These are just a sampling of cost-effective measures that can truly improve your security posture.

Several museum security directors around the world are actively investigating past thefts from their museums. Could you discuss this dual role of protector and investigator?

AA: While the security of the collection is my first priority, there is nothing I wish more than to recover the art stolen from the ISGM in 1990. I really look forward to the day when my job is solely protecting those 13 pieces of art, rather than finding them.

As much as this is true, I do think that any person who is charged with investigating crimes involving art, and at the same time protecting art, cannot help but have a heightened perspective on his security role. In the course of my work investigating the Gardner heist, I have done a great deal of research into art crime and the methodologies of the art criminal. Spending such an enormous amount of time on such an endeavor has made me more keenly aware of the vulnerabilities that exist at museums. So in this way, our current security posture, which I think is outstanding, has benefited from the work I have done on the investigation. I think that my colleagues would agree that there is much to be learned about the ways in which museum thefts occur and that these lessons learned are invaluable to current protection strategies.

What do you think is the future of art theft? Is it these "blitz" thefts we have seen lately, that seem to neutralize alarm-based security through surprise and speed? What do you think is the best way to protect against the future of art theft?

AA: Much work needs to be done in terms of awareness of the problem of art theft throughout the world. To this end, I think that the work of ARCA and other reputable organizations like the Museum Security Network are invaluable to putting a dent in the problem.

In terms of technology, I do believe that the future of art theft prevention holds great promise. I am especially excited about the prospect of deploying GPS technology to protect art. When one considers the success of Lojack in recovering stolen automobiles, it's easy to see the promise of secreting an imperceptible GPS device on a painting or object so that if it is indeed stolen, recovery methods will be greatly enhanced, especially in the crucial hours immediately following the crime.

DA: Short question, but not a short answer, I'm afraid. If criminals are prepared to take lives in order to commit their crimes, there is very little real defense, unless the works are guarded like bullion. This would clearly negate the intent and the ability to display great and iconic works, turning the museum into a sealed vault. It would reduce the number of works that could be shown. It could end up, in a very gloomy future world, as a virtual art gallery, with only images of the works on display. That is what we want to avoid. If you want to give public access to original artworks, there will be risk, and there is no real defense against a thief who is willing to kill in order to steal.

Chapter 13

Exercises in Futility: The Pursuit of Protecting Art

Stevan P. Layne

Museums spend millions on the acquisition of valuable artwork. Millions more are spent on the construction of beautiful structures to house collections, attract visitors, and exhibit and store their artworks. A fraction of these costs are reserved for electronic systems to protect the art, and even less for the annual budget to screen candidates for employment, train security staff, and monitor the daily activities of both staff and visitors.

Armed robberies of major collections make the news. Overnight burglaries, particularly those that might parallel movie depictions of the techniques, like the elaborate bypass of exotic alarms, always make the headlines. On the other hand, thefts from collections perpetrated by present or past staff members rarely make the news, unless well-known or exceptionally valuable art is involved.

In recent surveys of U.S. museums, most if not all of their recent thefts involved employees. If missing art is removed from storage, or any area of the museum other than the exhibit area, the chances of a nonemployee or contractor being involved are slim. Yet many museums fail to initiate the basic protection steps to reduce the vulnerability to internally related theft. These include, but are not limited to:

- Properly installed electronic intrusion detection devices, video surveillance, and exhibit protection alarms.
- Proper monitoring and response to surveillance systems and intrusion detection systems.
- Strict key control.

- Thorough preemployment screening of staff, volunteers, contractors, and vendors.
- Periodic post-employment checks with criminal records repositories.
- Consistent checks and balances by staff and external auditors.
- Positive package inspection at all incoming and outgoing access points, especially staff and contractor exits.

In the aftermath of many museum losses, it is found that employees involved with theft steal more than one object, and more often than on one occasion. Collusion among employee-related thieves is a rare occurrence. While regular full-time employees may have the best opportunities to steal, part-time employees, contractors, volunteers, and former employees are often involved. Anyone with unsupervised access to collections, access to keys and/or alarm codes, after-hours access to the facilities, or unmonitored access to storage areas or museum exits may be involved with losses.

In one little-publicized case, the museum hired an individual to serve as registrar. His credentials were self-manufactured, and his experience minimal. No one checked. Over a period of a couple of years, he systematically removed items from the collection, along with the corresponding accession card. He sold artifacts on the open market, until someone finally realized that collection items were missing. A few phone calls, prior to hiring, would have revealed numerous inconsistencies in the applicant's stated background.

In another case, a museum recognized for its highly sophisticated electronic systems and professional security force survived a potentially damaging incident. A security officer on night patrol was alerted to an alarm in a gallery, well after closing hours. Initial inspections found everything in order, and the alarm was logged as "false." There are no "false" alarms—only some that may be unfounded. Something makes alarms go off, whether caused by people, the environment, or, on rare occasions, faults with the device itself. This same alarm initiated a couple of times and the responding officer made a cursory inspection of the gallery each time, reporting the alarm as false. When the next shift took over, both the dispatcher and security officer briefed their relief, reporting a troublesome alarm in the involved gallery. The new shift, however, included a supervisor and trainee for the patrol function. Not long after the shift began, that same alarm initiated. This time, the supervisor led the trainee on a thorough search of the gallery. It was not long until an inebriated "visitor" was found passed out behind an exhibit. Each time the drunk had rolled over in his sleep, the motion-detector alarm had gone off. He had been there since the museum closed, several hours earlier. The lesson learned: Alarms alone cannot protect your property. It takes the astute efforts of a dedicated and alert staff, following consistent procedures to complete the protection picture.

We could fill page after page with "war stories" of incidents related to employee theft and/or failure to properly respond in the protection of museum collections. I am often amazed, but not surprised, to learn that staff members who steal do so for extended periods, without raising any suspicions, in spite of blatant acts. In one large facility, a financial manager consistently skimmed thousands of dollars annually from daily deposits. No one became suspicious when this mid-level manager bought expensive cars, took expensive overseas vacations, or even when he purchased a home that should have been out of reach for his salary level. He might still be there if an upset staff member had not "dropped the dime" to report irregularities—after what was determined to be years of losses.

The remedies, or sound prevention methods, are available to institutions of any size, scope, or budget. Museums take surprisingly few preventive measures until after the fact. That is closing the barn after the horses are gone—throwing up a few cameras, changing locks, and adding a few alarms are all Band-Aids on a gaping wound. You need to have a plan. We suggest a major long-term protection plan that encompasses every aspect of museum protection. Simply utilizing a generic checklist or online assessment guideline is better than doing nothing, but not by much. Each museum has a unique environment, to include physical makeup of the building and its surroundings, composition of the staff, composition of the collections, operating philosophies of the director, curators, registrar, and security manager, and the amount of emphasis placed on daily operational protection methods.

In smaller institutions, the duties of operations manager, security manager, HR manager, and facilities manager fall on one or two individuals. Expertise in the selection of electronic systems, preemployment screening, and training of staff are often left to vendors or contract agencies. Where there is no direct supervision by a knowledgeable administrator, gaps in the protection picture are widened.

What can you do to better protect your assets? How can you identify the potential thief among your trusted staff? What positive protection measures may be applied without damaging the museum's dedication to providing a quality experience for the visitor and an enjoyable working environment for staff?

These are the questions posed by astute directors and managers whenever change is in the wind. The following guidelines are suggested for most facilities. However, we recognize the need to tailor protection measures to the specific needs of the institution, related to factors previously stated.

THE MUSEUM AS BANK VAULT

Protect the building like you would a bank vault. Banks do not store money in containers that anyone may access. They tightly restrict access and regularly audit both practices and inventories. The museum needs to assure that its collections are housed in a facility that may withstand changes in temperature and humidity, pest infestations, attempts to penetrate the perimeter, and attempts by insiders to remove valuable assets. This means a sound application of physical barriers, special lighting, use of electronic systems, use of video surveillance, and both regular and irregular patrols.

SCREEN EVERYONE

A thorough background screen needs to be conducted for every employee, volunteer, and intern. This should include checks of criminal history records, credit checks, education verification, verification of previous employment, and character references. Any attempts at falsification of facts presented on the application should mean ineligibility. Background information that is impossible to verify should become suspect. A professional personal interview should be helpful in determining capabilities and character. Exit interviews for departing employees are also critical, to determine whether there might be any passive-aggression or scheming on the part of the departing employee that could lead to a future security incident.

DOUBLE-CHECK AND REORIENT

Do not assume that previous employers provided proper or necessary training. Rudimentary orientation and training for each position should be a part of the hiring process. Professional, scenario-based, classroom and field training are best. On-the-job, video, or correspondence training produces some results, but should be supplemental to a sound hands-on training program.

SELECT TAILORED ELECTRONIC SYSTEMS

Select the museum's electronic systems with the same care and scrutiny you would use to buy a new car or home. Know what you want before you start looking. Screen potential vendors by checking with existing clientele. Require competitive bidding to assist in the selection process. Assure that system contracts benefit the museum, as much or more than they benefit the vendor.

REEVALUATE POLICIES

Utilize proven policies, procedures, and operational guidelines. Policies governing visitors after hours, access to buildings and collections, substance abuse, use or handling of museum assets, key distribution and retrieval, vendor selection, money handling, and protection of assets should all be refined, reviewed, and in place.

PARTICIPATE IN THE PROFESSIONAL COMMUNITY

Participation in recognized professional organizations is recommended to network with peers, learn by others' mistakes, and gain by others' experimentation. ASIS, AAM, ARCA, IFCPP, ICMS, and regional security or museum protection organizations should be considered.

QUESTION VENDORS

Vendors and their employees should be required to present evidence of criminal history clearances before being allowed on the property. This is a standard practice and should be part of every contract.

BEWARE OF LOW BIDS

Selection of both proprietary and contract security officers is a task requiring attention to detail and knowledge of the industry as a whole. "Low bid" selection processes often result in low performance. Detailed specifications should require optimum standards in appearance, education, qualifications, and performance.

KEEP UP TO DATE WITH TOPICAL PUBLICATIONS

Review of topical publications is helpful. *Suggested Practices in Museum Security* is a generic guideline that outlines "what you ought to have." The *Cultural Property Protection Manual* is a guideline with draft policies, procedures, and checklists included. *Suggested Practices* is available through ASIS, and the *Protection Manual* is available through the IFCPP. Subscribing to professional journals on security, museums, and art crime is a good way to keep up to date.

AUDIT AND SELF-EVALUATE OFTEN

Special audits should be performed by both internal and external parties. External audits should utilize the services of persons not affiliated in any way with system or service vendors.

It is difficult to predict who will steal or aid someone in the commission of theft. Directors, curators, business managers, finance managers, registrars, security managers, security officers, volunteers, interns, contractors, vendors, and regular museum staff have all been involved in thefts. Anyone with the opportunity to remove valuable art and not get caught may take that opportunity.

Your protection program needs to reduce the opportunity to steal. Getting caught should be a distinct possibility, and severe penalties need to be in place to dissuade potential opportunistic criminals from trying. If there is no clear opportunity, there will be no crimes of opportunity.

Chapter 14

Security for Temporary Exhibitions: Regular, Customized, or Bespoke

Dick Drent

The world as we know it is changing, and with it our way of thinking alters, whether we like it or not. Terrorism is just one of the issues, along with increased crime rates and environmental problems that make us feel unsafe and aware of the potential dangers that surround us. These issues affect our way of living and our way of thinking. In this context, we may also reflect on worldwide changes in the field of museum security that have been taking place during the last decade.

The way we used to protect our cultural heritage, with a primary focus on the conservation element of protection, is no longer sufficient. There are more risks that endanger our heritage than ever before. We are forced to increase security measurements in a much more sophisticated way than we would like—and here the friction lies. It is one thing to discuss the necessary measures taken on organizational, constructional, and electronic security levels (also known as the OCE levels) with colleagues from the security field, but it is quite another thing explaining what is required, in this era of new dangers, to a board of trustees, to the museum's director, its conservators, the heads of its exhibitions, or other substantive decision makers in the field of cultural heritage.

Therefore, it is necessary for professionals in the field of art and art security to communicate with each other and to learn from the issues at hand. It is not about right or wrong, good or bad, nice or ugly. It is all about cooperation within a museum and between museums, to make the most beautiful exhibitions in the most secure way possible.

Here lies the key. If we can communicate on this level, with respect for the wishes, needs, and agendas of all the parties involved in running a museum, it will be much easier to get connected and get things done. One of the less-touted roles of a museum security director is that of ambassador between departments, to produce the best exhibitions at the lowest possible risk, while stepping on as few toes as possible and keeping everyone happy.

Within the security business, the way of thinking has changed. We now know how to secure our museums in the best way, and what is needed in order to do so. Having learned from past mistakes and successes, we as security directors can produce a better security system that is more effective and efficient than ever before. Our next challenge is to connect to the other substantive parts of the museum's organizational nucleus, endeavoring to make our security measures work within the context of the museum as a whole. The message is this: each department needs to step off from its island and work together for the improvement of the museum.

Of course, there are many roads that lead towards Rome, and therefore it is not to say that the method used at the Van Gogh Museum is the holy grail of security measures. But, arrogant as I may sound, as a security expert, I dare to say it is one of the better ways, and I can prove that it is working.

I am going to take you through the steps that we took at the Van Gogh Museum (to which I will refer as VGM), and will give you the results of our improved theories and practices in how to secure a museum and its individual exhibitions, either permanent or temporary. When it comes to your museums, it is up to you how you want to get it done. This is just one example that has proved successful. Each museum has its own peculiarities, and so any objective security measures may be taken as they are, customized, or even altered in major ways, "tailor-made" to each new institution.

THE VGM METHOD

The impact of 9/11 has led the management of the VGM to investigate the museum's security. In the summer of 2002, a security audit was conducted in the VGM. The results were astonishing. The VGM needed to seriously improve its security measures on all levels: organizational, constructional, and electronic. Plans to do so were well underway when, one day, reality caught up with us before we could close the circle.

In the early morning hours of December 7, 2002, thieves propped up a ladder against the rear of the museum, and climbed 15 feet to a first-story window. They smashed through the glass and gained entrance into the building. It took only minutes for the thieves to run to the main exhibition hall and steal two Van Gogh paintings, *View of the Sea at Scheveningen* and *Congregation Leaving the Reformed Church in Nuenen*, valued at €3 million. Even though the break-in immediately triggered an alarm, the police were not able to get to the museum in time to apprehend the robbers.

In December 2003, the police tracked down the two prime suspects, arrested them, and brought them to trial. The suspects were found guilty, and received four- and five-year sentences. Unfortunately, even though the men had been captured, the paintings still have not been retrieved. It is believed that the men exchanged the art works for a large sum of money.

The theft, of course, had a lot of consequences for the museum and its staff. The advice given in the security audit, specifically on the construction and electronic elements of the security, was taken, and new technology was installed in the following months. This included new digital CCTV recording, fences, burglary-proof glass, and additional security staff. We also started a 24/7 dog patrol around the museum, with two dogs on duty during the night. These measures were implemented directly after the burglary.

The VGM management, however, thought that these measures were not enough. Plans were made to further improve the OCE security measures. If the measures already taken had brought the VGM security to a standard acceptable level, the next plan was to take it to the next level.

Members from the security profession will understand that, although there is no international security standard, there are certain elements that large national art collections should expect to have in place in their security. The particulars will vary depending on the museum's security budget. I will discuss these particulars in terms of standard security measures, and then explore how they can be customized or tailor-made to meet the needs of various institutions.

The first step is to test every piece of construction and electronic security equipment that is to be installed in the museum. At the VGM, we tested these ourselves, something that I recommend security directors insist on doing, even when security subcontractors insist that their products have been extensively tested.

For example, protective glass has an international security standard that is based on the time it would take a person to break through it by using various tools. Ordinary glass might break with only one hammer blow. At the VGM, we accepted security glass only after we tested it ourselves—we were not satisfied with testing the glass in a laboratory with a hammer or an axe. We used the big boys, on loan from the police department, who were trained to enter a building in an unconventional way. We chose a testing area that was similar in arrangement and construction to the VGM premises, using the exact sizes of panes of glass that the museum was planning to install, and the same materials used in the museum for the window frames. We attacked the glass not only with regular "burglary" tools, but also with guns, explosives, welding techniques, driving a car through it, and so on.

If the security standard set by the glass company was that their security glass withstands 15 minutes of attempted break-in before it smashed, we wanted a 25-minute resistance. By insisting upon this before signing an expensive security contract with the glass manufacturer, we instigated our own, new security standard, and refused to accept anything less. We used similar testing techniques for the new fences, skylights, walls, and doors. The electronic security measures underwent similar testing by our staff.

The most important part of the security overhaul was the organizational element. The most expensive and ideal construction and electronic measures will not work without a good working security organization. A door, for example, will not close or stay closed if your guards are not trained and ready to act on an alarm. We wanted to go further than just training our guards to react to alarms in the proper way. Once an alarm is sounding, the incident is already well underway. We wanted our guards to prevent an alarm from going off by intercepting the incident before it occurs. This implied training guards to be *proactive* rather than *reactive.* Most times, museums rely primarily on construction and electronic measures and forget to train their guards. Within the VGM, the construction and electronic measures are there only to support the guards in doing their jobs.

THE O-SIDE: ORGANIZATIONAL IMPROVEMENTS

So how do you upgrade your O-side? How do you assemble a team, and how do you get them committed to the cause, protecting the cultural heritage at the highest level? Get them to be proactive instead of reactive.

The work of the guards in a museum used to be dismissed as a "necessary" optical job. That meant that the museum needed someone who the visitors could see, who simply wore a uniform to give the idea that an area was secure; but the guards were not necessarily meant to do anything more than keep, for instance, children from touching the paintings. The "job" of the guard was to react to certain incidents, from enforcing house rules ("no flash photos, please") to providing general information about the museum and its exhibitions to curious visitors. The guards back then were more like uniformed hosts than security personnel. Many museums employed guards who were not specifically trained or skilled, and were mostly students, volunteers, and retired former colleagues, catching up on crossword puzzles. It goes without saying that this was and is inadequate, and did not serve to improve the museum's security.

At the VGM, we began our new approach to security staff with a number of special training programs for guards. First of all, we no longer permitted volunteers to serve as security staff—every guard ought to be a trained, professional security guard. We expanded our staff from 40 guards to 70, and we now are growing to 100 guards. We no longer want subcontracted security companies—we want every guard we have to be a member of our museum's staff.

We also developed a new way of managing our guards.[1]

We use Social Competence Management as a steering tool. We want to see certain elements in our guards that increase their commitment to the museum they work for.

We therefore developed five elements that we want to see in all our guards, and we keep track of their progress over the course of their careers with us. These traits are:

1. Cooperation (working well with other staff)
2. Client services (working well with visitors)
3. Adjusting ability (reacting well to changes and new requests)
4. Commitment (to their careers and the museum)
5. Verbal presentation (whether they are presentable, articulate, polite)

Within these traits, there are examples of behavior that we want to see in our guards. If they do not yet have these skills, we train them in order to improve them. Our training includes communication, robbery actions, surveillance methods, and risk analysis. Offering training, and making the guards feel part of a team, results in a better job commitment.

The security management staff is similarly trained, and they supervise the guards to gauge their social competence. The management evaluations of guards, which once took five minutes, now last an hour. We sought to improve and increase the interaction between management and staff, increasing the sense of camaraderie and teamwork. These extended evaluation meetings have resulted in an improvement on quality of the service on the work floor, and an improved working atmosphere in the museum.

We delegate tasks and responsibilities to those guards who are able to handle them, including the creation of senior-guards, therefore providing our staff with opportunities to work toward promotions—an added incentive towards loyalty and dedication to the museum.

All new and old staff, in addition to the aforementioned on-site training, are trained in a variety of specialized skills. Such skills have been practiced during ORRI training.

ORRI TRAINING

ORRI stands for Observation, Recognition of behavior, Risk analysis, and Intervention.[2] This course was developed from tactics and techniques in law enforcement, borrowing heavily from the fields of surveillance, police infiltration, and SWAT. It includes the following elements:

Observation

In observation, we train the guards to understand the difference between seeing and watching. Seeing implies passivity, while watching implies seeing in order to gather information. We teach them to find the right spot to oversee a situation without being obtrusive, even in uniform. We go over how to approach a subject in a natural way, such as a visitor exhibiting suspicious behavior. The next step is getting the necessary information with which to make an informed decision about how to proceed. For instance, a good description of a potentially suspicious subject may be forwarded to the next post or to the control room for further action.

Recognition of Behavior

Recognition of behavior is the next step. We determined what exemplifies normal and abnormal behavior in a museum context. For example, in a square with 1,000 clothed people, you would immediately notice a naked person. But in a sauna, you would not. There, a person with clothes on will get your attention. If a guard knows what is normal, he can recognize what is abnormal behavior for museum-goers.

In a museum, abnormal behavior might consist of searching out CCTV cameras, showing an interest in the guards and how they do their rounds, peering behind the works of art, not looking at the art as they walk through the museum, and so on. These traits suggest hostile surveillance, and must be noted by guards. If guards are trained to be on the lookout for such behavior, it has the added bonus of giving them a proactive task, so they will be better prepared to react if the need arises.

Risk Analysis

When a guard has gathered the necessary information, he must make a risk analysis based on what he has observed, and how it differs from normal behavior. Is there an immediate threat, and if so, what should he do? Does he have enough information to warrant an intervention? If so, what kind of intervention should he choose? In this part of the training, we teach proper risk analysis, even for small incidents like food or drinks in an exhibition room, or photographing where it is not allowed.

Intervention

The risk analysis may lead the guard to an intervention. Here, the guard must choose if it will be a security intervention, or a host intervention. Security interventions are reserved for cases of a real risk or perceived immediate threat (for instance, a masked man enters the museum). A host intervention is a nonconfrontational initial step to gather more information on what may require a security intervention, to correct nonthreatening illegal behavior (e.g., eating in the gallery), or to help museum-goers.

This training is practical. We use actors in a "live" situation in an open museum, full of guests who are unaware that training is taking place. This makes the situation very realistic for the guards. Training amongst the public is an added dimension that has proven to be much more valuable than theoretical or off-site training. You cannot beat the real thing.

The VGM has given this training to every guard on staff and is developing an advanced course, at the request of the guards, which will further augment their training. The fact that the guards requested more training is testament to its success. The new ORRI course (ORRI-II) will incorporate profiling and communication.

There is no standard format to follow if you want to improve your security organization, as the needs of each institution are distinct. But there is a logical guide to getting started.

In order to achieve a regular, a customized, or even the bespoke forms of security that will be an ideal addition to your organization, I recommend the following:

- Audit your museum as objectively and thoroughly as possible, so that you can see all the risks and loopholes.
- Risks need to be presented to the decision makers (the board or director). Make them aware that it is their problem to solve—you are there to help, if they will let you.
- Write out potential scenarios as to where and how these risks can occur in your museum.
- Create measures at the organization, construction, or electronic levels that will function specifically to prevent or control these risks.
- Present the necessary budget for your recommended measures to the board. Make sure that you have decided whether your security measurements should be regular (along standard lines), customized (with some elements altered for the specific museum), or bespoke (for unusual situations and museums that require a reinvention of the regular measures).
- Repeat the evaluation of risk every year. New circumstances, situations, evaluations, and the real-life testing of existing measures can change your view on security. Do not rest on your laurels, but test and retest, anticipating problems and ways to beat your own security.

For future development of security management in a museum, I recommend:

- Stay on top of the O-side of your security organization.
- Compare subcontractors within your own region, country, and even worldwide. Do not settle for any action or product from subcontractors with which you are not completely comfortable (think of our glass testing as an example).
- Start cooperating with colleague museums on security issues. Learn from each other. The VGM started a joint venture with the Rijksmuseum, and that resulted in a newly built, state-of-the-art combined control room for the two museums. Other museums in Amsterdam and even from other parts of the Netherlands are very interested in joining this cooperation, pooling financial resources to improve the situation for all.
- Train not only the guards, but also the responsible people in your organization. Security management training for exhibition managers will give you a profit you would never believe.
- Work on an audit system with colleague museums, and let your museum be audited by a colleague. No one will be better at finding loopholes in your security than a security director at a nearby museum. You can help each other improve your respective museums, and make each other's jobs easier. This a safe and inexpensive way to test your security measures
- Do not be too shy or too proud to get help and advice from colleagues
- Establish a Research and Development section within your museum, specifically for security and facility management
- Make sure the position of the security manager is well placed within in your organization, preferably directly under the director or business-director.

In summation:

- Make sure your security organization is an intrinsic part of the total organization of your museum. It is not a security issue alone. It is a key issue for the entire museum.
- There must be a balance between the O, C, and E measurements
- There is never a state of perfection. You can always improve.
- Improve your organization: plan, do, act, check.
- And always remember: shit happens, so be prepared.

NOTES

1. Editor's Note: Among the essays in this section of the book, we can see a new set of criteria emerging on how best to protect museums, using entirely logical methods that may, nevertheless, sound radical because they differ from so much of the laissez-faire security that exists in most of the world's museums today, including major national galleries. Rather than summarize and reiterate what the essayists have expressed, I wish to draw the reader's attention to the overlap and mutual agreement among the essayists of new and critical implementations, many of which require no significant increase in budget.

2. Editor's Note: Note the similarity between the SPOT and BASS training to which Amore referred in Chapter 12, and this ORRI training which Drent describes here. They are two incarnations of the exact same principle, and they increase security significantly at no extra cost to the institution. ARCA recommends that such systems be employed by all institutions that house works of art, with particular relevance to underfinanced institutions, which cannot afford high-tech security measures.

PART V

Libraries and Archives

Chapter 15

The Quiet Crime: An Introduction to the World of Rare Book, Map, and Document Theft

Travis McDade

"Oh," Forbes Smiley said. "I forgot about that."

He was looking down at his jacket to where the police officer standing in front of him was pointing. There was a bulge caused by something in the inside pocket.

Smiley reached in and pulled out a rolled map. Unfurled, it was 20 cm × 16 cm and estimated to be worth $50,000.

Smiley explained to the officer that he had gotten the map from a dealer in London named Philip Burden, author of *The Mapping of North America, 1511–1670*. Then the two looked at the map, which had a portrait of its author, John Smith, the Admiral of New England, in the upper left-hand corner.

Mentioning the name Philip Burden might have meant something to those in the map business with whom Smiley ordinarily dealt, a talisman used to ward off suspicion in the face of lack of provenance. But that name did not mean much to most other people, and it certainly did not impress the officer, who immediately asked Smiley if he had any proof of the transaction.

Smiley admitted he did not. Then he reconsidered his earlier statement entirely and said that maybe he had gotten the map from someone else. He was not used to such scrutiny.

It was 3:00 PM on an early June afternoon. Smiley was 49 years old, married, and the father of a five-year-old boy. He was standing in the first-floor lobby of Yale University's Beinecke Library in New Haven, Connecticut, but he lived in the town of Chilmark, Massachusetts, a seaside community on Martha's Vineyard. Chilmark, incorporated in 1694, is one of North America's oldest permanent settlements. But the town was a bit too far south to appear on the map Smiley was about to hand over to the officer, which only went as far as Cape Cod. Besides, the map had been composed 80 years before the town of Chilmark officially existed.

When the map left Forbes Smiley's possession that day, it was the first step in a repatriation effort. Known to have stolen more than 100 separate maps from Yale, Harvard, the British Library, and others from among our most important cultural repositories, Smiley was not caught because of institutional integrity or stringent security. He was caught because dozens of easy thefts from libraries had allowed him to become careless. So at Yale that June day, he had not even noticed he had dropped a razor blade on the floor.

But someone else did.

Rare book, map, and document theft is a growth industry and is performed most often with the decidedly low-tech approach that worked so well for Smiley. A distinct subset of art theft, this crime has a rich tradition lately transformed by technology. Originally a crime of humble profits for a few dedicated thieves and dealers, the Internet, as it has for much art crime, has expanded the population of thieves and raised their salaries. It has also galvanized the resistance.

Once a few small thefts punctuated by an occasional blockbuster, these crimes served as a minor annoyance to libraries and archives. Now the recent trend of pilfering threatens to bleed our cultural heritage institutions dry. But there is some good news, too. Recent examples have shown that people are beginning to pay attention. And at the federal level of the American criminal justice system, at least, laws have evolved to combat this crime.

THE CRIME

Libraries and archives make theft easy. It is their nature. These institutions are designed to give access. Their mission is to get printed material into the hands of patrons, who sometimes bridle at the lightest scrutiny. This fact does not make security impossible, but it makes it harder than in museums or galleries, where patron expectations are different.

Security efforts in libraries and archives are typified by locked doors, tattle tape, and a single guard at the front. These meager measures reassure the public and salve the collective conscience, but they offer little protection from dedicated thieves—who are suddenly in great supply. While special collections are mostly well protected, the general collections of university libraries abound with valuable items. But expense, and the mission of these institutions, precludes proper security measures. For people who know what they are doing (and some who do not), this constitutes an almost limitless supply of valuable material at their fingertips.

In late June 1980, Robert Kindred squeezed through an unlocked men's room window to break into the main library at the University of Illinois at Urbana-Champaign. Bypassing the school's superior rare book collection—which *was* adequately protected—he ranged for two nights in the general stacks. In two trips, he managed to take more than a dozen large books, worth more than $20,000. The only thing keeping him from more thefts was the weight of the books he stole. Kindred did similar work at more than a dozen universities across the United States.

A few years later, Stephen Blumberg made Kindred's thefts look like misdemeanors. Blumberg bluffed, bullied, and snuck his way into library collections nationwide, exposing security as a farce. He used counterfeit or stolen IDs, purloined keys, and assumed identities. He broke locks, climbed in windows, and hid in elevator shafts.

These men had a few qualities in common: imagination, motivation, and the benefit of underprotected targets. What Daniel Spiegelman showed in the early 1990s was that, given enough time, the same sort of man can make his way into even a *well-protected* target.

Poking around the stacks at Columbia University's Butler Library, Spiegelman discovered that an abandoned dumbwaiter shaft rose from the open stacks to the closed stacks of the Rare Book and Manuscript Library (RBML). Spiegelman exploited this minor security flaw, making numerous trips inside the fortress-like RBML. He even got into "the vault," a supposedly super-secure area within the closed stacks. He covered his tracks so well that when the theft was finally discovered, everyone thought it was an inside job.[1]

But these three men are headline-making exceptions. Book thieves do not need great imagination or willingness to crawl into dark places. Every year, more thieves use mundane tactics—hiding in dim corners with razor blades, notebooks, or oversized coats—and walk right out the front door.

James Brubaker, a former schoolteacher, traveled extensively throughout the western United States, cutting maps and lithographs from library books—and sometimes taking the books themselves. He stole thousands of items before he was caught. James Shinn did almost exactly the same thing, though his travels took him farther afield, and his tastes were a little more refined. He particularly enjoyed cutting lithographs and prints of flora and fauna from old scientific journals. Both men, like petty shoplifters, relied mostly on lax security and large pockets.

Insider theft is the most popular recent trend in book, map, and document crime. In the past 10 years, scores of these crimes have been discovered—and the likelihood is that there are many more undiscovered. From library interns right up to directors—and all points in between—these thefts occur almost constantly.

David Breithaupt was a part-time night supervisor at Kenyon College's library. He managed to con janitors into giving him keys to the special collections during his book theft spree. Robert "Skeet" Willingham, Jr., on the other hand, was a published historian and the head of special collections at the University of Georgia, when he was stealing from, and destroying parts of, the collection he was charged with protecting. In the first half of 2008 alone, Lester Weber, Edward Renehan, Jr., and Daniel Lorello, all pleaded guilty to stealing items from the collections they administered. All three men sold these items to the highest bidder.

Books, maps, and archival documents are the low-hanging fruit of the art world. Unfortunately, very little can be done to change this, as long as libraries and archives remain open to researchers.

THE GRACE PERIOD

If ease of theft was not bad enough, there is a second component to library and archive thefts that make them even more appealing: a grace period.

Unlike thefts of major artwork, with thefts of books, maps, and documents, there is almost always a significant time lag between the crime and its discovery. If the thief, particularly an insider, knows how to cover his tracks, a crime might go undiscovered for years—or indefinitely. This, too, is just the nature of the institutions.

It was a book dealer in Philadelphia who informed the Rockland County Historical Society that Rebecca Streeter-Chen stole an 1823 copy of *Tanner's New American Atlas* from their vault. A collector of William Faulkner material from Connecticut called Dr. Lisa Speer at Southeast Missouri State University to tell her that a letter from their Faulkner collection was for sale on eBay. After map thief Forbes Smiley pleaded guilty, it was the FBI that informed some of the United States' most important cultural repositories of maps they had missing: some of them had no idea.

Columbia University's RBML was lucky that Consuelo Dutschke wanted to look at a certain Spanish manuscript when she did. If she had not, then Daniel Spiegelman would have had even more of a head start. No one noticed that the manuscript was missing from the vault, because Spiegelman purposely left behind its hollow preservation case. Dutschke glanced at the empty case numerous times in the days after Spiegelman stole it, but it was not until she actually pulled it off the shelf that she discovered the theft.

Rare books, maps, and archival documents sit waiting to be used. Unless they are of particular importance—or the library is subject to frequent inventories—these items are only discovered missing when the next person wants to use them. For many materials, this may mean years. This is particularly true with items such as atlases, books of fine art which, while cataloged as a whole, are not inventoried at the individual item level.

Compounding the problem, libraries and archives that do discover something missing do not immediately suspect the item has been stolen. The first reaction upon finding a gap in a collection is that it has been left out, checked out, or misplaced. Theft is often the very last possibility considered.

THE MARKET

Stealing a book, map, or document and getting it discreetly away from a library is not difficult. Getting paid is another matter. The largest problem for these thieves, as with most art theft, is the fence: turning theoretical value into cash. For libraries and archives, this used to be the good news.

Extremely rare and important books and maps have always been difficult to sell. Like major pieces of artwork, these items are too well known to be of value in any but an abstract sense. This fact has only grown more pronounced, in the Internet age. For instance, there is virtually no illicit market for a Gutenberg Bible or a Shakespeare first folio. Unless the theft is to fill an order for a collector, there is little incentive to steal very valuable books. (Ransoming works back to institutions, a scourge of the art world, has not yet come to the book world.) But items of moderate value are a very different story.

Twenty-five years ago, very little risk was involved in cold-selling moderately valued stolen items to an unknown book dealer. Unless the book dealer was picky about provenance, or suspicious by nature, a thief could fairly easily sell his stolen goods, armed only with a good cover story. (This usually amounted to faking an inheritance). Low-end book dealers, who are picky about provenance, and suspicious by nature, have never been plentiful.

Still, thieves could usually use a particular dealer only once, unless the dealer was in on the theft (another Yale thief, Benjamin Johnson, got in trouble after an dealer got suspicious that a college student had so many well-preserved and valuable materials that did not fit his cover story). That meant that thieves had to do a lot of traveling. Not only was this expensive and time-consuming, but it tended to multiply risk over time.

Eventually, an honest dealer might suspect something, or notice a library book stamp. With very few exceptions, the life of the professional book thief was an unprofitable grind.

Then came the Internet. Online auction sites cut out not only the middlemen, but also much of the expense and risk associated with selling stolen items. Internet commerce can be almost completely anonymous (or require a warrant to force disclosure of identity), and it does not require travel. On top of that, as long as the items being sold do not attract a lot of attention, there is very little risk. Even if the thief sells the stolen items for a few hundred dollars at a time, every cent is profit.

Daniel Lorello, an archivist at the New York State Library in Albany, is the perfect illustration of this modern thief: an educated, middle-aged, white male, with slight money problems. Working an archive, he stole small and obscure items, things he has referred to as "shit," that he didn't think his employer would miss, or that had yet to be cataloged. He liked to steal in the mornings, before his colleagues showed up. Because he had a key to the place, he was able to do so unhindered. He stole hundreds of items over the course of several years. No one questioned him, right up until he was caught. He had steady work—so he was neither bored nor poor. Instead, he stole because he needed money for small things like house renovations, credit card bills, and tuition. He started slowly, selling a couple of items here and there on eBay, to supplement his income. Pretty soon he had boxes of stolen items at his home, waiting to be sold.

This same basic script has been followed by dozens of men in the eBay era. Denning McTague, a summer intern at the National Archives and Records Administration (NARA), sold items of Americana professionally, until his business failed. Then he went back to school, and eventually gained insider access to NARA. He smuggled dozens of items out, hidden between the leaves in a yellow legal pad, and sold them on eBay.

James Brubaker, the retired schoolteacher who stole from libraries throughout the western United States, sold items for years at the online auction site. When law enforcement finally searched his house, there were several pieces already in envelopes, ready to be sent to buyers.

Archivist Lester Weber declared bankruptcy before leaving Iowa, and starting over afresh in Virginia. He kept out of financial trouble in his new home, in part by stealing from his employer, the Mariner's Museum. Over the course of five years of pilfering the collection he was charged to protect, Weber averaged $32,000 per year (all of it unreported), selling items on eBay. Not enough to fund a lavish lifestyle, to be sure, but enough to keep him and his wife in the black.

So, ironically, it is the least popular material that is most susceptible to theft. While major pieces are fairly secure, the small items that have yet to be fully mined by historians are more at risk than ever before.

THE PUNISHMENT

There are two lines of silver around this dark cloud. First, people are paying attention. Second, the law, if not society, is coming around.

McTague, Lorello, Brubaker, and Southeast Missouri State thief Robert Hardin Smith were all caught because attentive and skeptical buyers on eBay turned the men in. Spiegelman and Weber were caught when people connected the dots and started paying attention to the men. Smiley was nabbed not because Yale had their security cameras on—they did not—but because a librarian noticed the razor blade on the floor and became suspicious. In each case, as with most of these crimes, security failed miserably, and the institutions were bailed out only by attentive and responsible individuals.

In late 2002, American federal criminal law began treating these crimes with the seriousness they deserve. An addition to the federal sentencing guidelines, called the Cultural Heritage Resources Guideline,[2] ensures that the theft or destruction of items important to cultural heritage is punished as severely as, and often more severely than, other such items.

The four young men who tasered a special collections librarian at Kentucky's Transylvania University in an effort to steal an Audubon elephant folio, a first-edition *On the Origin of the Species* and other books, were each sentenced to a remarkable 87 months in federal prison. On appeal, this sentence was deemed too *low* and adjusted upwards.

Howard Harner and Denning McTague, both men who stole documents from the National Archives, were each sentenced to prison time. Harner got two years, McTague 15 months. While neither of those is a remarkably harsh sentence, they are an indication that the federal judiciary takes these matters seriously.

Unfortunately, at the American state level and abroad, the news is less encouraging. Rebecca Streeter-Chen, who stole an atlas worth tens of thousands of dollars from a collection she was meant to protect, was merely given probation by a state court in New York. Norman Buckley, a British man who stole several hundred thousand dollars worth of rare and antiquarian books, including a sixteenth-century Chaucer edition, was sentenced to a short jail term—and that was then suspended. These two typify the lenient treatment given to people outside the American federal system.

The main difference is that in the American federal system, judges have very little latitude to make lenient sentences. Once a person has been convicted or pleaded guilty to a crime against cultural heritage, they are almost guaranteed to get some jail time. In the American state system and abroad, this is generally not the case. Judges have immense latitude to take into account family issues, addictions, and—in the case of Buckley—heartbreak. (Buckley claimed he was distraught over the end of a long-term relationship, and that drove him to theft.)

But serious treatment has to start somewhere. Ideally, the actions of the American federal system will be noticed by judges and prosecutors in other venues, and these crimes will be met with the punishment their harm warrants. Spreading that message, though, might be a difficult in a society that tends to treat even the most serious library thefts as little more severe than expensive overdue books.

CONCLUSION

The Forbes Smiley case is a good example of the modern face of the crime. Smiley, an educated, well-connected man who was a familiar face at many libraries, stole with impunity for years until a single person noticed something amiss. Once alerted, the legal system and aggrieved institutions responded with vigor.

Smiley was charged at both the state and federal level and eventually sentenced to 42 months in a federal minimum security prison. (His lesser state sentence is being served concurrently.) Part of his plea agreement has been an effort to repatriate some of the maps he stole to their rightful owners, a task for which he showed tepid enthusiasm.

This is a paradigm our cultural repositories can live with. Libraries and archives are rightly uncomfortable with much of a lockdown mentality, particularly when it diminishes access granted to the overwhelming number of scrupulous and dedicated patrons.

So while the thefts are nearly impossible to prevent, society can make them too risky to attempt. An increase in serious criminal punishment coupled with a higher risk of detection in the marketplace will tip the risk-vs.-reward balance in favor of our public institutions. For their part, institutions can at least make a demonstrable show of security while at the same time publicizing thefts.

Helping prevent these sorts of thefts requires some strategy, but not a lot of money. Making the crime difficult, even if only slightly more difficult, often pays dividends. Small efforts, like proper key control and the inclusion of a few cameras, are very valuable. A single camera at library entrance often discourages theft simply because it lets thieves know someone is paying attention.

But maybe the single most important thing libraries can do is remove valuable and vulnerable items from their general collections into special collections. This is simply not practical in all cases, but the effort has three benefits. First, it protects those items that are put in the special collections. Second, it forces libraries and archives to survey their collections so that they know what they have. Third, it lets the staff know that the institution is concerned about the protection of the collection, and the staff will likely follow suit.

In the Internet age, no library or archive is safe. It used to be that a remote location or a humble collection size meant that committed thieves would not waste their time. But commitment has been taken out of the equation, and now every collection is a target.

As with most crime, being informed of the danger is the biggest part of the battle. Being willing to fight for the collection should follow naturally.

NOTES

1. For a more fulsome account of this crime and subsequent legal proceedings, see Travis McDade, *The Book Thief: The True Crimes of Daniel Spiegelman* (Westport, CT: Praeger, 2006).

2. The Cultural Heritage Resources Guideline is located at Section 2B1.5 of the *Federal Sentencing Guidelines.* Its official name is "Theft of, Damage to, or Destruction of Cultural Heritage Resources."

Chapter 16

Unexpected and Accessible: Threats to University Collections

John Kleberg

- Two million dollars worth of ancient coins were stolen from the campus of Harvard University in 1973. The final 5,000 coins from the theft, some dating from 6 BC to 3 AD, were recovered in April 1979.
- In March 1995, a vellum sheet from the Codex Argenteus, the famous Silver Bible, was stolen from a display in the library at the University of Uppsala, Sweden. The thieves, hooded men equipped with a hammer and tear gas, made off with the page while startled onlookers stood by.
- "The ownership of a spectacular ancient Egyptian tomb ornament, stolen from a small Pennsylvania college in the late 1970's and bought several years later by the Museum of Fine Arts in Boston, has been resolved after a year of contentious negotiations. The school, Lafayette College in Easton, has also filed suit against a former employee in connection with the theft . . . At the time, officials at Lafayette were unaware that the breastplate was missing. For years it had been displayed in the reading room of Lafayette's library. After a new library was built in 1961, however, it was placed in storage. 'We had no idea we didn't have it for six years,' said Robert I. Rotberg, Lafayette's president."[1]
- A former employee at the Kenyon College library in Gambier, Ohio, pleaded guilty to stealing more than $50,000 in rare books and documents from the collection over a two-year period and selling them on eBay.
- After a night of partying, students in an Ohio State University residence hall removed four watercolors from a building lobby and took them to their room, rationalizing their actions as compensation for financial assessments they thought unjustified. Three students were arrested and charged with

felony theft when the value of the previously unrecorded art was estimated at between $3,000 and $5,000 each. The case ended with restitution and diversion. The work was the product of a former faculty member for whom the residence hall was named, and who became a noted artist and teacher. A review of storage areas in the residence hall resulted in locating several more watercolors, long forgotten and never inventoried, which had been gifts to the university.

- Similarly, an 1884 portrait of Robert Browning, possibly the last painting of the poet, was displayed in a small liberal arts college library. The portrait was stolen in 2003 but went unnoticed for some time before police were alerted. It remains missing.

Colleges and universities around the world hold major collections of art and cultural artifacts. Collections may have been assembled by faculty members or university researchers, donated by benefactors, or acquired to enhance a collection or promote public interest in the institution. Items of particular value may also be acquired as part of an endowment or even as an investment to benefit future generations of scholars.

Even in relatively small private academic institutions, significant libraries and special collections are not unusual. They are, however, often underprotected from theft, vandalism, or accidental damage. While institutions may not be aware of their total assets, thieves often are. The open access of most educational institutions makes it easy to "case the joint."

Threats, damage, and theft in these university collections may not be reported. This phenomenon, which is also seen in some museums and private collections, is a misguided attempt to protect the institution's public image for fear of scaring off potential donors, or to advertise inadequate security, which might encourage future criminal opportunities. A "don't rock the boat" mentality might take over and discourage security enhancements that are expensive or altering to the "status quo."

Educational administrators may not consider or even realize the significance of their collections as substantial institutional assets, both educational as well as financial. Collections are often thought of as decorative, despite what might be multimillion-dollar contents, and are therefore often overlooked when considering security.

Campus collections are sometimes so vast and varied that the institutions lose track of what they own in the way of artistic pieces, historic artifacts, and rare printed materials. Items may not be properly cataloged, or even cataloged at all. The relative independence of faculty and departments to research, explore, and acquire items of value over time results in collections that are irregularly inventoried, protected to varying degrees, and administered without a coherent over-arching organizational approach. One campus might have a science museum, an ethnography museum, a rare books library, and two art museums, all run independently, with little or no dialogue between them.

Experience has demonstrated that such situations are not unusual in the United States. Most campus collections are insufficiently secured and exposed at a level that would be considered unsuitable for any facility designed for exhibition. Security staffs often face challenges in obtaining the financial resources essential to provide even the minimum protection needed to ensure that these valuable items remain available for future generations of researchers, scholars, and students.

As inadequately secured as are many American campus collections, still worse off are objects and artworks that fall outside of established collections, such as those that decorate hallways, offices, classrooms, and studies. An innovative program initiated a number of years ago by university police and security services at Ohio State University has promoted identification and protection of intrinsically valuable items that were located about the campus outside recognized collections. Administrative and academic members of various departments were educated about the importance of documenting and properly recording important and overlooked items. An interesting feature of the program, tagged "Reducing the Risk," is that it was developed by security staff rather than academic, arts instructional faculty, or financial administrators.

Three critical elements were put in place to promote a broader sensitivity and conscientiousness regarding the possessions of the university located outside cataloged collections. First, eye-catching promotional material about the program was printed and distributed to deans, department chairs, and directors, encouraging them to identify and record information about pertinent items in their areas. Second, a computerized database was created. This included images; detailed descriptions of items including medium, size, description, location, and condition; and any security measures in place. Also key was a determination of who had official custody of the object—essentially, who was responsible for caring for and protecting the item. Delegation of authority and responsibility is a powerful tool to encourage administrative action. Third, financial resources were allocated on an annual basis to provide, at no cost to the department or custodian, funds for restoration, security, or display protection of the items.

An example from early in the Reducing the Risk program illustrates the need. The geology library on the Ohio State campus is adorned by various oil paintings by noted artists representing various geological features. One of the paintings, *The Petrified Forest* (1904) by Thomas Moran, had been a gift to the university by the first president (a geology professor) and had been prominently displayed in the library for years. In a large gilt frame, the unsecured painting was appreciated by many, but few recognized the value. When inventoried and entered into the database for the program, it was found to have an estimated auction value of $3 million.

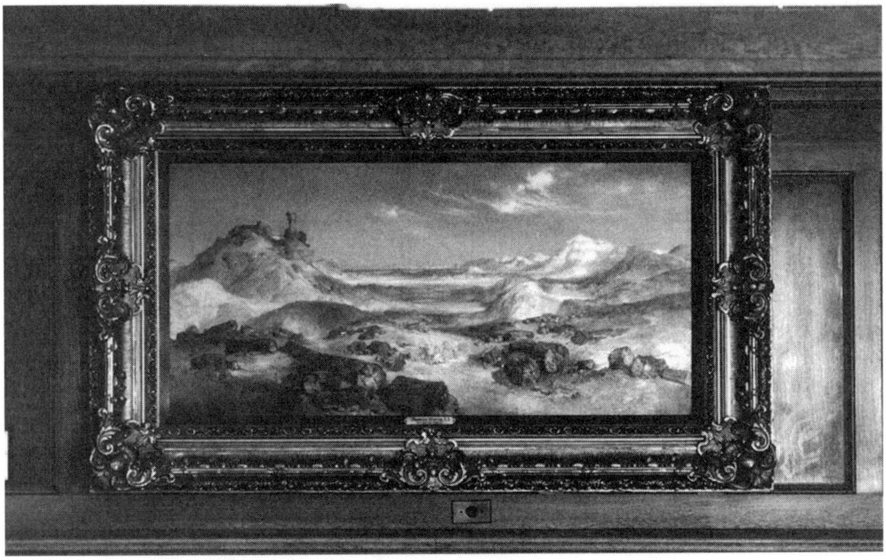

The Petrified Forest, Thomas Moran, N.A.
Images courtesy of the author and Photo Services: Ohio State University.

The painting was quickly provided with a security alarm and given some minor restorative work, at no expense to the library since they were the "unofficial custodian" of the piece. While many on campus did not recognize the presence of the painting, its location and subject matter were known to those familiar with the artist's work, as contact with a curator of a Moran exhibition in Washington, DC, demonstrated. Identifying this painting early on helped persuade university financial officers of the value of the project in protecting institutional assets.

A member of the university security team who was particularly interested in the project and willing to "evangelize" the program message, was given the task to identify items located throughout the University for inclusion in the database. The findings were remarkable. Major artistic works, artifacts of historic interest, paintings by minor artists who are locally cherished and valued, in addition to other items, were quickly identified. Items located now include oil paintings, watercolors, historic furniture, mineral specimens, Heisman trophies, Roman coins, outdoor sculpture, indoor sculpture, mosaics, cut glass art, WPA murals, antique medical equipment, eyewear collections in the College of Optometry, and even an historic beehive. The collective value is unknown; however, the paintings alone exceed tens of millions of dollars. The costs were minimal: about $5,000 to purchase software, digital photographic equipment, and printed materials, plus staff time. An annual appropriation of $5,000 was made for protection enhancements, which could be used without expense to individual department budgets.

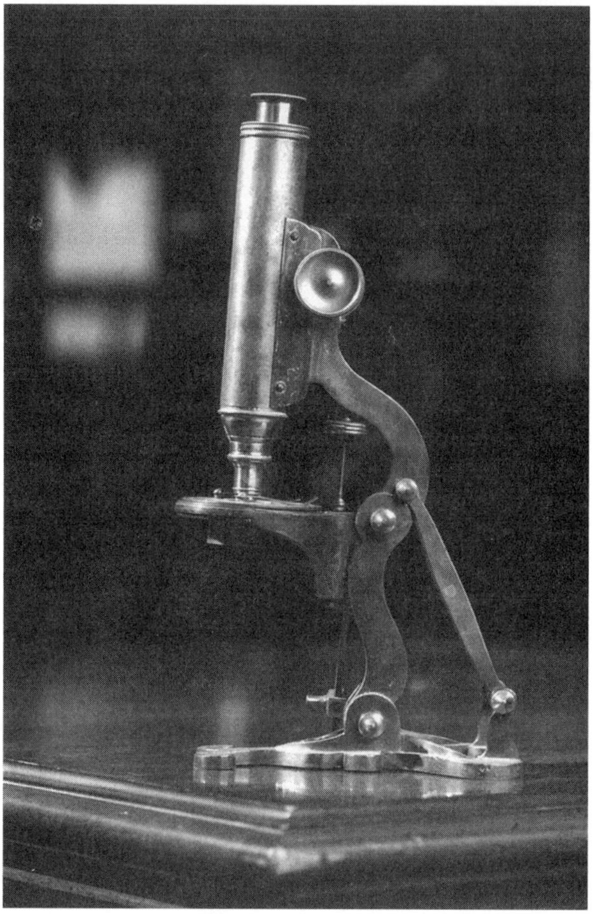

Microscope: Academic artifacts are numerous at colleges and universities and may be the object of antique thieves.

Images courtesy of the author and Photo Services: Ohio State University.

The program continues, and other educational centers have become interested in the Ohio State experience. Insurance underwriters also appreciated the contribution the effort made to providing essential data for adequate coverage.

An additional and somewhat unexpected benefit of the program has been the interest of local municipal police in the program. This has resulted in presentations about the importance of protecting and documenting collections to regional security directors as well as police officials and risk managers at colleges and universities. Two presentations have been made at national organization conferences. Alerting even local police patrol officers to the value of objects of art, when compared to an ATM

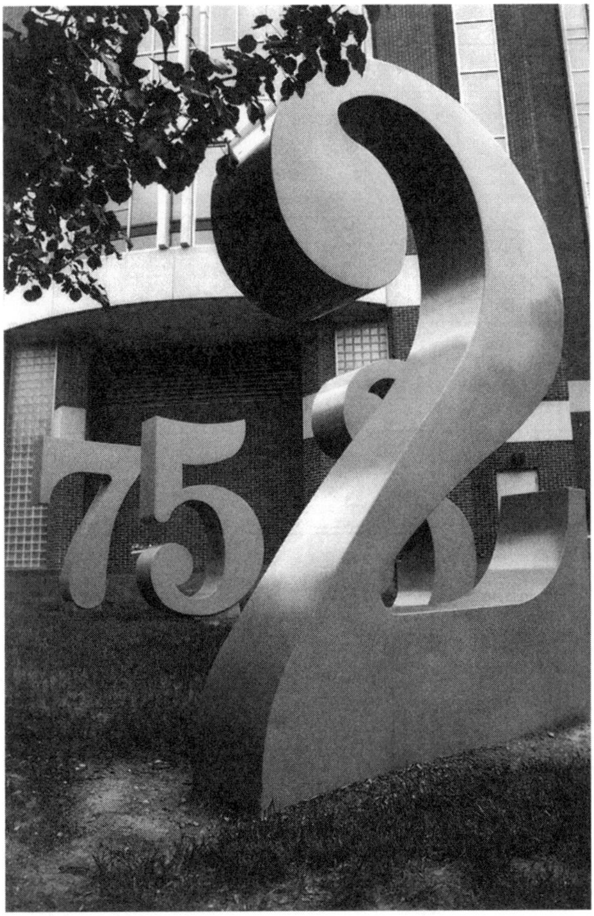

Garden of Constants: Public art is frequently found on campus. Thieves may target art for the material value of the object, or it may be subject to malicious defacing.

Images courtesy of the author and Photo Services: Ohio State University.

theft for example, has been helpful in promoting consciousness. From board rooms to public building lobbies to government facilities, the program has created as increased awareness of what was always there, but rarely protected because it was infrequently recognized for its value.

Such items are rarely comparable with the vast and highly valued items found in major museums or private collections. Nevertheless, many of these items, such as the Thomas Moran, are of considerable value. Locating and identifying unrecognized art works and preserving and protecting them against crime directed at such items is a crucial responsibility for campus personnel.

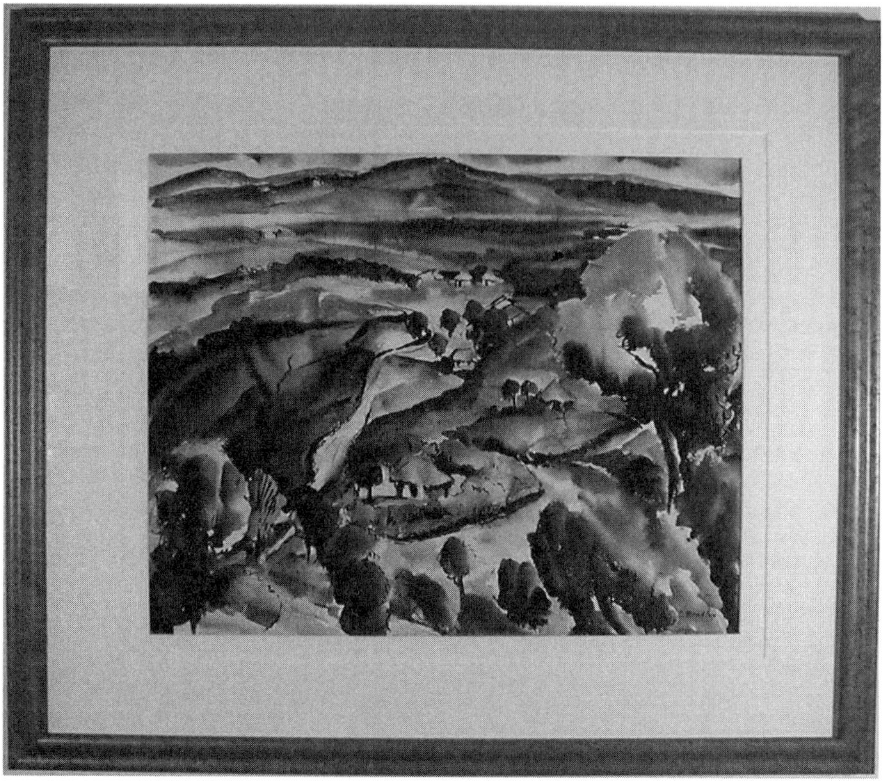

Mountain Huts, watercolor by Carolyn G. Bradley.
Photo by John Kleberg.

It is of critical importance to recognize the potential of loss should these uncataloged objects be stolen. The involvement of organized crime in much art theft is reason enough to protect artworks, so as not to fuel other activities in which they are engaged. But the academic, historical, cultural, and aesthetic value of such objects, particularly to the institutes of higher education that own them, is too often overlooked.

Student personal safety, potential terrorist acts, and disaster preparation and response occupy campus security, leaving art protection as an afterthought. Creative programs are required to inspire officials to take art protection seriously, and provide incentives to participate in programs such as the Ohio State project.

Chief financial officers and senior academic officials, as well as campus security and public safety managers, should encourage the identification, documentation, and valuation of these often unseen and noncataloged assets. While it may seem less than intriguing to many in security or university police forces, as noted in Edward Dolinck's *The Rescue Artist* while quoting Charles Hill of the London Metropolitan Police, "'The police won't say so,' remarks Charles Hill, 'but what they think is, What's so important about pictures, anyway?' " protecting cultural heritage in the custody of academic centers is an important and challenging duty.[2]

The implementation of such a program is simple:

1. Adopt an institutional policy on collections management. What will be collected, who may authorize acquisitions, what is appraisal process, who is custodian, what procedures will be followed, etc.
2. Determine what department is responsible for recordkeeping and assign responsibility.
3. Budget sufficient dollars to sustain the program of recording and monitoring works in the collection.
4. Ensure risk managers are included in the process to provide for adequate insurance protection.
5. Periodically review by internal audit the program and processes.

Since the founding of the University of Bologna, in 1088, colleges and universities have been centers of culture, history, and scholarship around the world. They have always been and continue to be the "home" of vast collections of cultural and artistic treasurers. Such collections must be protected.

NOTES

1. Carol Vogel, "A Happy Ending: Museum Keeps Stolen Artifact and College Gets Cash," *New York Times,* April 11, 1992.

2. Edward Dolnick, *The Rescue Artist* (New York: HarperCollins Perennial Edition, 2006).

Chapter 17

Bringing It All Back Home: Recovery of Stolen Special Collections Materials

Richard W. Oram
Ann Hartley

After a perpetrator is sentenced, victims of special collections theft may discover that their troubles are only beginning. That situation is particularly true if large numbers of stolen items reach the marketplace, or if recovered books and manuscripts have been stolen from more than one library. In the 1980s, prominent theft cases involving James Shinn and Stephen Blumberg resulted in the discovery of hundreds of stolen books that could not be easily identified. Despite tireless efforts by dedicated librarians, many books never found their way back to the owners.[1] In 1994, Daniel Spiegelman was arrested for the theft of incunabula, maps, and documents from Columbia University Library's Rare Book and Manuscript Library. Numerous items were located in his safe deposit boxes and other locations, but many years after Spiegelman's conviction, important items thought to have been stolen by him remain at large.[2]

Two recent cases of theft resulted in valuable materials reaching the market and required extensive recovery efforts. E. Forbes Smiley III removed at least 97 maps from Yale University, Harvard University, and several other prominent collections in the United States and United Kingdom; the thief was sentenced in 2006. In the Mimi Meyer case, some 400 books were stolen from the Harry Ransom Humanities Research Center, University of Texas at Austin; Meyer was sentenced and given three years' probation in 2004.[3] The legal concept of replevin (the right of a property owner to sue the current possessor for return of property) is often involved in the return of stolen goods to their rightful owner. However, in common archival use, the term most frequently refers to the recovery of alienated governmental records, which is not under consideration here. It is also worth noting that the scope of our article does not include the recovery of books and manuscripts seized by governments during wartime.

Law enforcement action in the immediate aftermath of the theft often leads to recovery of many stolen items. In the Smiley case, the thief was apprehended in the process of removing maps from books at Yale University. A quick response by law enforcement resulted in the recovery of many other items taken from various libraries over the next few months. At the time of Smiley's conviction in July 2006, the prosecutor told the court that 86 of the 97 stolen maps were in the possession of federal agents. A year later, most of the owners had been identified, and almost all the maps had been returned. Nevertheless, subsequent institutional inventories raised questions about whether he had stolen additional missing maps.[4] In the Meyer case, the FBI, with cooperation of the thief, inventoried her Chicago apartment and confiscated some 300 books stolen from Texas, which were returned to the Ransom Center a few days after sentencing; however, not all the stolen books in her possession were found by the FBI. Later discussions between the Ransom Center and Meyer resulted in her disgorging several more books and maps. The Austin office of the FBI did not offer assistance with the recovery of around 100 books—the exact number is still unknown—that Meyer had sold at auction from 1994 to 2000. The thefts had taken place nearly 15 years before sentencing (as opposed to no more than eight years in the Smiley case), and some of the books reached the marketplace a full decade before the recovery began. The reason given by the FBI was that any information it obtained from the auction houses was part of a grand jury investigation, and under federal law (Rule 6, Federal Rules of Criminal Procedure), such information is confidential. Once a library becomes aware of theft, law enforcement officers can obtain a search warrant; yet if the library does not immediately know what has been taken (which is probable without a thorough, up-to-the-minute inventory and evidence linking the suspect to the supposed theft), a search warrant cannot identify particular books to be sought. To protect citizens' constitutional rights against unreasonable searches and seizures, search warrants must be not only justified with probable cause, but also limited in scope.

Since many theft cases are resolved through plea bargains, institutional victims have an opportunity to obtain court-ordered restitution as part of the settlement. That money will be important in buying back any books sold to good-faith purchasers who are willing to return them for the price they paid. In the Meyer case, the U.S. District Court staff

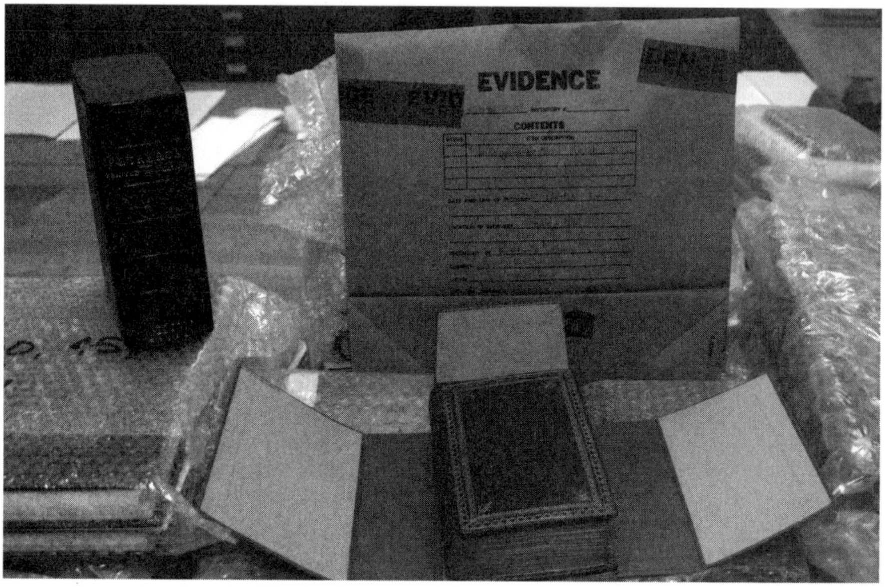

Il Petrarcha published by Aldus Manutius in 1514, a rare copy on vellum. Courtesy of the Harry Ransom Center.

requested an accounting of the books known to have been stolen and sold at auction. The Ransom Center was also asked to provide an estimate of the cost of identification and recovery efforts (which, in the final accounting, proved to be much too low). At sentencing, the judge simply set restitution as the sum of these figures, or $381,595. In the Smiley case, restitution to institutions and map dealers to cover their losses was initially set by the court at $1.9 million and later raised to $2.3 million, with the thief ordered to sell off some of his assets as part of a plea bargain. Since one of the reasons Smiley began stealing maps was to pay down a mountain of debt, the plaintiffs likely will not recover anything close to the full amount.[5] While financial restitution is obviously worth insisting upon, all too often the perpetrator lacks sufficient (or any) resources after paying legal bills, fines, and court costs. After sentencing, the thief may have nothing more valuable than information to help locate the stolen items; the victim institution should definitely seek an enforceable condition in the sentencing order or judgment that obligates the thief to cooperate.

THE RECOVERY PROCESS

For both practical and legal reasons, it is essential to begin the recovery process as quickly as possible after the discovery that materials are at large. Generally, the more time that has passed since the materials were stolen, the more times the property will have changed hands, and the more difficult the recovery effort will be. The importance of spreading the word about stolen items likely to have reached the market cannot be overstated. Informal, personal, and professional contacts should be alerted, and institutional notices must also be made, listing the stolen property. Police reports, insurance claims, notices in professional publications and discussion lists, entries on trade association Internet sites—all these efforts are important. The stolen items must be described in accurate, identifying detail. The theft victim needs to publish enough information so that a reasonably diligent person looking to buy a book would have notice that it has been stolen.[6] Fortunately, it is now generally accepted (at least in theory) that libraries have a clear ethical obligation to report thefts, or as Susan Allen has noted, "The question is no longer a question of whether to notify. Rather it has shifted to a question of who should do the notifying and who should be notified."[7] While administrators may resist transparency on the grounds that it may damage their institution's reputation, curators must strongly press the case for full disclosure.

Regrettably, as of 2008, all of the online registers for missing or stolen rare materials have serious limitations. For example, many auction houses typically recognize the Art Loss Register (ALR) as the definitive source of record on stolen items, including rare books and manuscripts; yet that listing is largely unknown outside the fine arts field, is little used outside of the United Kingdom, and is in no way comprehensive. Further, both searching and adding records to ALR require registration and the payment of fees, unless records are submitted through Interpol (not the easiest of tasks in practice, as the present writers discovered). The databases of the Antiquarian Booksellers Association of America (ABAA) and the International League of Antiquarian Booksellers (ILAB) are laudable in concept, but the ABAA database is still, at this writing, a relatively new effort that depends on the availability of staff time to keep the file current, and access to the ILAB database requires organizational membership.[8] The Library Security Officer (LSO) electronic mailing list and the "Incidents of Thefts" reports on the RBMS site are compiled from press reports and other sources, but often do not provide detailed listings of individual stolen items.

However, at this writing, the future for such registers is looking brighter. In 2008 a Web-based Missing Maps Database was inaugurated,[9] and curators, book trade representatives, staff from OCLC Online Computer Library Center (which maintains the WorldCat bibliographic database), and law enforcement gathered at the Getty Research Library in June 2008 to discuss the creation of a similar tool for missing rare books.

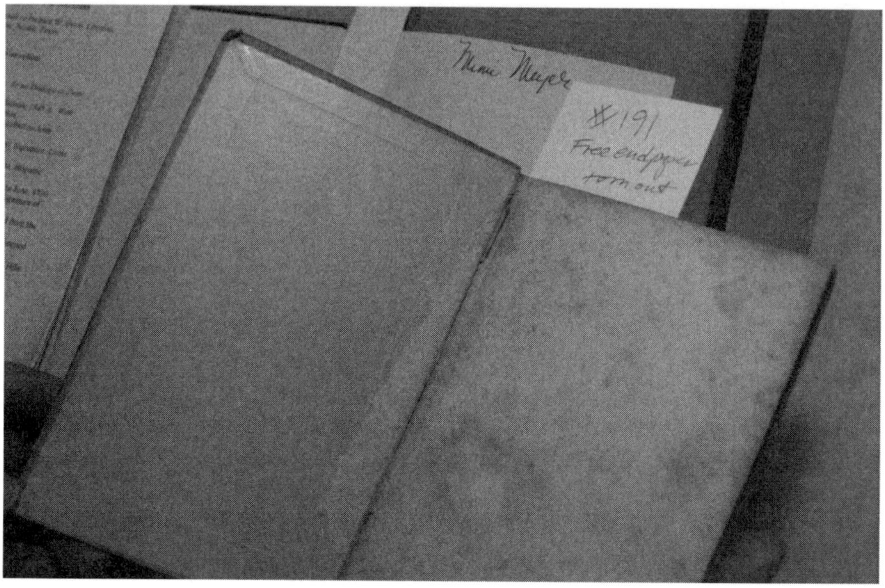

A stolen, mutilated book returned to the Harry Ransom Center.
Image courtesy of The Harry Ransom Humanities Research Center, The University of Texas at Austin.

Another part of the initial theft response involves an immediate report to the institution's risk management office and its insurer as well as continuing contact with them as the investigation proceeds. While many public institutions continue to "self-insure," it is becoming increasingly common for colleges and universities to take out fine arts insurance policies. Typically, those are designed to cover the institution in the event of a catastrophic loss, but there may be theft provisions as well. They will usually exclude losses resulting from "mysterious disappearance" (e.g., an inventory discloses that an item is missing from the collection, but it cannot be proven to have been stolen). Even when a loss results from a provable theft, the high deductibles required to keep premiums down, together with the relatively low values of most rare books and manuscripts (at least compared to works of art), may make it infeasible to claim. A highly desirable feature of fine arts insurance policies is the "buy-back provision." If the insurer does pay a claim and the stolen item is later located and returned, the original owner has the option of returning the settlement money and reclaiming the item; otherwise, the recovered item becomes by default the legal property of the insurance company, which has the option of selling it to recover its loss.[10] The Art Loss Web site of the Los Angeles Police Department notes that "Insisting upon a buy-back provision will not only ensure a victim's right to exercise this option, it will also obligate the insurance carrier to notify the victim if there is a recovery."[11]

Along with law enforcement and counsel, bookdealers are effective allies in tracking down and recovering stolen items. By and large, the book trade has a good record in collaborating with libraries to apprehend thieves and recover books; at a 2005 symposium on the recovery of stolen books, booksellers Ken Sanders and David Szewczyk reported on their identifications of suspicious materials offered for sale, which led to the arrest of the perpetrators, and cited other dealer involvement in successful sting operations.[12] The Code of Ethics of the Antiquarian Booksellers Association of America, the largest and most prominent trade association, specifically mandates cooperation with theft recovery:

> 3(b). An Association member shall make every effort to prevent the theft or distribution of stolen antiquarian books and related materials. An Association member shall cooperate with law enforcement authorities and the Associations' Board of Governors in the effort to recover and return stolen materials, and apprehend and prosecute those responsible for the theft, including, but not limited to, providing the names of the persons involved.[13]

Ideally, booksellers and librarians should present a unified front in resistance to the further distribution of stolen rare materials. In his book about the Spiegelman/Columbia theft case, Travis McDade takes the optimistic view that the "Book Community" of dealers and collectors greatly limits thieves' options when it comes to fencing rare materials, to the extent that they are "almost without exception" found out.[14] Nevertheless, the authors' experiences, as well as those of librarians involved in the Smiley case and other recovery efforts, suggest that the trade cannot be counted upon to "do the right thing" in every instance. Regrettably, a few members of the book trade take the narrow view that library thefts are primarily the result of lax security and thus exclusively a library problem.[15] Others cite their "obligation" to protect the identity and privacy of customers from probing victims of theft, although that is based more on the firm's relationship with the consignor than any statutory requirements.

More problematic is the fact that only a small portion of the trade is subject to the Code of Ethics of the ABAA, which is composed of established firms. Mom-and-pop storefronts selling used books on eBay and Amazon proliferate. Owners who have located stolen books or archival materials on online auctions have had difficulty getting the sites to intervene.[16] The laissez-faire environment of the Web thus tends to promote the unchecked distribution of stolen items, as well as those with suspect provenance. Auction houses—ineligible for ABAA membership—present a particular problem because they frequently insist on protecting their consignors' and purchasers' identity, even when there is overwhelming evidence that stolen material has passed through their rooms.[17]

HARD LESSONS

This is perhaps the most surprising and difficult lesson for victims of theft: owners generally have a *legal right* to return of their stolen property, but even if they are able to locate it, recovery is often problematic. If they do not know where the property is, or even that it has been stolen, it is obviously even more fraught with difficulty. Ideally, the thief would be in the position of being both fully cooperative and highly organized, having retained impeccable records about which materials were sold and to whom. If this is not the case (Meyer, though initially cooperative, suffered from severe memory lapses and had to be encouraged to remember where more stolen books in her possession were, and, as we have noted, it is impossible to be certain that Smiley identified all the maps he had taken), the library will have to approach the dealers and auction houses that can be identified. As the authors discovered, the recovery process involves complicated and highly specialized legal issues. Thus, at the outset, one will wish to seek the best legal advice, beginning with in-house counsel.

Unless the case is miraculously simple, the victimized institution may face numerous legal complications. To take one example: the theft occurs at an unknown date in the past in one state, the thief lives in another state by the time recovery is undertaken in earnest, the first buyer of the stolen book is in a third state and refuses to reveal any information about the purchase of the book by its customer, alleging "privacy" concerns (date, name and address of buyer, and price are fundamental facts needed to follow the trail of a stolen item). Other complications are likely to accrue. When considerable time has passed since the theft, a limitations defense may be made against the original owner's claim. The limitations statutes are unique to each state with respect to starting and tolling of the clock. In New York State, a suit for replevin must be filed within three years,[18] but the clock does not start until the owner has made demand on the possessor and the possessor has refused. This application of the "discovery rule" means that the owner of stolen property has three years after learning who possesses the property to demand return of the property and file a lawsuit if the demand is refused.[19] In California, similarly, a three-year statute of limitations "accrues upon discovery of the whereabouts of a stolen article of artistic significance."[20]

A second obstacle might center on the issue of ownership, assuming the current possessor of the stolen book bought it in good faith with no reason to know it was stolen. A third obstacle, even if the first two are overcome, may be "laches," a legal doctrine providing that when a plaintiff unreasonably delays pursuit of his rights and thereby causes undue prejudice to the defendant ("sits on his rights"), the plaintiff's claim will fail. Laches also requires that the victim institution use reasonable diligence in trying to recover its stolen property, which includes public notice of the theft.

Such complications involving differences in state laws are far from uncommon and almost ensure the need for a qualified lawyer. When international recovery is in question, counsel becomes essential. Paying a retainer to an appropriate law firm (probably one that has some relevant experience and is recognized by commercial dealers) shows a commitment to recovering stolen property and will not go unnoticed. Even if litigation is not being considered, the terminology and common practices related to recovery of stolen property will be familiar to a good lawyer, who can be very helpful in drafting and negotiating agreements incidental to cooperative transactions leading to recovery. Since New York and California are major centers for the book trade, if the victim institution has lost books in (or via) these states, retained lawyers need to be licensed and experienced in their courts. Determining which law applies to which aspect of a case is not at all simple, and it is difficult to discern even basic principles that would govern all case outcomes.

Laws in continental Europe tend to favor the good-faith purchaser of stolen property rather than the original owner who is the theft victim. The American "discovery rule" generally does not apply, so the limitations period starts and continues running regardless of whether the theft victim knows where his stolen property is. Tainted provenance can be cleansed, and stolen property may return to the legal art trade. Under French law, a theft victim has three years from the day the property was stolen to claim it from the person who holds it (if the person holds it in good faith; a person holding property in bad faith must wait for 30 years before a claim from the owner will be barred by limitations, but after that, even the bad-faith holder of stolen property may have good title in France.)[21] In Japan, someone who owns a stolen item for more than two years becomes the legal owner of the object. This fundamental legal and cultural conflict recently became an issue when the library of Christ Church College, Oxford, attempted to recover a stolen Vesalius that had migrated to Japan. The current owner, a Japanese school of dentistry, refused to repatriate the volume(s), citing that country's law and leading to a loud outcry in the Western world.

In common-law countries, by contrast, it is commonly said that, "a thief cannot pass good title." The fact that a stolen book, for example, was bought at auction by an innocent, bona fide purchaser who paid a fair price, does not clear the book's dubious provenance, and no buyer in the United States or England may obtain good title to the stolen book. However, as the saying goes, "Possession is nine-tenths of the law."

While a library may have a good replevin case against a British or American collector who bought a book stolen from the library, if the library does not know who possesses the book, or how to reach the possessor, in reality there will be no lawsuit and no recovery.

Even with its current location known and the law on one's side, recovery of a stolen book may be difficult and time-consuming. Even though the thief has confessed to stealing some books, the institution may have difficulty proving particular missing books were stolen, rather than mislaid. The practical significance is that the institution may be required to show the books were stolen before they can be listed on some registries. The initial approach can be made by a letter (a certified letter from the institution's attorney, or from outside counsel, shows the institution is serious) asserting ownership and requesting the return of an item. Sometimes a formal approach will be less productive than a softer, diplomatic effort of persuasion; fear of notoriety and disgrace within professional or cultural circles may be more effective than a threatened legal challenge, especially where evidentiary proof to support the challenge is difficult to obtain or weak.

An appeal for return is enhanced in most cases by an appeal to the purse. As previously noted, circumstances may not even allow for compensation of current owners. Although the Ransom Center had enough funds to compensate current owners for the amount they paid for books stolen by Meyer, the passage of time had resulted in considerable appreciation of the materials. (In one case, the current owner had purchased a book for a figure about 400 percent larger than the original auction hammer price received by Meyer a decade earlier). Getting a book dealer to participate in the compensation proposal may not be easy. The dealer not only stands to lose money, but also risks being discredited for having bought and sold stolen property.

At one time, the ABAA adopted a "Fair Play Resolution" recommending that a bookseller who sold a stolen item split the cost of compensation 50/50 with libraries, although according to a spokesperson, that is apparently no longer its official policy.[22] The 50/50 split is recommended by the Code of Conduct jointly produced by the UK booksellers' trade association and the Chartered Institute of Library and Information Professionals (CLIP, formerly the Library Association).[23] Obviously, that is only a guideline, and when the value of an item has risen substantially since leaving the hands of a dealer, the chances of such participation fall. If a book has changed hands several times since the theft, with a price increase at every step, the victim institution is faced with four bad choices: (1) trying to get every seller along the way to contribute to payment of the current possessor; (2) trying to persuade the first dealer who bought from the thief to split or share the price of recovery; (3) trying to persuade the current possessor to accept less than he paid for the book; or (4) paying whatever is necessary.

In the course of pursuing the Smiley maps and Meyer books, institutions discovered that while most private owners understandably had mixed feelings about returning stolen property, in the end most were happy to see the book returned to its rightful owner in exchange for the price they had paid; a few, unhappily, demanded additional compensation of one kind or another. In such cases, the library will need to decide how badly it wants the book back. The present authors believe that yielding to such demands is, in general, not a good practice, but each library must make up its own mind, taking into account the importance of the individual item and the funds available for what may be extended and expensive litigation. Legal fees and expenses in large metropolitan areas are extraordinarily high. Unless the victim institution seriously intends to file a lawsuit for recovery of its stolen book (after researching all relevant laws and facts), a threat to do so is unethical and will almost certainly not produce a good result.

CONCLUSION

The reader may reasonably conclude from this article that the recovery of stolen rare items is a slow, time-consuming, and sometimes frustrating and/or painful process requiring the utmost in patience and persistence.[24] Among the obstacles we have pointed to are the lack of reliable shared information about unrecovered stolen books and less than satisfactory channels of communication among the booktrade, law enforcement, and the curatorial community, as well as the lack of readily available sources of information regarding the complex legal issues. On the other hand, the experience provides curators with a fascinating, if unsought, tutorial in the law of replevin and the inner workings of law enforcement and the book trade. Those who have lived through it pray that it is a once-in-a-lifetime education.

NOTES

1. Capsule summaries of both theft cases may be found in Nicholas A. Basbanes, *A Gentle Madness: Bibliophiles, Bibliomanes, and the Eternal Passion for Books* (New York: Holt, 1995), 465–519.

2. The list may be found on the Web at http://www.columbia.edu/cu/lweb/data/indiv/rare/missing/. See also Travis McDade, *The Book Thief: The True Crimes of Daniel Spiegelman* (New York: Greenwood, 2006).

3. The Smiley map thefts received extensive national and international publicity; for links to articles, see http://www.maphistory.info/smileynews.html. For background on the less-publicized Meyer case, see the Ransom Center press

release at http://www.hrc.utexas.edu/news/press/2004/theft.html, and Margarite Annette Nathe, "A Learned Congress: A Closer Look at Book and Manuscript Thieves" (master's paper, School of Information and Library Science, University of North Carolina at Chapel Hill, 2005), 60–62.

4. This Web page contains links to maps that were found to be missing after inventories were conducted at various institutions: http://www.nymapsociety.org/MISSING/WORAM.HTM (accessed March 5, 2009).

5. See John Christoffersen, "Map Thief Ordered to Pay $2.3M," Boston.com, May 22, 2007, http://www.boston.com/news/education/higher/articles/2007/05/22/map_thief_ordered_to_pay_23m/ (accessed March 5, 2009).

6. Suggestions for responding to thefts may be found in the "RBMS/ACRL Guidelines for Security and Theft in Special Collections" (2009) on the RBMS Security Committee web site. For a useful but now dated list of sources to notify, see Susan M. Allen, "Theft in Libraries and Archives: What to Do During the Aftermath of a Theft," *Journal of Library Administration* 25 (1998): 6–9. The RBMS Security Committee web site maintains an updated list of such resources.

7. Allen, "Theft in Libraries and Archives," 6.

8. A brief historical overview: between 1989 and the early 2000s, the ABAA distributed so-called Pink Sheets with reports of stolen books to its members and others, but the system had obvious disadvantages and was discontinued in favor of e-mail reports to membership and the ABAA missing books database, which went live around 2005. In 1980, the BAMBAM (Bookline Alert—Missing Books and Manuscripts) computer system began as a pioneering effort to link booksellers, librarians, and law enforcement through a computer network, but it ceased to exist in 1992, before Web technology became available. Some of its records are at the Grolier Club. That database was unusual in that it also accepted listings for items that were simply "missing" as opposed to being demonstrably stolen.

9. http://www.missingmaps.info. The database's principal developer is Joel Kovarsky.

10. The relevant clause in the University of Texas System fine arts policy reads: "The Insured shall have the right to repurchase from the Company any property of the Insured that is recovered for the amount paid to the Insured for the loss, plus an amount which represents loss adjustment and recovery expenses."

11. http://www.lapdonline.org/art_theft_detail/content_basic_view/1476.

12. "Declared Lost," sponsored by Saving Antiquities for Everyone (SAFE) held in Boston, October 29, 2005. A similar conference was held in Wales in 2002; see Chris Fleet, "Report of the 'Responding to Theft' Seminar," held at the National Library of Wales (http://www.maphistory.info/aberseminar.html).

13. Note that the Code stipulates cooperation with law enforcement, and not necessarily with libraries or other original owners. According to an ABAA spokesperson, that is because the Association does not wish to be drawn into ownership disputes.

14. McDade, *The Book Thief*, 28. To be fair, McDade applies his generalization to large thefts. As a counterexample, some seven years elapsed between Mimi Meyer's first sale of stolen books and her discovery in 2001 by librarians and booksellers, despite the fact that many of the books she sold displayed obvious signs of tampering with bookplates and ownership markings. McDade's

observation would be valid if he had stated that most book thieves who fence large numbers of materials are found out—eventually.

15. At an RBMS Preconference seminar at Austin, Texas, June 22, 2006, an ABAA bookseller declared in a public forum that book thefts were the fault of libraries. See Exlibris archives, http://palimpsest.stanford.edu/byform/mailing-lists/exlibris/2006/09/msg00192.html. That perception is repeated by William Finnegan, "A Theft in the Library: The Case of the Missing Maps," *New Yorker*, October 17, 2005, who observed: "Dealers, in any case, habitually blame libraries for thefts. Librarians are not serious about security, they say" (89).

16. See, for example, Patrick Meighan, "Old Nashua Tax Ledger Sold on eBay Stirs up Legal Debate," *Nashua Telegraph*, July 6, 2007, http://www.nashuatelegraph.com/apps/pbcs.dll/article?AID=/20070706/NEWS01/207060373. According to the reporter, "The issue has raised concerns about not only the private sale of public records, but also about whether an effective mechanism exists for stopping an inappropriate auction on the popular on-line buying and selling site."

17. The Rules and Regulations of the City of New York (6 RCNY § 2-125 [a]) specify that an auctioneer must "furnish to any buyer, consignor or owner of an article, upon request, information as to the whereabouts of that article that comes into his or her possession or that is sold or offered for sale by him or her." In addition, "an auctioneer must keep a written record of all details of each sale including copies of advertisements; lot number, quantity, description and selling price of each lot; record of disbursements; and net amount sent to persons entitled to proceeds of sale for a period of six years from the date of the auction."

18. McKinney's CPLR 214(3).

19. Where replevin is sought against the party who converted the property, the action accrues on the date of conversion (*Sporn v. MCA Records*, 58 N.Y.2d 482, 488, 462 N.Y.S.2d 413, 448 N.E.2d 1324 [1983]). Where the action is brought against a party who purchased the property in good faith, for value and without notice of the conversion, the action accrues only upon the refusal of a demand for its return (*Menzel v. List*, 22 A.D.2d 647, 253 N.Y.S.2d 43 [1964]). This is "because a good-faith purchaser of stolen property commits no wrong, as a matter of substantive law, until he has first been advised of the plaintiff's claim to possession and given an opportunity to return the chattel" (*Guggenheim Found. v. Lubell*, 153 A.D.2d 143, 145, 550 N.Y.S.2d 618 [1990], affd. 77 N.Y.2d 311, 567 N.Y.S.2d 623, 569 N.E.2d 426 [1991]), 153 A.D.2d at 147, 550 N.Y.S.2d 618).

20. Cal. Code Civ. P § 338(c).

21. See *Warin v. Wildenstein & Co.*, 13 Misc.3d 1201(A), 824 N.Y.S.2d 759 (2006), *affirmed* 45 A.D.3d 459, 846 N.Y.S.2d 153 (2007).

22. John Jenkins, *Rare Books and Manuscript Thefts: A Security System for Librarians, Booksellers, and Collectors* (New York: ABAA, 1982): Section V. This guideline is no longer in force, according to an ABAA representative (e-mails to Oram of November 19 and 21, 2007).

23. *Theft of Books and Manuscripts from Libraries: An Advisory Code of Conduct for Booksellers and Librarians*, UK Library Association and the Antiquarian Booksellers Association, Section 6.2 (http://www.la-hq.org.uk/directory/prof_issues/tobam.html).

24. Paintings by Rufino Tamayo and Andy Warhol supposedly stolen over two decades ago recently resurfaced in Manhattan. See, for example, Edith

Honan, "New York Gallery Sues for Return of Stolen Warhol," *Reuters,* February 5, 2008, http://www.reuters.com/article/domesticNews/idUSN0528337820080205, and Melissa Grace, "SoHo Gallery Sues Unemployed Brooklyn Man, Christie's over Warhol Painting," *New York Daily News,* February 6, 2008, http://www.nydailynews.com/news/2008/02/06/2008-02-06_soho_gallery_sues_unemployed_brooklyn_ma.html.

PART VI

Law and War

Chapter 18

Art Theft: Heralds of Change in the International Legal Landscape

Judge Arthur Tompkins

INTRODUCTION

The journeys of the maps, including a cosmographic map from a 1482 edition of Ptolemy's *Geographia*, stolen from Madrid's National Library by Cesar Gomez Rivero, neatly encapsulate many of the problems besetting legal efforts to secure the return of stolen artworks. After the theft, the maps traveled across numerous borders and through many jurisdictions, most of which had different legal structures governing the fate of stolen art works. Eleven of the maps have been located in the United Kingdom, Australia, Argentina, and the United States; some have been returned, and others remain missing.[1]

Absent, perhaps, from the stories of the recovered maps are two of the significant hurdles commonly facing claimants for the return of stolen art—the sometimes lengthy passage of time since the original theft, and an unwillingness on the part of the eventual possessor of the work to return it voluntarily.

Much has been said and written, particularly since the Second World War, concerning these, and other, legal and practical obstacles confronting the dispossessed art owner (or their descendants) seeking restitution. Not the least of these hurdles are the differences in the way various legal systems deal with the contest between the good-faith purchaser, who pays a fair and reasonable (or at least defensible) price and who buys the work without notice or knowledge that it has been stolen, and the original legitimate owner. There has long been a reluctance on the part of legal systems to accord full force to the rules or judgments of another, foreign legal system, resulting in judicial discrepancies.

The purpose of this essay is to look both within, and outside, the somewhat bleak international legal landscape with regard to the restitution of stolen art. Many national legal systems are built on the traditional premise of the insularity of national justice systems, and thus are unwelcoming to cross-border claims for the return of property. This essay will seek to identify some discernible trends in disparate fields that are sufficient, in combination, to herald cautious optimism for the future. These include:

- The development, particularly since 1945, of a functioning international criminal law system, exemplified by the establishment and operation of the International Criminal Court.
- The increase in pan-European cooperation, in matters relating to criminal law.
- The simplification of the law relating to limitation periods[2] as a means of resisting a claim for the return of a stolen art work.
- The increasing willingness of national courts to recognize and enforce a foreign state's claim to items forming part of its national heritage.

When combined, these factors prepare fertile ground for the possible development of a consistent international jurisprudence relating to the return of stolen objects, which may be more conducive to successful claims in the future, or at least greater and welcome consistency in the treatment of such claims.

INTERNATIONAL CRIMINAL LAW

Traditionally, criminal law is premised on the existence of sovereign nation-states, as separate and independent entities. Such sovereign states enforce the criminal law, and deal with the consequences of its breach, within their own boundaries. In 1908, the author of one of the classic common law texts on the Conflicts of Laws, A. V. Dicey, was able to quote with approval an earlier commentator, who said:[3]

> The common law considers crimes as altogether local, and cognisable and punishable in the country where they are committed.

With relatively few exceptions, traditional criminal law does not have extraterritorial operation. In 1982, a leading judge in the English Court of Appeal stated:[4]

> No one has doubted that our courts will not entertain a suit brought by a foreign sovereign, directly or indirectly, to enforce the penal or revenue

> laws of that foreign state. We do not sit to collect taxes for another country or to inflict punishments for it.

That, however, is changing, albeit slowly and painfully. Professor André Tunc described it thus:[5]

> The story of the efforts to create a "world law" is sad: only disappointingly meagre results have been achieved ... Jurists have no other weapons than hearts, mouths and pens with which to oppose the frightening machines which crush bodies and minds.

Space permits but the briefest of overviews of the modern development of international criminal law. Its recent history[6] begins with the two tribunals established in Nuremburg by the Allied Powers between 1945 and 1949. The first, and perhaps better-known, tribunal indicted 24 major Nazi war criminals and resulted in 19 convictions (of which 12 led to death sentences) and 3 acquittals. The International Military Tribunal for the Far East tried 28 Japanese military and political leaders between 1946 and 1948. Twenty-three defendants were convicted, including three prime ministers. Seven received death sentences, and 16 were sentenced to life imprisonment.

There were no new developments in this arena for almost 50 years. Then, in May 1993, the International Criminal Tribunal for the former Yugoslavia was established to hear cases arising from the conflicts in that state during the 1990s, including the case against the former (now deceased) president, Slobodan Milošević.

This was followed soon after, in November 1994, by the creation by the United Nations' Security Council of the International Criminal Tribunal for Rwanda, with jurisdiction over acts of genocide and other serious war crimes committed within Rwanda, or by Rwandan citizens in nearby states, during 1994. Some years later, in 2002, the Hybrid International/Domestic Special Court for Sierra Leone was established to try those responsible for crimes committed during Sierra Leone's 10-year civil war, with trials opening on June 3, 2004. A similar tribunal is now operating in Cambodia, after a protracted and difficult gestation.

Most significantly, on March 11, 2003, the International Criminal Court held its inaugural sitting in The Hague, having been established pursuant to the Rome Statute of the International Criminal Court, which came into force on July 1, 2002. As an independent body created by an international treaty, it remains in permanent session.

In the absence of an effective international criminal law, criminals will continue to take advantage of national systems' deficiencies, including inconsistencies between such systems in respect to, for example, claims for the return of stolen property. International art theft is a paradigm example of such advantage-taking by criminals, which frequently sees stolen art transported to countries where national legal systems are perceived as more sympathetic to claims to retain such works, or which facilitate, willingly or not, the easier creation of false provenances, or indeed valid title, so as to foster such retention.

As a result of the above developments, international criminal law is now well established, albeit not without sometimes trenchant critics, as a permanent aspect of the world's international legal institutions. The relevant point, for present purposes, is that there now exists a functioning international criminal law, so that the resolution of criminal disputes by such a structure is now unremarkable. That acceptance bodes well for the future easier resolution of cross-border disputes involving stolen art works; when the exotic becomes commonplace, then the resolution of competing rights by reference to basic principles against an informed backdrop, rather than the creation of confusion and doubt arising from unfamiliarity and inconsistency, becomes more likely.

EUROPE

The Prum Convention, also known as the Schengen III Agreement, was signed in May 2005 by Germany, Spain, France, Luxembourg, the Netherlands, Austria, and Belgium. It was adopted into European Union regulations for the Schengen States in June 2007, and allows for extensive exchange of information and cooperation between the contracting states and certain others within the European Union, with respect to police and criminal justice matters. Its purpose was, as noted by the then–European Union's presidency, to "help to intensify cross border police co-operation."[7] It was incorporated into EU law at the meeting of the Brussels European Council in June 2007.

While to some extent, its provisions have been watered down during the incorporation process,[8] the signing of the original treaty, and its subsequent expansion and incorporation, is indicative of an increased level of willingness within European states to work across national borders in matters of criminal justice. As is so often encountered in law enforcement issues, the balance struck by policy makers between, on the one hand, valid civil liberties and privacy concerns and, on the other hand, the increased effectiveness of law enforcement, has by this process swung perceptibly in favor of the latter. The desirability or otherwise of that swing continues to be debated, but the result is that cross-border law enforcement within Europe has been both simplified and increased.

A parallel, but separate and more global, development is the establishment and operation of Interpol's DNA Gateway. This is instructive for the art world, in which computerized databases of stolen art are slowly developing, but are not yet sufficiently all-encompassing so as to present a single point of reference to determine whether a given art work is stolen or not. Since its introduction in 2003, and having gone online in 2004, Interpol's international but anonymous database of forensic DNA profiles has demonstrated the benefits that flow to international law enforcement from the computerized access to fundamental information. The database now contains approximately 70,000 forensic DNA profiles, derived both directly from individuals and from crime scenes, and submitted by 44 countries. This is but a tiny percentage of the total forensic DNA profiles held in national DNA databases (as at November 2007, probably totaling about 13 million), but the 150 matches involving 12 countries achieved by the Interpol DNA Gateway demonstrate the effectiveness of selected international sharing of such information. Compared to that database, the three major stolen art databases (operated by Interpol, the FBI, and the private-sector, for-profit Art Loss Register) have yet to achieve either pervasive international acceptance or, indeed, something approaching the perception of universality, which would give substance to their undoubted deterrent potential. But it is happening, and an increasingly all-encompassing computational capacity (so-called "cloud computing") may mean that such universality is within practical reach, given sufficient will and resources. The example of the Interpol DNA Gateway shows that it can be done.

THE LIMITATION CLOCK

When the return of stolen artworks is sought, the obstacle of limitation periods frequently arises. This is particularly so where stolen art has been out of circulation for many years, and where national law permits the final, good-faith owner to establish a valid claim after a period (usually three or six years, but not always) of uninterrupted possession:

> Overcoming a good-faith purchaser's state of limitations defence is often the owner's most significant hurdle.[9]

Recent English case law[10] confirms an early twentieth-century rule that both a demand that goods be returned, and an unequivocal refusal to return them, are required before the limitation clock will begin to tick. The leading 1911 case had stated:[11]

> The real owner . . . may have been deprived of control over his chattel for a hundred years, but it still remains his property, and an action will lie to recover it. . . . If there is a demand by the owner of the person in possession of the chattel and a refusal on the part of the latter to give it up, then in six years the remedy of the owner is barred.

A similar "demand and refusal" approach is taken in New York,[12] subject to a defense of unreasonable delay. If, upon demand, the possessor refuses or fails to respond, then the limitation period will not begin to run.

This reaffirmation of the importance of both a demand and a refusal is of particular relevance to the dispossessed owners of stolen artworks, who, sometimes many years after their theft, fortuitously discover their whereabouts only to find that they are in the hands of a person who purchased them in good faith, and who refuses to return them. The chaos, ill feeling, and disruption that such demands can create is illustrated by the well-documented case of two Egon Schiele paintings, owned by Austria and lent by the Leopold Foundation of Vienna to the Museum of Modern Art in New York in 1997, which, just before their impending departure from New York, were claimed by two families claiming ownership as heirs of original Jewish owners who had lost the paintings to the Nazis.[13] In common-law countries, where this rule applies,[14] the ultimate possessor, irrespective of how they came by the object, cannot safely assume that undisturbed possession for longer than three or six years, as applicable locally, will protect them from a claim for conversion or replevin. Rather, a demand must have been received, and unequivocally refused, and then the limitation period must expire, before such a claim will be statute barred. On the other hand, the dispossessed owner needs to make such a demand and, if an unequivocal refusal results, take action within the applicable limitation period, calculated from the date of the refusal.

The same position pertains with respect to looted antiquities, being historic items of cultural importance discovered and with no known owner,[15] which are generally treated by operation of local law as belonging to their state of origin, particularly upon illegal export. The limitation period will apply to claims by the originating state equally as to an individual litigant. Such claims are usually brought before the courts of the country where the item is located, but issues as to ownership and/or possession at the time of deprivation are determined by application of the laws of the country where the item was originally discovered and/or from which it was illegally exported, often by the local courts calling expert evidence as to the laws of the state of origin.

There is no easy or "right" solution to resolving the competing interests of the original, dispossessed owner, and the good-faith purchaser.[16] From time to time, commentators place faith in the continued development of the computerized databases, those referred to above and others, as a means of satisfying the requirement of appropriate diligence placed by the varying legal rules on both the original owner and good-faith purchaser. Pro forma reference to such databases, without more, or reference when the likelihood of the item in question being registered is slim or nonexistent,[17] will be only one non-determinative facet of the enquiry into the fundamental issue of honesty of purpose and deed. The clarity and relative simplicity of the demand and refusal rule, while triggering criticism from some quarters that the pendulum has swung too far in favor of the original owner, nevertheless is more likely, at least, to provide a clear-cut answer, and thus predictability of outcome, in place of continued inconsistency of result depending on the location (and sometimes the ethical preference) of the court before which the issue happens to come.

RECOGNITION OF NATIONAL HERITAGE

The English Court of Appeal has recently reaffirmed an express willingness to give effective substance to a state's "national heritage" laws. In *Iran v. Barakat Galleries*[18] Iran sought to recover 5,000-year-old antiquities (18 carved chlorite jars, bowls, and cups), which it said were part of its national heritage, unlawfully excavated, and exported.[19] Barakat Galleries, which had the objects at its London gallery, had purchased the objects in France, Germany, and Switzerland, and claimed good title to them under the laws of those countries. Before the English courts, Iran claimed, first, that it had title to the objects by operation of Iranian law, conferring on it a proprietary right to possession that arose when the objects were found, but not delivered to the state (but instead transferred out of the country). Secondly, Iran claimed that the English Court should enforce its law, so as to recognize and/or enforce that title. The Court of Appeal concluded in favor of Iran, finding that Iran had both a proprietary title to the objects entitling Iran to recover them from the gallery, or an immediate right to possession sufficient to found a claim against the gallery for conversion or wrongful interference with goods.

The Court then answered a previously unresolved question,[20] as to the English courts' willingness to recognize and enforce a foreign state's "penal, revenue or other public law." The Court concluded, in favor or Iran, that its claim was not, in any event, a claim to enforce a foreign penal or public law, and went on to express its view that there were strong public policy reasons favouring such a claim:

> In our judgement, there are positive reasons of policy why a claim by a state to recover antiquities which form part of its national heritage and which otherwise complies with the requirements of private international law should not be shut out by the general principle invoked by Barakat. Conversely, in our judgement it is certainly contrary to public policy for such claims to be shut out.[21]

The Court noted the various international treaties and agreements in force in this area, none of which directly affected the case before it, and went on to comment:

> [The treaties and agreements] illustrate the international acceptance of the desirability of protection of the national heritage. A refusal to recognise the title of a foreign state, conferred by its law, to antiquities unless they had come into the possession of such state, would in most cases render it

> impossible for this country to recognise any claim by such a state to recover antiquities unlawfully exported to this country.[22]

Thus, the Court signaled a clear view in favor of the repatriation of items comprising part of a country's national heritage, which is in keeping with the principles of, for example, the UNESCO Convention on the Means of Prohibiting and Preventing the Illicit Import, Export, and Transfer of Ownership of Cultural Property[23] and the UNIDROIT Convention on Stolen or Illegally Exported Cultural Objects.[24] Evident in that and other such conventions, and in the judgment in *Iran v. Barakat,* is an uncritical acceptance of the underlying assumption that such repatriation is a good thing, without close examination of the arguments challenging such an assumption, which assert that antiquities found, sometimes coincidentally, within present-day national borders do not inevitably or properly "belong" to such states:

> Antiquity cannot be owned. It is our common heritage as represented by and in antiquities and ancient texts and architecture ... That discrete antiquities have been found within the borders of a particular modern nation-state is a matter of chance. There is no natural and indelible connection between antiquities and modern nation-states. The battle over our ancient heritage today is over false claims of ownership. It is a matter simple of politics.[25]

CONCLUSION

Stolen art, like crime in general, is a universal problem without a universal solution. Just as debate rages as to the best means of addressing crime, so too, the debate will continue as how best to resolve the sometimes intractable disputes caused as stolen art disappears and then reappears, often far removed in time, place, and circumstance. Necessarily, such disputes will continue to come before national courts, operating as they do as part of the coercive power of the world's nation-states. Solutions will vary, but simplicity of approach and consistency of principle stand a better chance of producing, in the end, a just result, remembering always that justice is a relative and not an absolute concept, calling in its aid both context and shared or reconciled values, and furthermore that justice is determined and imposed against a backdrop not only of local conditions, but also international relationships. This essay has identified some optimistic signposts along the road to such simplicity and consistency. There is far still to travel.

NOTES

1. Eight were handed to an investigating Judge in Buenos Aires, two were recovered by the FBI in New York, two in Sydney, and one in London; four

items remain missing: see http://www.guardian.co.uk/world/2007/nov/12/spain.artnews (accessed October 15, 2008) and http://www.thinkspain.com/news-spain/13657/australia-returns-stolen-national-library-map (accessed October 15, 2008).

2. Defined time periods after which a claim cannot be brought.

3. A. V. Dicey, *A Digest of the Law of England with Reference to the Conflict of Laws*, 2nd ed. (London: Sweet & Maxwell, 1908), 207.

4. *Attorney-General of New Zealand v. Ortiz* [1984] AC 1; [1982] 3 All ER 432).

5. Foreword to A. T. von Mehren and J. R. Gordley, *The Civil Law System*, 2nd ed. (Boston: Little, Brown, 1977), vii.

6. Leaving aside, for present purposes, the League of Nations's Permanent Court of International Justice, and before that, the international anti–slave trade treaty-based courts.

7. Presidency Conclusions of the Brussels European Council (June 21–22, 2007) paragraph 25; available at http://www.consilium.europa.eu/ueDocs/cms_Data/docs/pressData/en/ec/94932.pdf (accessed October 15, 2008).

8. For example, by the deletion of the "hot pursuit" provisions, allowing cross-border transit by law enforcement officers in pursuit of offenders without prior agreement: see M. Burgess, "The Prüm Process: Playing or Abusing the System?" *European Security Review* 8, no. 34 (2007): 8–10.

9. R. S. Kaufman, *Art Law Handbook* (New York: Aspen Law & Business, 2000), 286, paragraph 5.01.

10. *Schwarzschild v. Harrods Ltd* [2008] EWHC 521 (QB); [2008] All ER 299).

11. *Clayton v. Le Roy* [1911–13] All ER Rep 284; [1911] 2 KB 1031 per Fletcher Moulton LJ.

12. *Solomon R. Guggenheim Foundation v. Lubell* 550 NYS 2d 618; aff'd 77 N.Y. 2d 311. 569 N.E.2d 426, 567 N.Y.S.2d 623 (1991).

13. The case, and the "chaotic result of multijurisdictional connections in art theft cases" is described in Reyhan, "A Chaotic Palette: Conflict of Laws in Litigation between Original Owners and Good-Faith Purchasers of Stolen Art," *Duke Law Journal* 50 (2001): 955, especially at 1029–34. It turned out that neither claimant had a legitimate claim.

14. Primarily the United Kingdom, the United States, Canada, Australia, and New Zealand.

15. For a consideration of the matters considered in this paragraph, see *Iran v. Barakat Galleries* [2008] 1 All ER 1177; [2007] EWCA Civ 1374.

16. "Good faith" here usually denotes, at its core, honesty and propriety—or, put another way, the absence of dishonesty or bad faith: see, e.g., *Mogridge v. Clapp* [1892] 3 Ch 382 at 391; *Street v. Derbyshire Unemployed Workers' Centre* [2004] EWCA Civ 964. The requirement of due diligence in ascertaining the provenance of an item, as referred to, for example, in Kaufman, *Art Law Handbook*, 475, paragraph 7.04, is more properly part of the evidentiary matrix adduced to establish the core characteristic of honesty.

17. Because of the nature and circumstances of its finding, e.g., the unearthing of a previously unknown antiquity and its immediate export through illicit channels.

18. *Iran v. Barakat Galleries* [2008] 1 All ER 1177; [2007] EWCA Civ 1374.

19. Barakat Galleries disputed the origin of the antiquities, however the correctness of Iran's assertions was assumed for the purposes of the argument on the preliminary issues before the Court.

20. Left unsettled by the House of Lords in *A–G of New Zealand v. Ortiz* [1984] AC 1; [1982] 3 All ER 432.

21. *Iran v. Barakat Galleries, supra,* at paragraph [154].

22. *Iran v. Barakat Galleries, supra,* at paragraph [163].

23. Passed at UNESCO's 1970 General Conference, in force from April 1972, and accepted or ratified by (to date) 116 countries.

24. Signed at Rome in 1995 and, after the required five ratifications, in force from 1998. To date, 40 countries have ratified the Convention.

25. J. Cuno, *Who Owns Antiquity? Museums and the Battle over Our Ancient Heritage* (Princeton, NJ: Princeton University Press, 2008), 20.

Chapter 19

Economic Woe, Art Theft, and Money Laundering: A Perfect Recipe

Dafydd Nelson

"Crunch": a word usually associated with a noise made while eating breakfast cereal, or, as one dictionary definition puts it, "to crush or grind noisily." However, the Oxford English Dictionary has recently given a new meaning to this word: "a severe shortage of money or credit."

The "credit crunch" has hit most world economies very hard of late. The situation involving Northern Rock,[1] the recently nationalized UK bank, comes to mind, as do the plummeting stock indices, as investor confidence reaches lows not seen for 15 years or more. But despite all the economic doom and gloom, the art trade remains, unsurprisingly, buoyant.

ART MAINTAINS VALUE

Art has always sold well, even during an economic downturn. As company share prices and real estate values plunge, works of art have a curious way of maintaining, and even gaining, value in dire times. For instance, The Royal Institute of Chartered Surveyors states that the art industry has maintained its level over the first quarter of 2008, even while the crunch has been particularly severe.[2] Why is this the case? Even when the world's economy is in recession, the "superrich" are eager to invest. Works of art by famous painters, for example, are unique objects that retain their value, even in rocky times.

The value of an artwork is derived from a combination of its perceived authenticity and perceived rarity. Even if the work is a fake, as long as it has been authenticated by an expert, its value is retained. Bear in mind that experts themselves may have an incentive to authenticate a work that is in fact a fake, where, for example, they are to receive a commission from any sale.[3] One of the great problems is that it may not be in the interests of professionals connected to the trade to discover that a work is a fake, or that money used to purchase a painting has been derived from criminal activity. If this happens they stand to lose millions.

For those who want to splash out the odd million, contemporary art is viewed as the must-have accessory. Charles Saatchi, for example, almost single-handedly created a market for the "Young British Artists" such as Damien Hirst, and is now investing in young Chinese artists.[4]

A work by the British graffiti spray-paint artist Banksy entitled *Laugh Now but One Day We Will Be in Charge* recently sold for £100,000. What is interesting about Banksy is that while his works are considered to be "art," and are cut out of the walls onto which they are sprayed in order to be sold, other graffiti spray painters are regarded as criminals and subjected to arrest.

ART CRIME ABOUNDS

At first glance, this appears to be great news for the art world. When times are good, everyone in the art world benefits. During depression, the art trade still remains afloat and prosperous. However, art crime abounds. Theft, looting in conflict zones, money laundering, and forgeries mean that dealers and purchasers need to be on their guard, particularly given that the art trade is still thriving and remains one of the few buoyant industries in a landscape of recession.

Insurance companies are so worried that the price of art will continue to rise and this, in turn, will spur more theft and related suspicious transactions, that they have increased premiums for the first time in 18 months, in the fall of 2008. The theft of works by Degas, Cezanne, Van Gogh, and Monet from the Büehrle Collection in Zurich[5] in February 2008 spurred a rise in premiums of approximately 10 percent by insurers such as Hiscox. Charles Dupplin, chairman of Hiscox's art and private client division, said "premiums will edge up for museums by up to 10%" because "there has been a marked increase in levels of activity of major art thefts driven in part by very large increases in the value of modern art."[6]

Of great concern to financial regulators is that the money gained from illicit criminal activity is being used to purchase works of art—art is therefore a means of laundering illicit funds. Criminals are using the safe investment of artworks to launder illicit funds and protect their ill-gained wealth even in an economic recession, because unlike real estate and such, authentic art retains its value. Certainly, there's no point in a hard-day's robbing, if you then lose most of the money by investing in property or in stocks that plunge in value. Therefore, this credit crunch period is prime time for theft, as well as activity that can fall into the category of money laundering. That criminals launder ill-gotten funds by buying artworks in times of recession should result in stricter observation on the part of dealers to determine the origins of funds with which buyers make purchases. But the art industry is loath to do anything that infringes upon the confidentiality code of conduct that has always been a part of the art world—and any stricter regulations would hurt business. We therefore see a situation in which the opaque transactions of the art industry can obscure and protect criminal funds, while the art trade will suffer if it seeks to regulate its own transactions.

A DODGY DEGAS DEAL

Examples of money-laundering schemes gone wrong in the art world are not uncommon. In June 2001, two New York City art dealers were reported to have been charged for conspiring to launder over $4 million worth of drug money by attempting to sell paintings claimed to be originals by Modigliani and Degas to a federal agent posing as a drug dealer. The *New York Times* reported that one of the dealers, Shirley D. Sack (a wholesaler of art and jewelry) had been attempting to sell a painting by Raphael in exchange for drug money or funds from organized crime figures.[7] Arnold K. Katzen, a principal of American European Art Associates, and Alan M. Stewart, a Connecticut art dealer, were also charged. Both Sack and Katzen were arrested in Boston at the Ritz Carlton Hotel, where they attempted to sell the Degas and Modigliani paintings. All three guilty parties were legitimate art dealers, involved in both legal and illegal activities.

In the art world, the line is often blurred. Above-board dealers may be involved in the occasional shady plot, and any one art transaction may have both legal and illegal elements to it. Take, for example, the much-publicized sale of the Gospel of Judas, a Coptic codex that, on the one hand, had been illegally looted and smuggled out of Egypt, but was then bought in a series of legitimate transactions between known dealers, collectors, and institutions. The transaction history of that one object included both criminal and legal interactions. Such examples are commonplace, particularly when dealing with antiquities, relatively few of which left their countries of origin legitimately.

Examples of art used to launder money abound. In March 2002, U.S. officials seized two paintings, a Goya and a 1924 work by Japanese artist Tsuguharu Foujita, that were being used by a Spanish money-launderer to settle a $10 million drug debt.[8] More recently, in June 2008, police searching thousands of safety deposit boxes seized at three London centers found nearly 14 million pounds as well as several stolen works of

Renaissance art. The premises were all owned by Safe Deposit Centres, a company set up some 20 years ago. Two directors of the company were arrested on suspicion of money laundering. In all, there are 10 safe deposit companies in London, all of which must be registered with the Financial Services Authority, as stated by the money-laundering regulations that came into force in December 2007.[9] These examples demonstrate that art is being used to launder illicit funds—and all of them occurred during tough economic climate periods, like those in 2001–2 and 2007–8.

MONEY-LAUNDERING REGULATIONS

Money laundering is a serious enough offense that it has been elevated in the public's eye to the category of "heinous crime."[10] Dealers and auction houses must take action to defend against money laundering, and are legally obliged to do so. But what exactly is money laundering? And how are we to guard against it?

In the United Kingdom, Her Majesty's Revenue and Customs (HMRC), the government arm responsible for the vast majority of money-laundering regulation, defines this activity as the "exchanging criminally-obtained money or other assets for 'clean' money or other assets with no obvious link to their criminal origins. This also covers money, however come by, which is used to fund terrorism."[11] This definition covers the purchase of an asset using money obtained from, for example, the sale of drugs, arms, or by insider trading on a stock exchange. All banks and law firms active in the property market train their staff to look out for suspicious sums of money that may be in the process of being laundered. The asset in question could be a piece of real estate, like a house, or, as described in an example above, the asset could be a painting by Degas.

From December 15, 2007, new law, in the form of the Money Laundering Regulations 2007, requires businesses to establish systems to prevent money laundering and to report transactions that, on the face of it, look suspicious. The problem with this is one of both economics and psychology. The financial industry and art trade wants to keep clients happy and keep money flowing in. By implementing the checks and safeguards required to intercept money-laundering attempts, businesses run the risk of both alienating clients and losing money from the transactions. Whether overt or subconscious, the tendency is to favor business and to not look too closely at potentially questionable deals. One can always claim ignorance if a dealer or financial institution is found to have been passively complicit in a money-laundering transaction.

The 2007 UK Regulations implemented the European Community's Third Money Laundering Directive,[12] a piece of legislation initiated and passed by the European lawmaking institutions that overarch European national governments. This pan-European approach means that money laundering is tackled in a uniform way among European Community member states. It is important to remember that money laundering does not apply just to one sector or jurisdiction, but is something that spreads across all forms of economic activity and cannot be contained within national boundaries.

Many traditional financial businesses, such as banks, building societies, and investment firms, come under these Regulations, as do legal professionals, accountants, and tax advisers. But dealers of high-value goods, defined as those who take a commission of €15,000 or more on any transaction, are also covered. Given that the average sought-after painting will cost millions of euros, and auction houses such as Christie's and Sotheby's rarely handle works of art worth less than £10,000, the art industry must also comply with this legislation.

HMRC has the responsibility for supervising high-value dealers. In order to comply with the Regulations, it is essential for the regulated business to perform a number of functions, which include registering with HMRC, paying an annual fee based on the number of premises used to trade, putting anti-money-laundering systems in place, and reporting any suspicious transactions. Anti-money-laundering controls are policies and procedures that allow a business to assess the risks that its day-to-day activities will be used by criminals to launder money, through verifying customers' identity and monitoring customers' business activities. HMRC does not mandate what risk-based measures should be in place for businesses: it is for senior managers to decide on a reasonable approach which balances the costs to customers with a realistic assessment of the risks involved.

HMRC states that policies and procedures covering the following should be put in place:

- Customer due diligence measures and ongoing monitoring
- Reporting
- Recordkeeping
- Internal control
- Risk assessment and management
- Monitoring and management of compliance
- Internal communication of such policies and procedures

These measures are to be applied on a "risk-sensitive" basis, meaning that businesses must use their judgment to assess the risks of money laundering and decide on the level of ID verification, enquiry, and monitoring that is reasonable given the businesses activities. ID verification is termed "customer due diligence." This requires the verification of customer identity through documents, data, or information obtained from a reliable and independent source. Obtaining details of a customer's source of funds is an essential element to satisfying money-laundering regulation requirements—but the source is not always clear.

Of comfort to would-be buyers who crave anonymity is that there is no requirement to make the ID information public and, therefore, the only people who need be satisfied of identity and source of funds is the auction house itself. However, if a business is caught failing to comply with the Regulations, severe consequences could result. HMRC can impose civil penalties, such as fines, and a business can lose its registration with HMRC. If this occurs, and a business continues to trade, then criminal prosecution can result.

Due diligence requirements vary depending on the circumstances of the transaction. For example, where you have an occasional transactions where there is no business relationship and the value of the deal is of €15,000 (£9,000) or more, and where there are no "significantly higher than usual" risk factors present, HMRC requires that you "obtain and verify ID documents, data or info" and "where appropriate, identify and verify details of the beneficial owner." It is up to the individual business to determine the risk factor of each transaction. Where additional risk factors are present, for example, when an art dealer sells a painting to a buyer through an intermediary (a non-face-to-face transaction), HMRC guidance says you should "obtain additional evidence of identification and/or apply supplementary measures to verify the documents supplied. Consider undertaking the first transaction through a bank account in the customer's name."[13] It should be noted that the details of these decisions are internal to the businesses, and therefore the government relies to a great extent on the businesses monitoring themselves.

The requirement to take all of these measures may seem a little odd. What if a customer wants to remain anonymous? The art trade has a unspoken code of anonymity, making it the least transparent multibillion-dollar market in the world. In fact, the annual value of the international art trade is estimated to be in the tens of billions of dollars. Out of this, something like $6 billion a year falls into the pockets of organized criminals, making art crime the third highest-grossing annual criminal trade in the world, behind only drugs and arms.[14]

In short, individual businesses—in this case, art dealers—are left to police themselves along the HMRC and EU guidelines. The strict policing required to curb money laundering through art purchase would poison the well from which the art trade drinks, risking the alienation of clients and the loss of business.

THE WAY FORWARD

Auction houses must be extremely vigilant when accepting even relatively small sums of money from buyers of artworks. Ensuring that money-laundering regulation requirements are satisfied is an essential part of the day-to-day running of such establishments.

But unsurprisingly, this runs counter to the interests of the art trade. Dealers would lose millions if they discovered anything untoward. It is therefore not in the best interests of the art trade to look too hard at their transactions. As long as a business can claim to have checked, so as not to run afoul of the HMRC or other relevant European commissions, the art trade will overlook all but the most overt attempts at money laundering, and criminals will continue to profit through art deals, particularly in times of recession.

It will likely take an external, independent regulatory body through which all art transactions must be run, requiring some active proof that the funds used for purchase came from legitimate sources, in order to impede money laundering through art purchases. While the HMRC and EU have set up good guidelines, the enforcement is left up to the trade being regulated, requiring a level of self-policing that is practically improbable to hope for.

The establishment of an independent, perhaps international anti-money-laundering agency specifically to monitor the art trade is a method that law enforcement agencies would do well to consider.[15] An independent agency with an art-specific focus could be what is needed, and would surely not be a waste of resources, given the large sums involved. Such an agency could be either nationally or EU-sponsored. Given the international nature of the art trade and art crime, and art crime's considerable support of the other activities in which organized crime is involved, some action must be taken.

NOTES

1. Northern Rock describes itself as a "specialized lender, whose core business is the provision of UK residential mortgages." Its focus on mortgages meant that institutional lenders became reluctant to lend to it in the wake of the U.S. subprime crisis during the summer of 2007. The bank was reliant on this source of finance, and once it dried up, the Bank of England had to step in and supply liquidity in its function as "lender of last resort." With no viable private-sector bailout forthcoming, the UK government decided that the best course of action would be to temporarily nationalize the bank until the business was ready again to be taken into private hands.

2. See the 2008 Quarter 1 report from RICS at http://www.rics.org/Knowledgezone/Economiccommentary/aas_q12008_220408.htm.

3. See artinfo.com at http://www.artinfo.com/news/story/28263/buyer-beware/.

4. See "Charles Saatchi Draws Chinese Artists to His Gallery's Retooled Web Site," *International Herald Tribune*, March 13, 2007, http://www.iht.com/articles/2007/03/13/news/artists.php.

5. The works stolen were *Poppies Near Vétheuil* by Claude Monet, *Count Lepic and His Daughters* by Edgar Degas, *Blossoming Chestnut Branch* by Vincent Van Gogh, and *Boy in a Red Waistcoat* by Paul Cézanne. The theft took place on Sunday, February 10, 2008, and the estimated worth of the paintings stolen stands at $163 million.

6. See Yvette Essen, "Cost of Insuring Art Rises after Robberies," *Daily Telegraph*, February 25, 2008, http://www.telegraph.co.uk/money/main.jhtml?xml=/money/2008/02/25/cnart125.xml.

7. See "Money Laundering Charges for Art Dealers," *New York Times*, June 2, 2001, http://query.nytimes.com/gst/fullpage.html?res=9900EEDB173FF931A35755C0A9679C8B63.

8. David Adams, "Bristling Art Dealer Paints Herself as a Victim," *St. Petersburg Times*, June 18, 2003, http://www.sptimes.com/2003/06/18/Worldandnation/Bristling_art_dealer_.shtml.

9. See David Pallister, "Art, Jewels and £14m Cash Seized in Deposit Box Centre Raids," *The Guardian*, June 5, 2008, http://www.guardian.co.uk/uk/2008/jun/05/ukcrime.

10. See Rob Norton, "In Defense of Money Laundering," *Fortune* 27, September 1999, http://money.cnn.com/magazines/fortune/fortune_archive/1999/09/27/266170/index.htm.

11. See HM Revenue and Customs Web site, http://www.hmrc.gov.uk/mlr/beginners.htm.

12. Directive 2005/60/EC is available at http://eur-lex.europa.eu/LexUriServ/LexUriServ.do?uri=OJ:L:2005:309:0015:0036:EN:PDF.

13. See HMRC due diligence guidance at http://www.hmrc.gov.uk/mlr/mlr8.htm#4b.

14. See Noah Charney, "Buyer Beware," ARTINFO, August 11, 2008, http://www.artinfo.com/news/story/28263/buyer-beware/.

15. It should be noted that the nearest existing agency to an independent art regulator, the Art Loss Register, is a for-profit institution, the major shareholders of which include auction houses such as Christie's and Sotheby's. Therefore, their activities will be in the interests of their shareholders, and they do not serve as an independent regulatory body. A governmental or EU institution, with no ties to any for-profit arm of the art community, is needed in order to produce unbiased, beneficial results which, de facto, will impede the profits of the art trade.

Chapter 20

The Artifacts of Wartime Art Crime: Evidence for a Model of the Evolving Clout of Cultural Property in Foreign Affairs

Erik Nemeth

INTRODUCTION: TIME INTENSIFIES THE MEANING OF WARTIME ART CRIME

As a distinct type of art crime, wartime abuses against cultural property present risks that persist beyond a particular battle or conflict. Plunder of fine art during World War II, looting of antiquities during the Cold War era, and the burgeoning illicit trade in art in the post–Cold War period each contributed a new dimension to art crime. Without adequate attention to restitution or repatriation, and without commensurate indemnification, the abuses against art objects in each wartime period retain political significance. One half-century after the illicit act, paintings plundered from Jewish collections still carry the stigma of ethnic cleansing and induce high-profile legal cases. Antiquities acquired through exploitation of developing nations during *détente*[1] force museums to assume defensive postures in order to protect their collections. In the post–Cold War period, security threats posed by transnational organized crime and terrorism further politicized art crime. Specifically, use of stolen paintings as collateral in narcotics trafficking, and the targeting of religious monuments in political violence, implicates art crime as a threat to international security. The mounting political and security risks across wartime periods compound the relevance of art crime to foreign affairs.

Wartime art crime differs fundamentally from individual thefts of fine art. The scale of theft, and interrelation with foreign affairs, create a distinct type of art crime. Whether part of a campaign of conquest, such as during World War II, or a consequence of competing political interests, such as during the Cold War, wartime art crime occurs on a scale that touches hundreds, thousands, and millions of pieces of art. As part of foreign policy or precipitated by political decisions, wartime art crime creates a role for stolen artworks in foreign relations. The association of plundered Jewish collections with the Holocaust, and the looting of antiquities from nations in which Western powers competed with the Soviet Union for political influence, demonstrated direct and indirect integrations of art crime into foreign affairs. The scale of wartime art crime also expands the time frame, or life span, of restitution. The time required to locate and identify the large volume of artworks originally stolen, or destroyed, during wartime results in the interrelation of restitution and postwar foreign affairs. The history of restitution of artworks plundered during World War II creates a case study for the accruing political clout of wartime art crime. In the same time frame, controversies over the ownership of cultural property looted during the Cold War era reveal a recurring pattern with calls for repatriation. Juxtaposition of the processes for restitution of Nazi plunder and for the repatriation of antiquities looted during the Cold War era compounds the political clout of art crime that, in turn, motivated trafficking in, and destruction of, cultural property in the post–Cold War period.

The large scale and inherent political significance of wartime art crime have long-term ramifications in foreign affairs. A deliberate program to plunder fine art that parallels a military campaign, collateral damage to archaeological sites during armed conflict, or looting of antiquities that precipitates from military incursion, all constitute wartime art crime. As an integral part of military conquest, and enabled by the chaos of combat, wartime art crime occurs across wide geographic regions in the theater of war and affects a range of individuals and institutions incidental to the conflict. In parallel with the broad impact, the ideologies of aggressors, and power struggles in the aftermath of military action, politicize wartime abuses against cultural property.

The large-scale, politically charged nature of wartime art crime has created persistent controversies in foreign relations. Plunder that occurred at the time of the Napoleonic Wars created controversies that have lasted two centuries. Egyptian cultural artifacts in the Louvre remain a point of contention, and the "Elgin Marbles" in the British Museum have become a metaphor for debates over the ownership of cultural property. Such debates, in combination with growing concern for the destruction of cultural property during armed conflict, as epitomized during World War I, led to a series of international conventions. The conventions politicized the plunder of World War II and looting during the Cold War era, which, in turn, added to the legacy of controversies over possession of national treasures and privately owned artworks. The resilience of motivations to pursue repatriation, and the viability of claims for restitutions decades after the plunder, demonstrate that the poignancy of wartime art crime does not dissipate and that, perhaps in time, the art objects embody the politics of the past conflict.

CAUSE AND CONSEQUENCE: MOTIVES SHIFT, BUT CONTROVERSIES PERSIST

While unauthorized movement of artworks consistently creates controversies over ownership, the motives for plunder shift from one conflict to the next. Beyond the obvious material profit from pillaging in the wake of conquest, a combination of political, religious, entrepreneurial, and *cultural* motives have added an ideological complexity to the material value of looting. At least since Roman times, parading captured artworks has symbolized conquest to the citizens of the victorious nation.[2] In the Middle Ages, motivations to seek out cultural artifacts, such as beneath the site of the Temple of King Solomon, included a perceived religious power of the objects in question.[3] In conquests of the New World, plunder of Native American riches took the form of entrepreneurism.[4] Colonialism enabled a potentially less aggressive "accretion" of native antiquities to private and public collections of imperial nations,[5] but World War I[6] and World War II[7] realized a return to violent destruction and displacement of cultural property in Europe on a massive scale. In retrospect, each historical period displayed new reasons to exploit the cultural heritage of the conquered nation or oppressed ethnic group. Building on the basic desire to acquire material wealth, the exploitation of artworks shifted from an afterthought of military conquest, to a strategic objective in campaigns to enrich national patrimony and to define and impose ideologies.

Tactical Exploitation of Cultural Property in Sync with Military Action

Not unlike the conquests of Alexander the Great and the Roman Empire, the expansion of the Third Reich included plunder of fine art and cultural artifacts of conquered territories. Distinctions lie less in the extent of plunder, and the intent of cultural domination, than in the integration of organized plunder within a military campaign. Empires in antiquity may have leveraged symbolic value in cultural domination *after* military victory, but campaigns of conquest in the nineteenth and twentieth centuries *began* with exploitation of cultural property. In the case of the conquest of Persepolis, historians debate the degree of premeditation shown by Alexander, in his destruction of the palace of Xerxes.[8] While by the time of Napoleon, artworks served as point of negotiation for Italian dukes who sought clemency.[9]

Prior to 1939, the National Socialists already leveraged art to gain cultural control and to generate funding for the war. In the late 1920s, Alfred Rosenberg founded an organization to uphold a German aesthetic and protect German culture from the "corruption" of the Impressionists and Expressionists. In 1933, Dr. Paul Joseph Goebbels implemented the cultural politics with the burning of books by Jewish intellectuals and the removal of modern art from German museums.[10] The movement continued into World War II with the confiscation of *Entartetekunst* ("degenerate art") from museums, galleries, and private collections in annexed and occupied territories throughout Europe. Disposal of "degenerate art" included both destruction and sale. The Nazi authorities enlisted the services of professionals in the art market to identify and manage the sale of the more valuable artworks. Dealers, such as Karl Haberstock, organized the sale of artworks, such as the auction at the Fischer Gallery of Lucerne, Switzerland, in 1939. The proceeds either financed the purchase of desired artworks or fed into the Nazi military campaign.[11]

After mandating a definition of fine art, Adolf Hitler, Hermann Göring, and Heinrich Himmler proceeded to amass artworks for both personal collections and the planned *Führermuseum* in Linz, Austria.[12] Initial phases of acquisition targeted the artworks of Jewish collectors. Property laws that persecuted Jewish citizens as part of the ethnic cleansing of the Holocaust enabled the National Socialist Party to acquire prized artworks in Germany and annexed territories. With the *Anschluss*[13] and *Kristallnacht,*[14] personnel of the *Sicherheitsdienst,*[15] *Schutzstaffel,*[16] and *Gestapo*[17] sought out, and detained, wealthy Jewish collectors in Vienna, such as members of the Rothschild family, who then negotiated freedom by relinquishing artworks. In the plunder of territories conquered by force, the Nazi authorities needed to circumvent preexisting international conventions, such as the 1907 Hague Convention (IV) on the Laws of War, which prohibits looting in Articles 46 and 47. Alfred Rosenberg established the *Einsatzstab Reichsleiter Rosenberg*[18] (ERR), which pursued acquisition of artworks outside of military operations. Operations in France leveraged civil service personnel to locate and confiscate Jewish collections, and the ERR exploited the neutrality of Switzerland to engage civilian art professionals who overtly organized exchanges of confiscated paintings.[19] Covert tactics of disguising art historians as soldiers, and claiming artworks for scientific purposes, represented attempts to conceal wartime plunder. Recruiting civil service personnel, through embassies in occupied territories, to locate and confiscate Jewish collections represented another thinly veiled tactic of "legitimate" looting. Together, the plunder initiated directly by Hitler and through the ERR rivaled the scale of the Nazi military conquest. Through the campaign against "degenerate art," confiscation of "enemy" art collections, and "nonmilitary plunder," the Nazi regime exploited cultural property prior to, and then in lock step with, the military campaign of the Third Reich.

While the Nazi authorities sought to circumvent the prohibition of wartime plunder, the Soviet authorities pursued wartime acquisitions in the name of reparations.[20] Soviet forces plundered with the premeditated intent of regaining material and cultural losses incurred by the *Wehrmacht* (German armed forces) in Soviet territories. To compensate for destroyed artworks, Joseph Stalin intended to acquire pieces for display in the Pushkin Museum, and other public collections. Enlistment of prominent artists and scholars to evaluate the cultural losses, and to identify artworks of commensurate value in German-occupied territories, illuminates the forethought of plunder. The removal of the friezes of the Pergamon Altar in Berlin, and the seizure of entire collections, such as paintings from the Dresden Gallery, illustrate the scale of plunder. Despite attempts to justify the acquisitions, the Soviet covert deployment of art historians as soldiers suggests a realization of the questionable legitimacy of reparations in the form of cultural property, and the extensive involvement of security-intelligence services (such as the NKVD and MGB) suggests an interest in concealing the acquisition of so-called trophy art.

Throughout the initiative, individuals of high rank and ordinary soldiers further compromised the spirit of reparations by exploiting the situation for personal gain. General Ivan Serov, who held responsibility for the NKVD in occupied Germany, apparently absconded with the crown of the King of the Belgians from a collection of trophy art.[21] The disregard for international agreements against wartime plunder cast a long shadow on the acquisitions. In the case of Nazi plunder, an association with ethnic cleansing tainted the illicitly acquired artworks to the extent that calls for restitution still hold meaning more than a half-century later.

Lasting Consequences of Wartime Art Crime: Artworks at Large Lead to Phases of Resolving Ownership

The sheer number of art objects displaced during wartime, and the confusion inherent to war, complicate and prolong restitution. As experienced in World War II, the process of sorting out the rightful owners of plundered artworks, or compensating the heirs of victims, can span decades. With such duration, the life span of resolving wartime art crime comprises phases—recovery, return, revitalization, redefinition—of restitution. The efforts of restitution in response to the plunder of World War II have thus far formed three phases.

- Recovery of cultural property displaced during a war occurs during and immediately following the wartime period.
- Return of artworks to the victims of plunder may already begin during the wartime period and continues into the period following the war.
- Subsequent events in foreign affairs either directly or indirectly revitalize issues in restitution.

Evolving perceptions of the value of cultural property, and accompanying international conventions, allude to a fourth phase that may realize redefinition of the basis for restitution. The decades following the plunder of World War II have provided a case study for recovery, return, revitalization, and redefinition. The looting of antiquities during the Cold War era provides a second case study for the corresponding phases of repatriation, and abuses of cultural property in the post–Cold War period have elicited phases of indemnification. Figure 20.1 illustrates the common phases of resolution of wartime art crime and introduces examples that a later section will reference.

In the atmosphere of a long history of conventions on wartime protection of cultural property,[22] nations attempt to mitigate controversy over possession of cultural property during, and immediately following, military action. In an initial phase of recovery, Allied forces responded to the mass plunder in Europe during World War II by ferreting out and recovering caches of art that the Nazi authorities had secreted in hundreds of locations[23] Transporting the artworks to central collecting points and managing the return of cultural property to nations and individuals formed a second phase of restitution. In the aftermath of war, realizations about the intricacies of reuniting art with rightful owners became apparent. Following World War II, restitution of cultural property created political conflicts between Western Allies, in addition to the growing tensions between the United States and the Soviet Union.

With time, subsequent incidents in foreign affairs require a reexamination of the concept of restitution. In the case of Nazi plunder, the fall of the Berlin Wall led to a third phase of restitution. The opening of communication with the former East bloc enabled investigations into outstanding assets in bank accounts, gold deposits, and life insurance policies of victims of the Holocaust, which in turn revitalized pursuit of restitution of Nazi-plundered art. The political successes of restitution and the high market value of returned artworks suggest an inevitable fourth phase, which will redefine the motives and basis for pursuing restitution.

Looting of antiquities during the Cold War era created a case study for phases of repatriation. In the late 1960s, testimony of archaeologists exposed the unauthorized movement of cultural artifacts from nations with emerging and developing economies to so-called collecting nations.[24] The scale of looting made antiquities the preferred plunder of

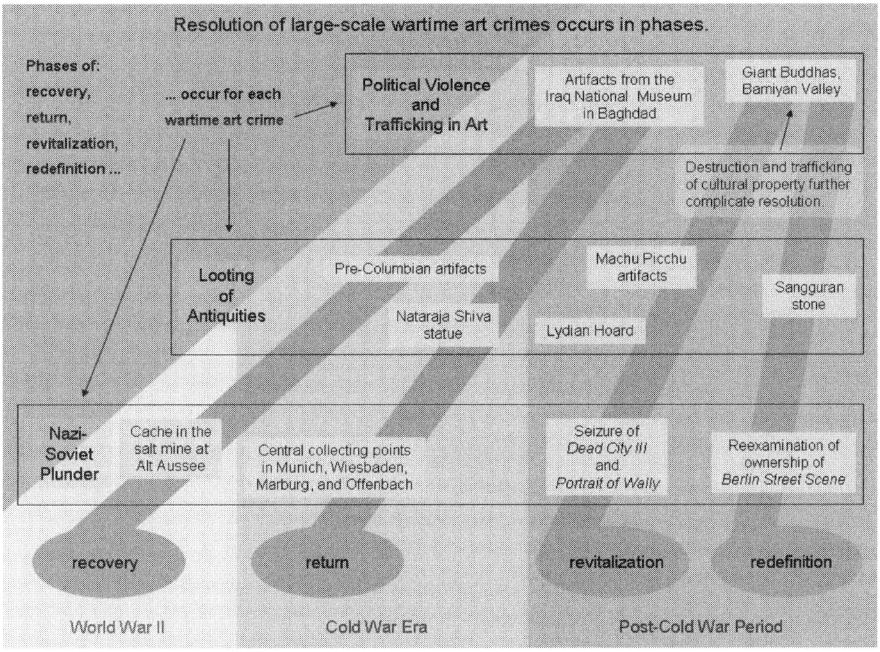

Figure 20.1 Phases of Resolution

The phases of recovery, return, revitalization, and redefinition recur for the wartime art crimes of World War II, the Cold War era, and the post–Cold War period. Restitution of Nazi plunder began during World War II and continues into the post–Cold War period. Repatriation of looted antiquities began during the Cold War era and also continues into the post–Cold War period. Resolution of the preceding wartime art crimes predicts that destruction of cultural property and trafficking in art of the post–Cold War period will require phases of indemnification. (Diagram courtesy of the contributor.)

the Cold War era.[25] In comparison to the phases of restitution that followed the plunder of World War II, looted cultural artifacts of the Cold War era have entered a second phase of repatriation with an indication of following phases. In the first phase, academic studies assessed the problem of looting, and law enforcement agencies tracked down and prosecuted citizens involved in trafficking. As in World War II, the scale of looting prior to exposure of a problem had already created a large volume of illicitly acquired objects. But unlike the ceasing of Nazi plunder with the end of World War II, the looting of antiquities continued past the end of the Cold War.

In the second phase, so-called source nations of the antiquities have effectively challenged powerful collecting nations. Influential individuals (such as Norton Simon, who agreed to return a prized Nataraja Shiva statue to India in the 1970s), museums (like the Metropolitan Museum of Art, which agreed to return the Lydian Hoard to Turkey in the 1990s), and universities (like Yale, which agreed to return artifacts of Machu Picchu to Peru in 2007) have complied with the requests and demands of the nations of origin. The phases that continue to extend the life span of restitution for Nazi-plundered artworks suggest that looted antiquities from the Cold War era will experience revitalization and redefinition of movements for repatriation. Further, the political ramifications of the art crimes of World War II augur an evolving significance of looted antiquities in foreign affairs.

POSTWAR RAMIFICATIONS OF WARTIME ART CRIME

After a conflict has subsided, the international influences and private motivations that induce each phase of restitution define a model for the political clout of objects of wartime art crime. The phases of restitution following World War II and phases of repatriation resulting from the Cold War era create political goodwill, consensus, leverage, and cachet, which develop the meaning of cultural property in foreign affairs (Figure 20.2). In the midst of conflict, nations garner political goodwill by devoting resources toward the protection and recovery of cultural property. When the scale of wartime art crime extends the process of restitution into the postwar period, nations strategically diffuse liability for the displaced art objects by gaining international consensus through conventions and treaties. After the implementation of treaties, nations and private parties leverage the political clout of cultural property to pursue individual cases for the return of specific art objects. The potential for returned objects to contribute to national patrimony or individual financial gain lends cachet to restitution. With each restitution and resale, plundered art objects accrue political clout as opposed to diminishing in the consciousness of the international community. The model for the phases of resolution of wartime art crime also provides insight into the evolving significance of the displaced cultural property in foreign affairs.

World War II—Wartime Plunder Begets a Model for Restitution

Plunder of art by the Nazi and Soviet authorities during World War II precipitated restitution of artworks that continued into the new millennium. Against a backdrop of the destruction of historic sites caused by aerial bombardment across Europe and the ethnic targeting of Jewish collections during the Holocaust, plundered art became a medium for diplomacy. The Western Allies acknowledged the symbolic value of restitution in consideration of the destruction of Germany and Nazi-occupied territories.[26] As part of the effort of goodwill, the first phase of restitution, recovery, began before the end of the war. The United States established

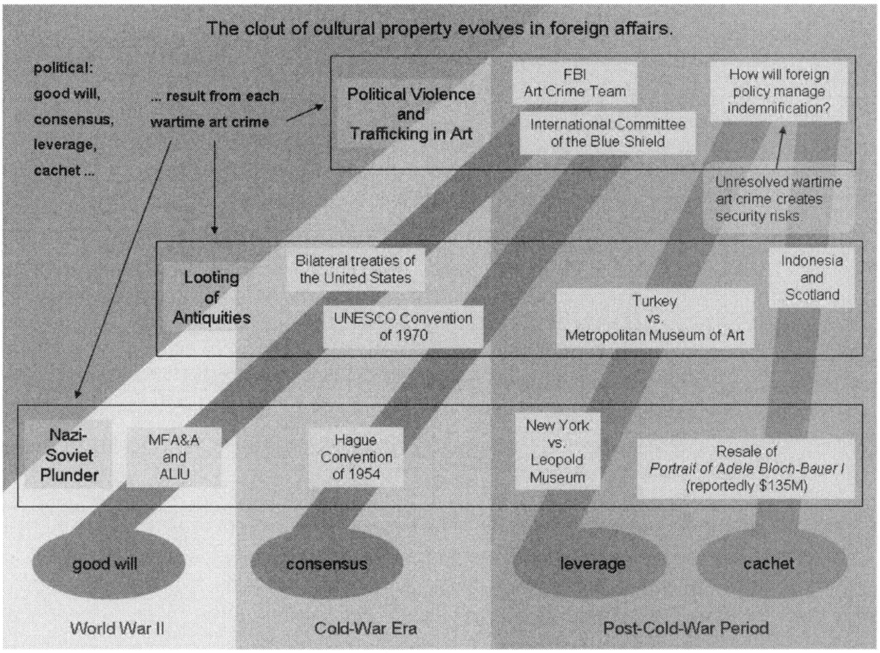

Figure 20.2 Political Clout of Cultural Property

Political meaning develops in parallel with the phases of resolution of wartime art crime. Nazi and Soviet plunder of World War II created opportunities to garner good will through recovery and reparations, while the process of restitution led to consensus though international conventions in the Cold War era. In the post–Cold War period, unresolved cases offered points of political leverage and added to the cachet of cultural property tainted by wartime art crime. Antiquities looted during the Cold War era acquired similar political clout with each phase of repatriation. Following the model, the art crimes of the post–Cold War period have created opportunities for good will and consensus, but also present risks as impacted nations seek indemnification. (Diagram courtesy of the contributor.)

the Roberts Commission in 1943, which joined efforts for restitution by commissions in England and France in 1944.[27] As part of the recovery effort, the U.S. Army formed the Monuments, Fine Art, and Archives (MFA&A) branch in 1943, and the Office of Strategic Services formed the Art Looting Investigation Unit (ALIU) in 1944. The MFA&A managed the recovery of artworks from caches such as the salt mine at Alt Aussee, while the ALIU conducted interrogations to decipher the networks that had executed the plunder. The MFA&A organized the recovered objects at central collecting points in Munich, Wiesbaden, Marburg, and Offenbach as part of a process for returning cultural property to the rightful owners.

The Soviet authorities also endeavored to find artworks in Germany and Nazi-occupied territories. Seeking reparations for destruction by the *Wehrmacht,* Stalin authorized a campaign to compensate the Soviet people for the cultural losses of the war. "Trophy brigades" secured and transferred renowned antiquities and works of fine art. Examples include the aforementioned friezes of the Pergamon Altar, shipped from Berlin to Leningrad,[28] and Old Master paintings, such as the *Sistine Madonna* by Raphael, moved from Dresden to Moscow. Although Stalin authorized acquisitions only for national patrimony, officers and soldiers secretly looted artworks.[29] In contrast, while individuals of the armed forces of the United States, England, and France may have looted for personal gain, the policy of the Western Allies focused on the return of cultural property. With quite opposite interpretations of "restitution," the Western Allies and the Soviet authorities both realized political opportunities that resulted from wartime abuses of cultural property.

Despite the success of efforts to recover plundered artworks, and to compensate for destruction of cultural property, the large scale of wartime art crime, and the conceptual complexity of restitution, left questions about outstanding artworks that lingered into the Cold War era. In the second phase of restitution, Western Allies faced the challenge of assuming responsibility for return of displaced cultural property. Aside from the challenge of returning millions of pieces of art from central collecting points, the Western Allies contended with separating the restitution of cultural property from the repatriation and indemnification of material assets, such as industrial equipment. For example, the Netherlands and Belgium faced the challenge of balancing the importance of cultural heritage and the importance of regaining economic viability, while France pushed for absolute recovery of cultural property.[30] On the eastern front, Soviet authorities celebrated the return of artworks to East Germany in the 1950s (such as the *Sistine Madonna* and the friezes of the Pergamon Altar)[31] but also elected to retain other works for display in the Hermitage and the Pushkin museums.

The deteriorating relationship between the United States and the Soviet Union manifested in decreasing cooperation on restitution with Russia and nations of the Soviet bloc. Whether controversy over rights to cultural property agitated relations or broader political controversies over the governance of Germany affected restitution, cultural property had acquired tangible importance in foreign affairs. Closure of the collecting points, in the late 1940s and early 1950s, and the resolution of the Soviet Union to retain trophy art as reparations, brought the second phase of restitution to an end. But the remaining volume of displaced artworks reinforced a need for wartime protection of cultural property.

Through UNESCO, at The Hague in 1954, international recognition of the art crime of World War II manifested in the *Convention for the*

Protection of Cultural Property in the Event of Armed Conflict (Hague Convention of 1954). The convention complemented the first two phases of restitution by providing nations with an opportunity to demonstrate consensus on a commitment to curbing wartime art crime. The commitment, however, could obligate parties to relinquish cultural property and had the potential to indirectly limit defense strategies. Specifically, strategies that rely on weaponry that causes widespread damage would inevitably violate the conditions of the Hague Convention of 1954. As a result, not all nations participated. In contrast to the relative positions on restitution of art plundered during World War II, the United States did not accede, while the Soviet Union ratified the Hague Convention of 1954. By the end of the Cold War, over 70 nations had either acceded to or ratified the convention.[32]

Along with opening east-west commerce, the fall of the Berlin Wall allowed a flow of information on the financial assets of victims of the Holocaust. Discovery of bank accounts, life-insurance policies, and gold deposits belonging to ethnically persecuted individuals initiated a movement of indemnification in the 1990s that led to revitalization of restitution of artworks plundered during World War II.[33] In 1998, the Washington Conference on Holocaust-Era Assets illustrated an international intent to return cultural property and reinforced the third phase of restitution. The same year, the state of New York seized two paintings, *Dead City III* and *Portrait of Wally*, which the Leopold Museum of Vienna, Austria, had loaned to the Museum of Modern Art for an exhibition on works by Egon Schiele.[34] A district attorney questioned the provenance of the paintings and therefore the right of the Leopold Museum to claim ownership. The possibility for state agencies and individuals to challenge foreign institutions, coupled with an expanding art market, revitalized motivations to pursue restitution of Nazi plundered art and demonstrated the political leverage of unresolved wartime art crime.

A steady rise in the art market over the course of the Cold War era created a financial incentive that complemented the already politically charged nature of artworks that acquired a tainted provenance in association with the Holocaust. As the result of such questionable provenance, the Austrian State Gallery returned five paintings by Gustav Klimt to an individual in Southern California after a successful claim of restitution. Upon return in 2006, one of the paintings, *Portrait of Adele Bloch-Bauer I*, reportedly sold for a record high of $135 million in the global art market, which professionals estimated as greater than $50 billion that year.[35] The resale of *Portrait of Adele Bloch-Bauer I* introduced financial gain as a significant motive for challenging the ownership of artworks from the Nazi era of plunder and thereby added to the political cachet of restitution. Such a motive corresponds with the report of venture capitalists speculating on restitution cases.[36]

By contrast, Soviet authorities demonstrated tenacity in retaining trophy art as national patrimony. Even when a head of state attempted to bargain the return of artworks in political negotiations, security services might intervene to retain the artworks in question.[37] The evolving political cachet and growing financial value of artworks plundered during World War II added to the dynamics of restitution. The possibility of returned paintings commanding record prices upon resale suggested that a tainted provenance contributes to the market value of an artwork. The financial motive not only added to the revitalization of restitution, but also inspired scrutiny of reportedly legitimate transfers of ownership during the Nazi era. In a rather high-profile case, an heir of Alfred Hess, who collected German expressionist art after World War I, challenged the Brücke Museum of Berlin over the ownership of *Berlin Street Scene* by Ernst Ludwig Kirchner. Inspired by the Washington Conference of 1998, the case had basis despite evidence that the widow of Hess sold the painting prior to World War II. After return, *Berlin Street Scene* auctioned for $38 million in 2006.[38] The protracted but successful case indicated a redefinition of the basis for claims of restitution.

The Cold War: Looting of Antiquities Begets a Model for Repatriation

While the movement of cultural artifacts from "source nations" to "collecting nations" had origins prior to World War II, an expanding art market fueled a marked demand for antiquities during the Cold War era. A complex system created a flow of cultural artifacts from developing nations of Latin America, Africa, and Asia.[39] The coincidence of the sources of coveted cultural artifacts and the battleground of political conflict between the United States and the Soviet Union made looting of antiquities a wartime art crime that created a legacy for repatriation in the twenty-first century.

A seminal paper by Clemency Coggins in 1969 led to a new awareness of the scale of the art crime. Coggins itemized looted Mayan artifacts and linked individual objects to collections in the United States.[40] In 1970, as a "peacetime" complement to the Hague Convention of 1954, UNESCO established the *Convention on the Means of Prohibiting and Preventing the Illicit Import, Export and Transfer of Ownership of Cultural Property* (UNESCO Convention of 1970). By virtue of demonstrating international acknowledgment of the problem of looting of cultural property outside of military conflict, the convention provided an opportunity for signatories to garner goodwill and achieve consensus on the problem of looting. The first two phases of repatriation followed, with the prosecution of dealers and private collectors to recover objects and then the return of objects to nations of origin. In the 1980s, U.S. customs detected pre-

Columbian artifacts and returned the smuggled cultural objects to Peru.[41] In contrast to the restitution of Nazi plunder en masse, successful recovery and return of cultural artifacts occurred on a case-by-case basis, but still built on the precedent of restitution of World War II. Just as the plunder of World War II heightened awareness of provenance of fine art, looting of the Cold War era increased the onus of due diligence[42] for the collector of antiquities. The United States recognized the political liability by responding internationally in the form of bilateral treaties with nations such as Peru (1981) during the Cold War era and subsequently more globally with nations such as Mali (1997), Cyprus (2002), and Cambodia (2003). The successful prosecution of individuals within the United States, and the establishment of bilateral treaties, led to a third phase of repatriation in the post–Cold War period.

Acquisitions conducted in "good faith"[43] during the Cold War era appear differently through the lens of due diligence in the post–Cold War period. In the atmosphere of revitalized restitution of plunder from World War II, source nations of antiquities find leverage to challenge the holdings of esteemed museums. As mentioned above, Turkey secured the return of the Lydian Hoard from the Metropolitan Museum of Art in New York in the 1990s. Subsequent cases brought by the Italian government against the Metropolitan Museum of Art and other museums such as the J. Paul Getty Museum in Los Angeles, California, resulted in significant returns, in both the number of and the archaeological importance of the objects,[44] and also led to investigations of private collectors.[45] Public trials and investigations that result in the return of antiquities lend cachet to repatriation and establish a precedent for nations with emerging and developing economies to challenge the holdings of both the public and private collections in affluent nations.

With a renewed momentum for repatriation, requests by nations such as Ethiopia, Indonesia, and Tajikistan for return of cultural artifacts from Great Britain illustrate the growing potential for movement of cultural property from collecting nations back to source nations. Reportedly, Indonesia has requested the return of the Sangguran stone, a column dated the tenth century AD with Javanese inscriptions, from Scotland.[46] Ironically, the cultural property that an imperial power acquired as a symbol of dominance now provides a medium through which a former colony might exert political influence. The newfound political-economic value of antiquities promises to redefine the basis of repatriation and to create new motivations to exploit cultural property. As the plunder of World War II and the looting of the Cold War era worked through phases of restitution and repatriation, the rise of transnational terrorism and organized crime in the post–Cold War period introduced a new type of art crime.

The Post–Cold War: Transnational Terrorism and Art Crime, a Third Instance of the Model?

Ethnically motivated wartime destruction of historic buildings in the Balkans (1990s), targeting of religious monuments by the Taliban in Afghanistan (2001), and nationwide looting of archaeological sites and museums in the midst of military intervention in Iraq (2003), each represent cases of wartime art crime in the post–Cold War period. The Hague Convention of 1954 criminalized the destruction of historic buildings and religious monuments in the Yugoslav wars, and the UNESCO Convention of 1970 criminalized the widespread looting of cultural artifacts in the aftermath of military intervention in Afghanistan and Iraq. In addition to repeating past offenses of plunder and destruction, all three cases expanded the concept of wartime art crime.

Thinly veiled as collateral damage, the destruction of historic bridges, mosques, synagogues, and churches during the Yugoslav wars exemplified the tactic of cultural cleansing, in a broader campaign of ethnic cleansing.[47] The religious statement of the wanton destruction of the giant Buddhas of the Bamiyan Valley in Afghanistan occurred outside of a particular battle or armed conflict with the Taliban. Looting of the Iraq National Museum in Baghdad showed signs of organized crime, and reports suggest that insurgents traffic antiquities to fund operations.[48] Abuses against cultural property that occur in the context of war, but independently from a particular military objective, suggest that the twenty-first-century security threats of terrorist groups, insurgencies, and transnational organized crime exploit the political meaning and financial value of cultural property in a new type of wartime art crime.

In the post–Cold War period, the resolution of wartime art crime faces new complications. Utter destruction of religious monuments prevents restoration. The dispersal of looted cultural artifacts into the art market[49] complicates recovery and repatriation. UN missions to rebuild mosques in Bosnia, and to return objects to the Iraq National Museum in Baghdad, represent initial phases of indemnification, but the missions address only a fraction of the overall destruction and looting. Religious conflict creates violent opposition to the reconstruction of places of prayer, as has occurred with mosques in Bosnia. The ideological implications of rebuilding religious monuments add to the political liability of wartime art crime, as experienced in efforts to gauge the feasibility of rebuilding the Bamiyan Buddhas.[50] While such conflicts hinder an initial phase of indemnification, transnational terrorism and organized crime expand on art crime to innovate in the destruction of "the other" and profit from unguarded cultural patrimony. The developing crime-terror nexus[51] may further enable a symbiosis of religiously motivated destruction and opportunistic looting of cultural property that may, in turn, provide opportunities to exploit subsequent questions of indemnification. In combining the cultural cleansing of World War II and the large-scale looting of the Cold War era, art crime of the post–Cold War period promises to require as least as many phases of resolution that have the potential to create security risks.

As suggested by the successive phases of restitution from World War II and repatriation from the Cold War era, the political liability of art crime in the post–Cold War period will increase the significance of indemnification in foreign affairs. Reminiscent of the MFA&A and ALIU, the United States responded in 2004 with the formation of the Art Crime Team within the Federal Bureau of Investigation. While such efforts garner goodwill in the recovery of looted objects, how will nations incident to permanent losses of cultural property manage indemnification in the post–Cold War period? An effective strategy will include prevention. Nongovernmental organizations such as the International Committee of the Blue Shield (ICBS) demonstrate a consensus on the value of protecting cultural property in wartime.[52] Through the participation of committees from nations such as Australia, France, and Madagascar, the ICBS has the expertise and well-rounded perspective for preventing wartime art crime. With the benefit of insight into the financial influence behind the restitution of Nazi plunder, and witnessing the growing efficacy with which nations with emerging and developing economies challenge economic powers over possession of looted antiquities, governments have an opportunity to adjust foreign policy to leverage indemnification and capitalize on the cachet of cultural property.[53] As a starting point, past phases of restitution and repatriation provide a basis for predictive analyses, to mitigate and potentially forestall the political consequences of wartime art crime of the post–Cold War period.

CONCLUSION: FORESTALLING WARTIME ART CRIME

In a succession of phases, broad restitution of artworks plundered during World War II led to specific cases in which individuals challenged national institutions. Artworks returned through such cases have come to command a high market value. Repatriation of antiquities looted during the Cold War era followed a similar course, with source nations challenging prominent institutions in collecting nations over the possession of cultural property. The ability of private parties and emerging nations to challenge institutions in developed nations illustrates the political-economic value of cultural property. The phases of restitution and repatriation from both wartime periods have predictive value for the phases of indemnification that may follow from art crimes of the post–Cold War period.

In the prior two wartime periods, recovery of artworks allowed restitution of paintings or repatriation of antiquities to serve as a means of demonstrating respect for the rightful owner. In foreign relations, cultural objects became a medium of diplomacy. But in the wake of destruction in the Balkans and the disappearance of cultural artifacts from West Asia into the antiquities market, what will remain as objects of mediation? As the international community recognizes the extent and scale of the crimes against cultural property in the post–Cold War period, individual nations may identify and quantify the losses to cultural heritage to form a basis for indemnification. Acknowledging the potential significance of the indemnification in foreign relations, the United States and the nations of the European Union can draw on experiences of the cause and effect of the treatment of cultural property during war.

The stance of Western nations in relation to wartime art crime has shifted over the three wartime periods (Figure 20.3). In World War II, Western Allies assertively reacted as rescuers in response to plunder by the Nazi regime. During the Cold War, political interests of Western powers exposed nations with emerging and developing economies and thereby passively increased awareness of the unexploited cultural patrimony. Consequently, institutional and individual collectors in developed nations motivated trafficking of antiquities. In the post–Cold War period, military intervention of Western powers has made protection of cultural property a limited priority despite the threats of reactive political violence and looting in the chaotic aftermath of combat. Thus, the stance of nations such as the United States has shifted, while the associated political risks compound with the persistence of cases for restitution of fine art, the increasing pressure for repatriation of antiquities, and the need for indemnification of destroyed cultural property.

In World War II, Western nations proactively sought political goodwill abroad by initiating restitution in the victimized nations. During the Cold War era, developed nations needed to assume a defensive posture against accusations of looted developing nations. The increasing financial volume of the art market in general compounds the significance of cultural property in foreign affairs, and the potential for the provenance of plunder to increase the market value of affected artworks emphasizes the political-economic ramifications of wartime art crime. Consequently, in the post–Cold War period, military intervention that enables destruction of and trafficking in cultural property of ethnic and religious significance automatically incurs political liability in foreign relations.

Anticipation of phases of indemnification and recognition of the accrued political clout of cultural property create an opportunity for predictive analysis in the post–Cold War period. Based on experiences from World War II and the Cold War, nations like the United States can devise strategies to mitigate the ramifications of destruction in Afghanistan and Iraq and thereby forestall the security risks posed by political violence against religious monuments and trafficking in antiquities. Learning

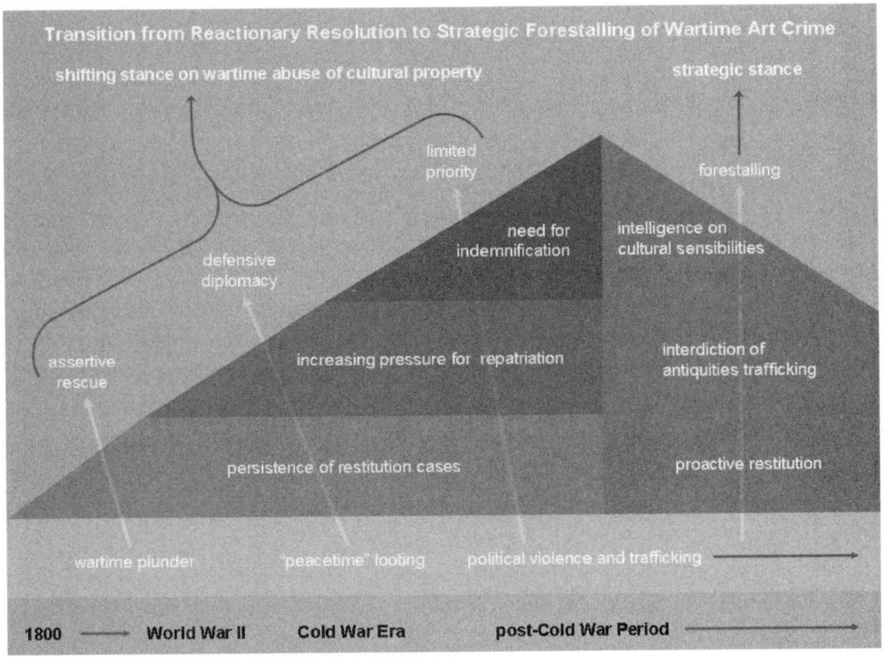

Figure 20.3 Towards a Strategic Stance on Wartime Art Crime

A shifting stance on wartime abuse of cultural property results in unresolved wartime art crimes. The persistence of cases for restitution of Nazi plunder, an increasing pressure for repatriation of antiquities looted during the Cold War era, and the need for indemnification of destruction of cultural property in the post–Cold War period combine to create mounting political clout and security risks. As a strategy, nations might proactively resolve past wartime art crimes and apply intelligence to forestall risks associated with abuses against cultural property. (Diagram courtesy of the contributor.)

from the positive effects of the MFA&A in World War II, the United States can mitigate political backlash by proactively initiating projects that recognize and demonstrate a sense of responsibility for the historic buildings, religious monuments, and artworks that military intervention puts at risk.

Acting to investigate the looting of the Iraq National Museum in Baghdad had positive results in that the return of pieces garnered international recognition. Initiating conservation projects for sites of archaeological significance may yield similar political goodwill. The success of the ALIU, in deciphering the networks that plundered art in the Third Reich, and the effectiveness of intelligence agencies in the Cold War indicate a wherewithal for analyzing trafficking in antiquities in the post–Cold War period. Devising intelligence strategies to infiltrate trafficking networks would not only forestall looting, but also provide insight into the security risks of the crime-terror nexus. In combination, proactive restitution for Nazi-plundered art, continued vigilance on interdiction of trafficking in antiquities, and intelligence on the cultural sensibilities of groups and governments abroad form a strategic stance of mitigating wartime art crime. Such a policy would recognize and leverage the evolving clout of cultural property in foreign affairs.

NOTES

1. *Détente* refers to the period of the late 1960s to the early 1980s, which realized a reduction in the tension between the Soviet Union and the United States.

2. Mary Beard, "Captives on Parade," chap. 4 in *The Roman Triumph* (Cambridge, MA: Belknap Press of Harvard University Press, 2007).

3. Steven Sora, *The Lost Treasure of the Knights Templar: Solving the Oak Island Mystery* (Rochester, VT: Destiny Books, 1999), 122–39.

4. Henry Morton Robinson, *Stout Cortez: A Biography of the Spanish Conquest* (London: The Century Company, 1931), 28–39, 330.

5. John Henry Merryman, "Introduction," in *Imperialism, Art and Restitution*, ed. John Henry Merryman (New York: Cambridge University Press, 2006), 1, 9–10.

6. Alan Kramer, *Dynamic of Destruction: Culture and Mass Killing in the First World War* (New York: Oxford University Press, 2007), chap. 1 and 2.

7. Elizabeth Simpson, ed., *The Spoils of War—World War II and Its Aftermath: The Loss, Reappearance, and Recovery of Cultural Property* (New York: Harry N. Abrams, 1997), part 2.

8. Lewis V. Cummings, *Alexander the Great* (Boston: Houghton Mifflin, 1940), 246.

9. Richard H. Horne, Denis Auguste Marie Raffet, and Horace Vernet, *The History of Napoleon* (London: R. Tyas, 1841), 48–49.

10. Peter Adam, *Art of the Third Reich* (New York: Harry N. Abrams, 1992), 33, 52.

11. Lynn H. Nicholas, *The Rape of Europa: The Fate of Europe's Treasures in the Third Reich and the Second World War* (New York: Alfred A. Knopf, 1994), 2, 4–5, 25.

12. Jonathan Petropoulos, *Art as Politics in the Third Reich* (Chapel Hill and London: University of North Carolina Press, 1996), chap. 5.

13. The *Anschluss* ("annexation") refers to the annexation of Austria by Nazi Germany on March 12, 1938, and represented the movement towards reunification of German-speaking lands.

14. *Kristallnacht* ("Crystal Night," or "The Night of Broken Glass") refers to the early morning of November 10, 1938, when an enormous number of shop windows were broken in persecution of Jewish merchants in German-controlled territories. Escalated physical violence by Nazi authorities against Jewish citizens on that day has come to mark the beginning of the Holocaust.

15. The *Sicherheitsdienst* (SD, "Security Service") provided state and foreign intelligence services for the Nazi regime.

16. The *Schutzstaffel* (SS, "Protective Squadron") refers to an elite group of troops led by Heinrich Himmler to protect Nazi officials. The SS also worked in

tandem with the German army to persecute Jewish citizens of conquered territories.

17. The *Gestapo* (*Geheime Staatspolizei,* "Secret State Police") acted overtly, such as in suppressing student protests, and covertly, such as in capturing foreign intelligence agents, to counter threats to the Nazi regime.

18. In the 1930s, *Einsatzstab Reichsleiter Rosenberg* (ERR) had the responsibility of collecting Jewish cultural material within Germany with the intent of forming an institute for intellectual study. Cultural material came to include artworks from the collections of Jewish citizens in Germany, and during World War II, the responsibilities of the ERR expanded to include the acquisition of all art in conquered territories.

19. Hector Feliciano, *The Lost Museum: The Nazi Conspiracy to Steal the World's Greatest Works of Art* (New York: Basic Books, 1995), 4–5, 156–57.

20. Konstantin Akinsha, Grigorii Kozlov, and Sylvia Hochfeld, *Stolen Treasure: The Hunt for the World's Lost Masterpieces* (London: Weidenfeld & Nicolson, 1995), 21, 22.

21. Zhores A. Medvedev and Roy A. Medvedev, *The Unknown Stalin* (New York: I. B. Tauris, 2003), 74.

22. Jiri Toman, *The Protection of Cultural Property in the Event of Armed Conflict* (Hants, England: Dartmouth Publishing Co., 1996), 7–19.

23. Thomas Carr Howe, Jr., *Salt Mines and Castles: The Discovery and Restitution of Looted European Art* (Indianapolis, IN: Bobbs-Merrill, 1946), 20.

24. In this context, "collecting nations" refers to the United States, the United Kingdom, France, Germany, and other developed nations with cultural institutions and individuals who direct substantive financial resources towards the acquisition of antiquities from abroad.

25. Karl E. Meyer, *The Plundered Past* (London: Hamish Hamilton, 1974), 12.

26. David Roxan and Ken Wanstall, *The Rape of Art: The Story of Hitler's Plunder of the Great Masterpieces of Europe* (New York: Coward-McCann, Inc., 1965), preface.

27. Marie Hamon, "Spoliation and Recovery of Cultural Property in France, 1940–94," in *The Spoils of War,* ed. Elizabeth Simpson (New York: Harry N. Abrams, Inc., 1997), 63–66.

28. Antiquities Collection, *The Altar of Pergamon* (Berlin: Berlin State Museum, 1981), "The Discovery and Reconstruction of the Great Altar."

29. Wilfried Fiedler, "Legal Issues Bearing on the Restitution of German Cultural Property in Russia," in *The Spoils of War,* ed. Elizabeth Simpson (New York: Harry N. Abrams, Inc., 1997), 177.

30. Michael J. Kurtz, "Conflict and Cooperation: The Politics of Restitution in the Cold War," chap. 9 in *America and the Return of Nazi Contraband: The Recovery of Europe's Cultural Treasures* (New York: Cambridge University Press, 2006).

31. Elazar Barkan, *The Guilt of Nations: Restitution and Negotiating Historical Injustices* (Baltimore: Johns Hopkins University Press, 2001), 84.

32. UNESCO, *States Parties to the Convention for the Protection of Cultural Property in the Event of Armed Conflict 1954,* The Hague, 2007, http://portal.unesco.org/la/convention.asp?KO=13637&language=E.

33. Michael J. Bazyler, *Holocaust Justice: The Battle for Restitution in America's Courts* (New York: New York University Press, 2003), xi–xii.

34. William D. Cohan, "Unraveling the Mystery of *Dead City,*" *ARTnews* 107, no. 4 (2008): 114–23.

35. Eileen Kinsella, "$25 Billion and Counting," *ARTnews* 107, no. 5 (2008): 122–31.

36. Georgina Adam, "The Nazi Bounty Hunters," New York/London, *Art Newspaper,* December 2006, 1, 4.

37. Konstantin Akinsha, Grigorii Kozlov, and Sylvia Hochfeld, *Beautiful Loot: The Soviet Plunder of Europe's Art Treasures* (New York: Random House, 1995), 243–44.

38. Staff, "Traders of the Lost Art," Berlin, *Irish Times,* December 19, 2006, 12.

39. Bonnie Burnham, *The Art Crisis* (New York: St. Martin's Press, 1975), part 2, "The Antiquities Crisis," 87–187.

40. Paul M. Bator, "An Essay on the International Trade in Art," *Stanford Law Review* 34, no. 2 (1982): 277–80.

41. Jo Ann Lewis, "Peru's Lost World's: 700 Art Treasures Find Their Way Home," Washington DC, *Washington Post,* August 5, 1982, Style, D1.

42. Due diligence is an investigation or audit of a potential investment. In the case of antiquities, due diligence refers to the responsibility of the collector to ascertain the history of ownership of the object of interest.

43. In a good-faith acquisition, the buyer believes that the object has not been stolen and that the history of ownership is intact.

44. Elisabetta Povoledo, "Italy Showcases Its Returned Treasures," Rome, *International Herald Tribune,* December 21, 2007, 10.

45. Elisabetta Povoledo, "Collector Returns Art Italy Says Was Looted," New York, *New York Times,* January 18, 2008, 1.

46. Staff, "Indonesia Negotiates Return of Ancient Stone from Scotland," Jakarta, *Agence France Presse,* January 24, 2008.

47. Robert Bevan, "Cultural Cleansing: Who Remembers the Armenians," chap. 2 in *The Destruction of Memory: Architecture at War* (London: Reaktion Books, 2006).

48. Matthew Bogdanos, "The Terrorist in the Art Gallery," *New York Times,* December 10, 2005, 15.

49. Neil Brodie, "The Western Market in Iraqi Antiquities," in *Antiquities under Siege: Cultural Heritage Protection after the Iraq War,* ed. Lawrence Rothfield (Lanham, MD: Rowman and Littlefield, 2008), 63–73.

50. A. Gruen, F. Remondino, and L. Zhang, "Computer Reconstruction and Modeling of the Great Buddha Statue in Bamiyan, Afghanistan," in *Proceedings of the XIXth International Symposium CIPA 2003: New Perspectives to Save Cultural Heritage (30 September–4 October 2003)* (Antalya, Turkey: CIPA 2003 Organizing Committee, 2003).

51. Chester G. Oehme III, "Terrorists, Insurgents, and Criminals—Growing Nexus?," *Studies in Conflict & Terrorism* 31, no. 1 (2008): 80–93.

52. Corine Wegener, "Assignment Blue Shield: The Looting of the Iraq Museum and Cultural Property at War," in *Antiquities under Siege: Cultural Heritage Protection after the Iraq War,* ed. Lawrence Rothfield (Lanham, MD: Rowman and Littlefield, 2008), 163–73.

53. Patty Gerstenblith and Katharyn Hanson, "Congressional Responses to the Looting of Iraq's Cultural Property," in *Antiquities under Siege: Cultural Heritage Protection after the Iraq War,* ed. Lawrence Rothfield (Lanham, MD: Rowman and Littlefield, 2008), 103–15.

Afterword

Why Masterpieces Matter: Some Dogmatic Reflections

John Stubbs

. . . thou knowest the people, that they are set on mischief. For they said unto me, Make us gods, which shall go before us.

Exodus 32.22–23.[1]

QUAESTIO

Where does our fascination with beautiful things come from? Or rather, what makes us obsessed with beautifully made things, with the exceptional objects we describe as "masterpieces"?

One of the very few statements about human life that can claim objectivity is that beauty is a subjective element in our lives. One person's Persian rug is another's leopard-skin bedspread. The same relativity is true of different ages and cultures.

With the eye of the beholder beadily monitoring anything we might say about beauty in and of itself, we should perhaps speak instead of beauty's symbolic value, and, working from that, whatever it is that beautiful things represent.

PATRIARCHS

Mighty works of what we now call art have always been powerful objects, but in early civilizations, the great work of art was more than a great work of art can be any more. It was something to be worshipped. It was an idol; it was a god.

As the book of Exodus (chapter 32) records, while Moses was debating on Sinai with a singular, omniscient deity which no plastic form could be said to embody or contain, and thus one with theoretically unlimited power over the psyches of its believers, the Israelites below reverted to what they knew best. Frightened by the storm above the mountain, leaderless, they needed a totem and a protector, and so:

> the people gathered themselves together unto Aaron, and said unto him, Up, make us gods, which shall go before us; for as for this Moses, the man that brought us up out of the land of Egypt, we wot not what is become of him.

Aaron told the women of Israel to bring him their earrings, and the jewelery was smelted down to create the idol of the golden calf. "And they said, These be thy gods, O Israel, which brought thee up out of the land of Egypt."

As non-godless readers will probably remember, Moses's rage at the people's idolatry, on descending wearily from his conversation with God on the mountain, was not entirely consistent with either his prior or his later actions. When the Ark of the Covenant was created to rest in the Holy of Holies within the Tabernacle bearing the commandments, the Israelites really got something much better than their paltry calf. The Ark, and the larger structure of the Tabernacle itself, provided an über-totem with atomically destructive capabilities. It was also an item of extreme, elaborate beauty, crafted of acacia wood overlaid with gold, with two exquisite statuettes of cherubim covering the lid.

The God who emerged on Mount Sinai (and elsewhere in other world religions), God as a formless, omnipresent, and omniscient but transcendent entity, was probably the single greatest invention in the history of power. This God makes us desire to make masterpieces of our lives, to do the very best with the materials at our disposal. It is an unfortunate rule that the less tangible God is, the less finite are his requirements, and the more they extend from external forms of worship and conformity to the innermost layers of thought. The integration of God into the psyche perfected during the Reformation dispensed with the need for an idea of God at all to discipline human behavior. With the Enlightenment, God dissolved into the fabric of the mind itself, ensuring that we run now on automatic, without formal dictation from the beyond.

Yet even from the moment (or one of the moments) when that process began, with the greatest dictation of all, the inscription of the Ten Commandments, the power held by beautiful objects, or objects people agreed were beautiful, was still too great to lose. So the Israelites had their Ark, as Medieval Catholics later had their relics and altarpieces. Such objects are invested now with a lesser kind of sacredness, the kind attributed to masterworks of art. These works retain a huge, if more symbolic potency.

There was a conspicuously modern aspect to what contemporary artists might blasphemously call the "installation" of Moses's Ark of the Covenant. This was the element of exclusivity. The Ark rested in the Holy of Holies, the forbidden and most exalted section of the Tabernacle, which High Priests themselves could enter on only one day in the year.

COLLECTORS

So, to return to our opening question—what is it about beautifully made things that fascinates? It is hardly difficult to see why certain people should wish to possess objects such as the Ark.

Collecting is a common human activity. People avidly pursue or save up for things they think are special. Not so long afterwards, in many cases, the object of desire becomes indistinguishable from the rest of one's things. It merges into other stuff. In time, it may even become part of one's clutter, mere junk. Yet by then, fresh objects have taken its place in the phosphorous glow of our wishes.

The greater one's wealth and power, the more exclusive the object one is able to possess. People seem to think their stuff says a lot about them, and a lot depends on how exclusive it is—i.e., how many others are realistically able to own such things. In one sense, the theft of priceless art breaks this rule. When a penniless thief gets away with a masterpiece, he breaks the world's hierarchy of collections. He comes to own something that, for other collectors, he has no right to possess.

Penniless thieves, admittedly, with the means to outwit the security systems of a major museum or a magnate's home, are few and far between. Art is stolen on behalf of those individuals or, more often these days, syndicates with the means of paying for it. In that respect, there is no real difference between the theft of a masterpiece and its sale in an auction house. It is taken out of common view, into a personal Holy of Holies, is lost to most of the world, and the principle of exclusivity is upheld.

Possession, collectors reason, distinguishes them. By possessing something special, collectors take charge of its exclusivity. They trammel it up; it becomes an attribute of who they are. It can, as for John Fowles's fictitious, Huysmanian collector Count De Deukans, comprise an alternative to the world itself, an arena allowing mastery, a precinct of pure choice. Admittedly, De Deukans, in *The Magus,* turns out to be an invention of Fowles's magician, Conchis, but Conchis makes him credible largely because the insight about the nature of the collector holds true. De Deukans kills himself when his chateau is burned down by a servant, and his collection is lost. Though few would go to this last extreme, Ronald Storrs, the aesthetically and ethnically sensitive governor of British Cyprus, admitted in his memoirs of empire, *Orientations,* that he was never quite the same after his collection of artefacts and manuscripts was destroyed in a riot on the island.[2]

Psychologists have often said that collecting, when it becomes pathological, is a means of completing or perfecting oneself. Collectors, that is, can be enslaved by magical thinking about their rarities, since they are obliged to believe that the items comprising their collections are masterpieces of sufficient magnitude to overawe worshippers.

When collectors come to own works that would and perhaps should otherwise have a place in one of the world's great museums, the greater the danger of thraldom becomes. Each multimillion-dollar or euro acquisition aggrandizes them and their collection further, takes them closer to a perfect ownership of all they consider worth owning. Yet the acquisition is also more than implicitly a criticism of the collection as it was before the purchase. By comparison to what it is now, with its latest addition, the collection was poor and, by that logic, since there will always be something which can be added to improve it, the collection *still is* poor. Even the collector who ticks off everything on his shopping list is doomed to both a significant lack and an incomprehensible excess, a surplus that makes his marvelous stuff cheap to him, junk. Anyone who has amassed piles and piles of stickers in the hope of filling the last few spaces in an album will know how such a person feels. But really, the last thing one wants is to complete the collection, because where is there to go from there?

This is admittedly a rather harsh, possibly envious depiction of the collector's lot, and if I was a collector of great art, I am sure I would have softened it considerably. But it by no means excludes benign motivation, a highly developed sense of the aesthetic, even magnanimity, on the part of the wealthy who buy or commission works of art. Where would we be without the Medicis; and who could wish that the Guggenheim Museum in Venice did not exist? We rely on collectors to preserve artworks and support artists.

It may also be true that we need collectors to tell us what the masterpieces are and to collect them for us. They bring the golden calves if not the Arks of our time into being. Would the artists who received Lord Saatchi's patronage in the 1980s and 90s have attracted such critical attention without him? The great collectors decide for the rest of us what is exclusive and exceptional, and give us the limited privilege of deriding or envying them.

JOURNEYMEN

Why should those who do not have or want great collections care about things that great collectors and their experts designate masterpieces? Why *do* they care?

They would agree there is something special about art. They are amazed by the lifelike, by the re-rendering of reality; yet also beguiled by the abstract, the purely tonal or textural. They see the bird in a Brancusi sculpture, but something more, something to do with what it reveals about the bird shape, the flightiness of metal itself, the mirrored surface as deep as the world around it. They agree there is something special to such objects, but establishing what that element might be is another matter. The mega-philosopher and Nazi Martin Heidegger set out to find the essence of that special something in his essay, "The Origin of the Work of Art." He had little more to offer, in the end, than a manipulation of terms he had been playing with for the previous 20 years. The work of art, it transpires, is a being that discloses the fundamental undisclosedness of Being itself.[3]

It is easy, then, to get knotted up when you try saying what art is and what makes it special, worth celebrating and preserving. Yet most people on the planet also have or know of things they find beautiful, and have critical (even abusive views) of things that others consider works of beauty. In asking what it is those things represent, we perhaps do not need to say more than "something special." An exceptionally made thing, a masterpiece, constitutes and represents something exceptional, and that is a powerful thing in any culture.

Naturally, those who get to consummate or innovate a form of statuary, revolutionize a cinematic genre or develop a wholly different way of layering paint are rather few and far between. Yet the experience of trying to produce a masterpiece is not at all confined to such historically rare people. Few who try to make something they can call progress in life are exempt from the desire to accomplish something admirable in their field of endeavor; and few are unfortunate enough not to have some achievement they can look back on as a kind of personal masterpiece.

Masterpieces are always associated with difficulty, with a long slog for an uncertain reward. In medieval and early modern Europe, the masterpiece, the *chef d'oeuvre,* was the piece of work a journeyman had to complete in order to become a master of his guild. A journeyman was a trained craftsman without a permanent base or a shop of his own. He was hired for the short term, and could frequently be dismissed with a day's notice. He was required to be peripatetic. Although properly, his title in English did not signify "journey" (rather the French for "day," *la journée*), he was forced to be a roving soul. A journeyman could often only return to his hometown having completed periods of service for masters in a number of other cities. When other highly specific conditions had been fulfilled, he could apply to carry out his masterpiece for the masters, the execution of which was hampered by further obstructive requirements and time regulations. Most prohibitive of all, for many, was the hefty gift or bribe the guild also demanded, informally or by statute.

A journeyman who reached the point of even contemplating his masterpiece was already doing well. Those related to members of supposedly baser professions, such as executioners or shepherds, were in general barred from guild membership by default. Those who were qualified to join faced a long apprenticeship, indentured for at least three years and sometimes as many as 10, before they reached the rank of journeyman. The households of craftsmen and merchants were invariably run on austere lines and suffocating religious principles: little wonder that Europe's apprentices, notably in London, were prone to run wild on public holidays.

Historians have more or less unanimously concluded that the system was a fix, a way of keeping the numbers down in the guilds and controlling competition. One could always set up shop on one's own without joining the guild, but that was a risky venture, lacking the safety of numbers and the seal of official approval that always sways a customer. Moreover, the operation was openly rigged: besides the terrible obstacles facing a journeyman, the sons, nephews, and sons-in-law of existing masters were promoted above them automatically on finishing their apprenticeships. Circumstance and nepotism barred the journeyman's progress.

The majority accepted their lot, and settled down as best they could with the best master they could find. In terms of proficiency, there was generally nothing to tell between the two classes of masters and journeymen. A stock folk-image, indeed, is of the diligent apprentice or journeyman, and the lazy, exploitative master. In time the leaders of industry saw what an impediment the arrangement was to trade: in the meantime, the journeyman would look forward to a better future for his sons by marrying the master's daughter.

The masterpiece, if it got through the judging process, was to be prized grimly, since it cost the earth. But most of us still remain journeymen, usually by choice: even if we enjoy our jobs, they may not give us the chance of becoming masters, and many decide it is not worth the sacrifice. So we turn to masterpieces that have nothing to do with our work.

MOMENTS OF EXCEPTION

These masterpieces are the fruits of times when we are not our usual selves, or the people we turn out to be later in life, when we experience what the poets of antiquity decided was a divine fury, *enthusiasmus,* or "possession by the god." They often come quite early on, when we can still dream of doing anything.

Into this class of feat falls playing for the school team, winding the class bully, perfecting a dangerous flip on a skateboard. The experience itself varies entirely from person to person. My father would sometimes speak with a certain pride of the drawings he did of zygapophyses in biology class at school. Zygapophyses are the four lateral projections in the neural arch of a vertebra, the hooks onto which nerve and muscle are attached. My father did no further work in biology, of a formal academic kind at least, beyond the age of 16, yet it satisfied him to have recorded such a structure as the zygapophysis—unthought of yet fundamental, so important, now I think of it, to a solid upstanding backbone—with his own hand. The drawings themselves were, of course, long lost by the time I heard anything about them. But they occupy a place in his mind's private gallery, where they will always represent whatever it is they represent to him.

The point is that most of us have a collection of such treasures. Whether or not life is poorer without them is another question, since they can often distract us from the greater and more substantial good things that structure and support daily existence. Dwelling too long on them can give someone a hungry look. They need keeping in proportion, since in daily practical terms, they hardly matter at all.

But they are part of the reason why world-class masterpieces matter, and why it matters if they are stolen or destroyed. Just as our personal moments of exception say something about ourselves and those close to us, exceptional works of art say something about us all. We like to think of ourselves as being different in some way, and so we are: no two of us are identical any more than a single person can be wholly singular. So long as human life persists, humans will persist in trying to think of it as special. Artistic masterpieces come under a category of feats that gratify the need to think that way, and so we endow them with their peculiar symbolic meaning.

LIFE AS MASTERPIECE

There is an additional sense in which the masterpiece represents what we try making of life itself. The philosopher Renata Salecl has recently observed how contemporary men and women with the means and leisure to do so regard their careers, looks, health, and family plans as they would an ongoing art project.[4] Indeed, over many centuries, people have developed the habit of viewing their lives as ongoing works of art, or the processes that go into producing such works, with their personal biographies, unwritten in the case of the vast majority of human beings, comprising the finished work. Countless generations were brought up on a book of saints of one kind or other, from the great medieval catalogs of the canonized to John Fox's *Book of Martyrs.* The guilty modern preoccupation with biography reflects a continuing desire to gain an entry for ourselves among the pages of such volumes.

The idea of making a masterpiece of life itself is a loose, composite analogy, not a tidy comparison of symmetrical elements, and uncountable individuals have contributed to it in their own way. The politician or commander sees his statue in the square, and physically prepares the sources ready for the history of his life to be written down. The hero looks forward to his death as his masterpiece; or, in the heroic narratives relayed by the action movies of the last 20 years, the moment of his escaping what should and normally would be certain death, in the hail of bullets that peppers every visible and near-lying object except the protagonist running in plain view of the gunner, or the countless falls he survives through one reinforced-glass window after another. Artists await competent judgement of how they used the available materials, while naturally dismissing any biographical interpretation of their work as ignorant and inadequate—for literary and artistic biography threatens the mystique of the work quite as much as it fosters the cult of the person.

Yet those outside what we might call "masterpiece professions" think of their lives as artworks too, often merely by looking back, by noticing patterns and conferring shape on experience. Without reading a page of Hegel, they observe the events that granted growth and self-realization, and the tendencies or misfortunes that obstructed it. They consider the elements—genetic, familial, cultural, experiential—that composed them. Everyone, probably, faces (or hides from) difficult questions in their last years: what have you actually done with your time, and how did you feel while you were living it? Did you spend enough time with the kids and the others who mattered? Do you have a stock of sensations from positive memories? Did you, that is to say, live?

They come to consider how close their life came to being a masterpiece, and in fact, all those with the good luck to win or be given some autonomy are entitled to do so. The people whom transactional psychotherapists—the followers of Eric Berne—bluntly but perhaps accurately label "winners" are those who can look back and feel pleased with what they experienced and did, no matter how small that might be in any grand scheme of things. They are the ones who see in the half-empty glass the sign of having taken refreshment. The "losers" are those for whom their achievements, no matter how great, will never seem enough, and hoard their remaining half-full glass until closing time.

One's masterpiece, then, is closely allied to who one is in particular: it *is* one's life. Or conversely, it is what one's life failed to be.

THE DISAPPEARANCE OF MASTERPIECES

Why should it matter when masterpieces are destroyed? The short, simple answer is that such destruction strikes at the very heart of the specialness we try nursing in ourselves individually and collectively. But the question is worth exploring further.

If you think about it, the loss or theft of an artwork should mean very little so long as a good copy has been made of it. In a seminal twentieth-century essay, "The Work of Art in the Age of Mechanical Reproduction," Walter Benjamin discussed the impact of photographic and other reproductive technologies on art, and indeed on reality. The advent of film, he argued, transfigured the very nature of aesthetic experience. Mass reproduction left art vulnerable to political exploitation, and, reciprocally, politics prone to "aestheticization." Politics as art form was an integral element, for Benjamin, of fascism. Yet with regard to the older plastic forms of art, as Benjamin observed early on in his essay, and as artists, aesthetes, and art historians would violently agree, with comments on unforgeable brushstrokes and chisel work, the idea of a true copy is illusory. With a copy, one loses the "presence" of the work itself in time and space, and the history of which it is a wordless record. Traditionally, a copy also constitutes a diminution of the original, and the further it is from the original, the lesser it is.

This need not be true: the sense of diminution, as with most things, probably depends on the glass being half-full or half-empty. Benjamin, for example, followed a similar line of argument in an essay on translation. Something in the original language, he said, would always be lost by a translation; but he implied something could also be gained. So too a gifted, frustrated apprentice might work a new hidden element, an extra luster, into a replica that the original did not possess. To put it neutrally, copying or translating simply produces something different.[5]

As a student, I visited the cast gallery in the Victoria and Albert Museum in London. The contents of this vast chamber, wonderfully cool on the baking summer day I went there, are castings taken from hundreds of feats of statuary from around the world. They include Michelangelo's *David,* the facades of ancient temples, and the 100-foot column of friezes depicting the victories of the emperor Trajan. It is a vast silo of masterpieces, something between a waiting room and a white elephant stall. Afterwards, I wrote an enthusiastic poem, no masterpiece itself unfortunately, in which I tried saying that what was intrinsically wonderful about the casts was their in-between-ness. They were neither here nor there. "They stand in dislocation from the time and space / I browse in, and their own." That aspect struck me then as something profoundly artistic, something perhaps uncopiable, in its own right. The casts had more than the pathos of death masks.

But even supposing a true copy were possible; supposing there was such a machine as a matter replicator, which could reproduce an original down to the last atom (physics suggests that strange things would happen if one attempted replication at the subatomic level), including even the faintest imprint time has left upon it, would it matter then if the original were destroyed?

As I suggested at the outset, the crucial question is what the beautifully made thing represents, not what a certain person, even the greatest expert, finds beautiful about it. It is certainly a sentimental question, but it is one of great power.

The masterpiece is uncaptureable because we like to think we are uncaptureable, uncloneable ourselves. Our cultures have been urging us to think this way since the idea of the great individual, be it the Homeric hero, the biblical prophet, the Platonic sage, or the Plutarchan exemplar, took hold of the imagination millennia ago. Probably the fixation is a by-product too of the physical isolation of our minds. As an attribute of that fixation, the masterpiece represents both the summation of what we are, and the moments when we exceed ourselves.

The creation of masterpieces depends on a mixture of things. A necessary ingredient is diligence in a given field, over many, many years, as the artist becomes ready to consummate and innovate the field: even naturals such as Mozart had long childhoods of constant application. The masterpiece then needs the love that such persistence requires; a measure of talent, or genetic predisposition; as well as something still harder to predict or define, an unconscious or random factor, a shot of chaos, the accident of paint or stone, that can change everything. To return momentarily to great collectors, it is likely that the near-impossible compound is what they would most like to own—and what most could tell them for no charge at all can never be stolen or bought.

The disappearance of a masterpiece makes us confront the prospect of our dreams' extinction. Fabulous things will probably always go missing, through accident or act of malice. One consolation is that when they do, they remain fabulous in myth. Another is that masterpieces are in truth relatively plentiful, and we can choose our own to admire: there is no one golden calf, or one Ark of the Tabernacle, on which to concentrate our worship. There is an uncounted number, and the level of interest and care these works attract, in workshops and on Web sites alike, suggests that many will always find a critic and curator.

PROUST

Scanty attention and even less homage has been paid here to a tradition of great modern thought, ranging from the works of Hegel to those of Adorno. Considerable injustice has also doubtless been done to the subtlety of the one or two arguments within that tradition that have been mentioned. But, as my title warned at the outset, these have been dogmatic reflections.

The *fille rouge* of these paragraphs has been not that life resembles art or that art redeems life, but that the way we tend to feel about art resembles what we try making of life itself. In total, it is little more than a suggestion that the importance we attach to the masterpiece, regardless of the qualitative distinctions that aesthetics seeks to impose or understand, differs little from the care and love we invest in the commonplace.

The single greatest modern authority for this hypothesis is Marcel Proust. Living, for Proust, is itself an art, and the greatest masterpiece of all, one that takes a lifetime of its own, is making sense of it. Negotiating a crowded room, looking out of a hotel window, passing someone on the street, trigger acts of mental creation for Proust, imponderably rich and fraught with meaning. Not everyone, of course, can set down their impressions like a Marcel Proust. Yet few can read far into Proust without recognizing a great many of his impressions as their own, as he extrapolates in a seemingly infinite variety of forms from the "I" of his narrator to the "we" that includes his readers.

Proust is so impossibly, even claustrophobically subtle that there is little option than to be blunt and dogmatic with him in return. This, I think, is what Samuel Beckett was getting at, in his book on Proust (1931), when he refused to be drawn into analyzing quotations and instead just wrote down what he thought—albeit in an elusive and stubbornly ambiguous, Proustian fashion of his own. The Monty Python comics hit the nail on the head when they came up with their world championship in "summing up the works of Marcel Proust in one sentence." This is all one can do, until the sentences mount up into their thousands.

My single and unoriginal dogmatic sentence on Proust would be that he demonstrates, with astonishing variation, how life is always out of step with conscious thought. Or, to put it another way, he keeps showing how reality wrong-foots anticipation and preparation in all their emotional forms, from to the expectancy of pleasure, from calculation to presumption. The Proustian memory follows a similar principle: it is never what we would expect that recalls the full evocative force of the event or period we remember. The true, time-regaining moment of recall comes, usually uninvited, from a source wholly outside the scope of prediction or contrivance.

Proust and his narrator believe in the idea of masterpieces, and have highly elaborated views on how truly great works of art must prove themselves over time. But the Proustian conception of time, in which life never does the thing you think it will or want it to, has some difficult implications for the concept of a masterpiece. If Proust is right, going back to view the great painting that first hit you with the wonder of art is not the way to regain that sense of wonder. Masterpieces stop meaning what they did at first: the heart-stopping phrase of a certain sonata, for Monsieur Swann, no longer hits him with the idealistic emotions he felt when he first heard it, but merely recalls for him the cafés and salons he frequented at the time, and the skies above them. He is not dissatisfied by that.

Masterpieces occupy a point of resistance to the thought-thwarting action of time. They stay the same, unless they are stolen or lost, but what they evoke for any one person is in ongoing flux. When Proust's narrator goes on holiday, in the second volume of *In Search of Lost Time,* he suffers two great initial traumas. Firstly, his highly elaborated preconceptions of what his destination will be like are shattered upon his arrival; and secondly, he then has to cope with the hostile and alienating strangeness of his actual surroundings. This ordeal stems, he argues, from the networks of association one constructs around the objects and locations among which daily life takes place. We make ourselves in terms of the spell that Habit slowly casts over the things about us.

One can, one does, come to terms with change; it is how that happens which Proust explores so exhaustively. As Marcel realizes in one of the volume's most searching meditations, such transitions involve a death of the self one has fashioned in a familiar place, surrounded by familiar people and things. Our deepest fear, in considering this loss, is not the loss itself or the death of the current self it brings about, but the idea of what we will be when we have accepted the change and modified ourselves accordingly. We will no longer be ourselves. It is inconceivable to think that we shall merely have grown to recognize a new set of coordinates, a wider ambit of being. The perimeters of the present are always too tight to keep the past with us; the wholeness of what we call "the self" is always too stifling to keep our whole experience at the front of the mind.[6]

This, by extension, is what makes mourners cling to their grief, instead of expiating sorrow and moving on in life. It is also integral to the emotional core of our feelings about masterpieces. Each of us collects his or her moments of exception, just as each generation makes its decisions on what delights and enlightens it, what best reflects its preoccupations. Our masterpieces, in somewhat Pharaonic fashion, are the things we would like to take with us on the journey to the afterlife, to store up all we have learned and enjoyed, and to see us through the homesickness, the disorientation, the bewilderment of being in time; to help us enjoy that experience, in fact. They may, in the end, not really be the things that matter: but they put us in touch with the things that do.[7]

NOTES

1. Scriptural quotations in this essay are from the King James Bible.
2. On Storrs, see Jan Morris, *Farewell the Trumpets: An Imperial Retreat* (repr. 1998), 390–395.
3. The essay is collected in Martin Heidegger, *Basic Writings,* ed. David Farrell Krell (repr. 1993).
4. Professor Salecl's exploration of this point arises from her ongoing work on what she has named "The Tyranny of Choice." I am grateful to her for sharing this work in progress with me.
5. Both "The Work of Art in the Age of Mechanical Reproduction" and "The Task of the Translator" can be found in the selection of Walter Benjamin's essays, *Illuminations,* trans. Harry Zorn (repr. 1999).

6. The passage in question can be found in *In Search of Lost Time,* volume 2: *Within A Budding Grove* trans. C. K. Scott Moncrieff, Terence Kilmartin and D. J. Enright (repr. 1996), 286–88.

7. The author would like to thank Noah Charney, Renata Salecl, and Katja Šugman for conversation and non-dogmatic comments, and Matej Acetto for discussions, some time ago now, on his essay on "Law and Beauty."

Selected Bibliography

This list is in no way comprehensive, and only represents bibliographies as provided by individual essayists. More citations may be found in the endnotes, and a more extensive bibliography for this collection may be found online, at http://www.artcrime.info. To facilitate future art crime scholarship, comprehensive bibliographies with annotations will be published on ARCA's Web site and in the first two issues of *The Journal of Art Crime.*

Adam, Georgina. "The Nazi Bounty Hunters." *Art Newspaper* (New York/London), December 2006, 1, 4.

Adam, Peter. *Art of the Third Reich.* New York: Harry N. Abrams, Inc., 1992.

Akinsha, Konstantin, Grigorii Kozlov, and Sylvia Hochfeld. *Beautiful Loot: The Soviet Plunder of Europe's Art Treasures,* 243–44. New York: Random House, 1995.

Alder, C. "The Illicit Traffic in Asian Antiquities." Paper for the Australian Registrars Committee Conference. http://www.savingantiquities.org/pdf/Asian.pdf (accessed March 4, 2009).

Bailey, Anthony. *Responses to Rembrandt: Who Painted the Polish Rider? A Controversy Considered.* New York: Timken Publishers, 1994.

Baker, Paul. "Policing Fakes." Paper delivered at the conference sponsored by the Australian Institute of Criminology, Sydney, December 2–7, 1999.

Barkan, Elazar. *The Guilt of Nations: Restitution and Negotiating Historical Injustices,* 84. Baltimore: Johns Hopkins University Press, 2001.

Barkham, Patrick. "Dealer Convicted of Fraud as the Aboriginal Art World Fights Back." *The Guardian,* February 24, 2001, 1.

Bator, Paul M. "An Essay on the International Trade in Art." *Stanford Law Review* 34, no. 2 (1982): Introduction, 277–80.

———. *The International Trade in Art.* Chicago: University of Chicago Press, 1983.

Bazyler, Michael J. *Holocaust Justice: The Battle for Restitution in America's Courts.* New York: New York University Press, 2003.

Beard, Mary. *The Roman Triumph.* Cambridge, MA: Belknap Press of Harvard University Press, 2007.

Bevan, Robert. *The Destruction of Memory: Architecture at War.* London: Reaktion Books, 2006.

Boardman, J., and D. Finn. *The Parthenon and Its Sculptures.* London: Thames and Hudson, 1985.

Bogdanos, Matthew. "The Terrorist in the Art Gallery," *New York Times,* December 10, 2005, 15.

Brodie, Neil. "The Western Market in Iraqi Antiquities." In *Antiquities under Siege: Cultural Heritage Protection after the Iraq War,* edited by Lawrence Rothfield, 63–73. Lanham, MD: Rowman and Littlefield Publishers, Inc., 2008.

Brodie, Neil, Jenny Doole, and Colin Renfrew, ed. *Trade in Illicit Antiquities: The Destruction of the World's Archaeological Heritage.* Cambridge: McDonald Institute, 2001.

Brodie, Neil, Jenny Doole, and Peter Watson. *Stealing History: The Illicit Trade in Cultural Material.* Cambridge: McDonald Institute for Archaeological Research, 2000.

Brommer, F. *The Sculptures of the Parthenon. Metopes, Frieze, Pediments, Cult-Statue.* London: Thames & Hudson, 1979.

Brown, D. "MacGregor, William (1848–1937)." In *Oxford Dictionary of National Biography,* edited by H. C. G. Matthew and Brian Harrison. Oxford: Oxford University Press, 2004. http://www.oxforddnb.com/view/article/73478 (accessed February 15, 2005).

Burnham, Bonnie. *The Art Crisis.* New York: St. Martin's Press, 1975.

Catterall, Lee. *The Great Dali Art Fraud and Other Deceptions.* Fort Lee, NJ: Barricade Press, 1992.

Chanin, Eileen. *Collecting Art: Masterpieces, Markets and Money.* Roseville, NSW: Craftsman House, 1990.

Chi, J., and J. Gaunt. *Greek Bronze Vessels from the Collection of Shelby White and Leon Levy.* Atlanta, GA: Michael C. Carlos Museum, Emory University, 2005.

China Heritage Project. *China Heritage Newsletter* 1 (March 2005). http://www.chinaheritagenewsletter.org (accessed March 4, 2009).

Chippindale, C., and D. W. J. Gill. "Material Consequences of Contemporary Classical Collecting." *American Journal of Archaeology* 104 (2000): 463–511.

Cohan, William D. "Unraveling the Mystery of *Dead City.*" *ARTnews* 107, no. 4 (2008): 114–23.

Conklin, John. *Art Crime.* Westport, CT: Praeger, 1994.

Crowell, Todd. "A Farewell to Antiques." *Asiaweek,* 1997. http://www-cgi.cnn.com/ASIANOW/asiaweek/97/0509/nat4.html (accessed March 4, 2009).

Darracott, J., ed. *All for Art: The Ricketts and Shannon Collection.* Cambridge: Cambridge University Press, 1979.

Darracott, J. *The World of Charles Ricketts.* London: Eyre Methuen, 1980.

Elia, R. J. "Analysis of the Looting, Selling, and Collecting of Apulian Red-figure Vases: A Quantitative Approach." In Brodie, Doole, and Renfrew, *Trade in Illicit Antiquities,* 145–53. Cambridge: McDonald Institute, 2001.

Exhibition Catalog. *A Passion for Antiquities: Ancient Art from the Collection of Barbara and Lawrence Fleischman.* Malibu, CA: J. Paul Getty Museum in association with the Cleveland Museum of Art, 1994.

Fagan, B. *The Rape of the Nile: Tomb Robbers, Tourists, and Archaeologists in Egypt.* 3rd ed. Boulder, CO: Westview Press, 2004.

Feliciano, Hector. *The Lost Museum: The Nazi Conspiracy to Steal the World's Greatest Works of Art.* New York: Basic Books, 1995.

Fiedler, Wilfried. "Legal Issues Bearing on the Restitution of German Cultural Property in Russia." In *The Spoils of War,* edited by Elizabeth Simpson, 177. New York: Harry N. Abrams, Inc., 1997.

Fitz Gibbon, K., ed. *Who Owns the Past? Cultural Policy, Cultural Property, and the Law.* New Brunswick, NJ: Rutgers University Press/American Council for Cultural Policy, 2005.

Flescher, Sharon. "The International Foundation for Art Research." In Spencer, *The Expert versus the Object,* 95–102. Oxford: Oxford University Press, 2004.

Gill, D. W. J. "Recent Acquisitions by the Fitzwilliam Museum, Cambridge, 1871–1989." *Journal of Hellenic Studies* 110 (1990): 290–94.

———. *Donors and Former Owners of Greek and Roman Antiquities in the Fitzwilliam Museum, Cambridge.* Cambridge: Fitzwilliam Museum, 1992.

———. "Sotheby's, Sleaze and Subterfuge: Inside the Antiquities Trade." *Antiquity* 71 (1997): 468–71

———. "Winifred Lamb and the Fitzwilliam Museum." In *Classics in 19th and 20th Century Cambridge: Curriculum, Culture and Community,* edited by C. Stray, 135–56. Cambridge Philological Society supplementary volume, no. 24. Cambridge: Cambridge Philological Society, 1999.

Gill, D. W. J., and C. Chippindale. "From Boston to Rome: Reflections on Returning Antiquities." *International Journal of Cultural Property* 13 (2006): 311–31.

———. "From Malibu to Rome: Further Developments on the Return of Antiquities." *International Journal of Cultural Property* 14 (2007a): 205–40.

———. "The Illicit Antiquities Scandal: What It Has Done to Classical Archaeology Collections." *American Journal of Archaeology* 111 (2007b): 571–74.

———. "South Italian Pottery in the Museum of Fine Arts, Boston, Acquired since 1983." *Journal of Field Archaeology* (2009).

Gluckman, R. "Re-made in China: The Fine Art of Fakery." *IFAR Journal,* Spring 2000, 10.

Guardian. "Faker Who Flooded Art World Jailed for 6 Years." *The Guardian,* February 16, 1999. http://www.guardian.co.uk/uk/1999/feb.16/5/print.

Hamon, Marie. "Spoliation and Recovery of Cultural Property in France, 1940–94." In *The Spoils of War,* edited by Elizabeth Simpson, 63–66. New York: Harry N. Abrams, Inc., 1997.

Hebborn, Eric. *The Art Forger's Handbook.* London: Cassell, 1997.

Hills, Ben. "Judge Gives Go Ahead to Sell 1,000 Fake Paintings." *Sydney Morning Herald,* May 23, 2002.

Horne, Richard H., Denis Auguste Marie Raffet, and Horace Vernet. *The History of Napoleon.* London: R. Tyas, 1841.

Hoving, Thomas. *False Impressions: The Hunt for Big-Time Art Fakes.* New York: Simon & Schuster, 1997.

Howe, Thomas Carr, Jr. *Salt Mines and Castles: The Discovery and Restitution of Looted European Art.* Indianapolis, IN: Bobbs-Merrill Company, 1946.

Howland, R. H., ed. "The Destiny of the Parthenon Marbles." Proceedings from a seminar held at the Corcoran Gallery of Art, Washington, DC, February 13, 1999. Washington, DC: Society for the Preservation of the Greek Heritage, 2000.

"Indonesia Negotiates Return of Ancient Stone from Scotland." *Agence France Presse,* January 24, 2008.

Innes, Brian. *Fakes and Forgeries: The True Crime Story of History's Greatest Deceptions.* London: Amber Books, 2005.

Irving, Clifford. *Fake! The Story of Elmyr de Hory the Greatest Art Forger of Our Time.* New York: McGraw-Hill, 1969.

Jameson, M. H., C. N. Runnels, and T. van Andel. *A Greek Countryside: The Southern Argolid from Prehistory to the Present Day.* Stanford, CA: Stanford University Press, 1994.

Jenkins, I. *The Parthenon Frieze.* London: British Museum Press, 1994.

———. *Cleaning and Controversy: The Parthenon Sculptures 1811–1939.* The British Museum Occasional Paper, vol. 146. London: British Museum Press, 2001.

Jenkins, I., and K. Sloan. *Vases and Volcanoes: Sir William Hamilton and His Collection.* London: British Museum Press, 1996.

Kahn, Jeremy. "Chinese Quandary: Art or Plunder?" *New York Times,* October 18, 2006. http://www.iht.com/articles/2006/10/18/news/art.php (accessed March 4, 2009).

Kaufman, J. E. "The Illicit Trade: US Considers China's Request for Import Restrictions." *The Art Newspaper.* 2005.http://nyartsmagazine.com/index.php?option=com_content&task=view&id=1842&itemid=164

Keating, Thomas, Frank Norman, and Geraldine Norman. *The Fakes's Progress: Being the Cautionary History of the Master Painter & Simulator Mr Tom Keating.* London: Hutchinson, 1997.

Kinsella, Eileen. "$25 Billion and Counting." *ARTnews* 107, no. 5 (2008): 122–31.

Koldehoff, Nora, and Stefan Koldehoff. *Aktenzeichen Kunst—Die spektakulàrsten Kunstdiebstähle der Welt.* Cologne: DuMont, 2004.

Kramer, Alan. *Dynamic of Destruction: Culture and Mass Killing in the First World War.* New York: Oxford University Press, 2007.

Kurtz, Michael J. "Conflict and Cooperation: The Politics of Restitution in the Cold War." Chap. 9 in *America and the Return of Nazi Contraband: The Recovery of Europe's Cultural Treasures.* New York: Cambridge University Press, 2006.

Kurz, Otto. *Fakes.* New York: Dover, 1967.

Landesman, Peter. "A 20th-Century Master Scam." *New York Times Magazine,* July 18, 1999. http://query.nytimes.com/gst/fullpage.html?res=9401E1DF11 3CF93BA25754C0A96F958260.

Lanham, David, Mark Weinberg, Kenneth Brown, and George Ryan. *Criminal Fraud.* Sydney: Law Book Company, 1987.

Lewis, Jo Ann. "Peru's Lost World's; 700 Art Treasures Find Their Way Home." *Washington Post,* August 5, 1982, Style, D1.

Lubina, K. "Is that Ming Vase Precious or Just Ordinary?" *Art Loss Review* 196 (November–December 2006).

Luce, H. C. "Copying Chinese Paintings: Flattery or Forgery?" *IFAR Journal,* Spring 2000.

Mackenzie, S. R. M. "Regulating the Market in Illicit Antiquities." Paper for the Australian Institute of Criminology, Sydney, September 2002. http://www.aic.gov.au/publications/tandi/ti239.pdf (accessed March 4, 2009).

———. "Dig a Bit Deeper: Law, Regulation and the Illicit Antiquities Market." *British Journal of Criminology* 45, no. 3 (2005): 249–68.

McLeave, Hugh. *Rogues in the Gallery: The Modern Plague of Art Thefts.* Boston: Godine, 1981.

Mead, R. "Den of Antiquity: The Met and the Antiquities Market." *New Yorker,* April 9, 2007, 52–61.

Mee, C. B., and H. A. Forbes, eds. *A Rough and Rocky Place: The Landscape and Settlement History of the Methana Peninsula, Greece.* Results of the Methana Survey Project sponsored by the British School at Athens and the University of Liverpool. Liverpool: Liverpool University Press, 1997.

Merryman, John Henry. "Two Ways of Thinking about Cultural Property." *American Journal of International Law* 80 (1986): 831–53. http://www.jstor.org/pss/2202065 (accessed March 4, 2009).

———. *Imperialism, Art and Restitution.* New York: Cambridge University Press, 2006.

Meyer, Karl E. *The Plundered Past.* London: Hamish Hamilton, 1974.

Middlemas, Robert Keith. *The Double Market: Art Theft and Art Thieves.* Westmead: Saxon House, 1975.

Miles, Margaret. *Art as Plunder: The Ancient Origins of Debate about Cultural Property.* New York: Cambridge University Press, 2008.

Murphy, J. D. "Plunder and Preservation: Cultural Property Law and Practice in the People's Republic of China." Oxford: Oxford University Press, 1995.

National Gallery of Victoria. "Not a Forgery, but Not a Van Gogh." *Gallery Magazine,* September–October 2007.

Nicholas, Lynn H. *The Rape of Europa: The Fate of Europe's Treasures in the Third Reich and the Second World War.* New York: Alfred A. Knopf, 1994.

Norman, Geraldine. "Art Trading and Art Faking." In Keating, Norman, and Norman. *The Fakes's Progress,* 197–262. London: Hutchinson, 1997.

O'Connor, Francis V. "Authenticating the Attribution of Art: Connoisseurship and the Law in the Judging of Forgeries, Copies and False Attributions." In Spencer, *The Expert versus the Object,* 3–27. Oxford: Oxford University Press, 2004.

Oehme, Chester G., III. "Terrorists, Insurgents, and Criminals—Growing Nexus?" *Studies in Conflict & Terrorism* 31, no. 1 (2008): 80–93.

Ortiz, G. "Overview and Assessment after Fifty Years of Collecting in a Changing World." In Robson, Treadwell, and Gosden, *Who Owns Objects?* 15–32. Oxford: Oxbow, 2006.

Özgen, I., and J. Öztürk. *The Lydian Treasure: Heritage Recovered.* Istanbul: Ministry of Culture, General Directorate of Monuments and Museums, 1996.

Parcak, S. "Satellite Remote Sensing Methods for Monitoring Archaeological Tells in the Middle East." *Journal of Field Archaeology* 32 (2007): 65–81.

Pastore, G. "The Looting of Archaeological Sites in Italy." In *Trade in Illicit Antiquities: The Destruction of the World's Archaeological Heritage,* edited by N. Brodie, J. Doole, and C. Renfrew, 155–60. McDonald Institute Monographs. Cambridge: McDonald Institute, 2001.

Perticarari, L., and A. M. Giuntani. *I segreti di un tombarolo.* Milan: Rusconi, 1986.

Petropoulos, Jonathan. *Art as Politics in the Third Reich.* Chapel Hill: University of North Carolina Press, 1996.

Picón, C. A., J. R. Mertens, E. J. Milleker, C. S. Lightfoot, and S. Hemingway. *Art of the Classical World in the Metropolitan Museum of Art: Greece, Cyprus, Etruria, Rome.* New York: The Metropolitan Museum of Art, 2007.

Pitman, Joanna. *The Raphael Trail: The Secret History of One of the World's Most Precious Works of Art.* London: Random House, 2006.

Polk, K. "Unveiling Secrets & Lies: Examining Threats to Collections of Art."2001. http://amol.org.au/arc/papers/S&LKenneth_Polk.pdf.

Porter, Liz. "Art Imitating Art." *Sunday Age,* December 2, 2007, 18.

Povoledo, Elisabetta. "Italy Showcases Its Returned Treasures." *International Herald Tribune,* December 21, 2007, 10.

———. "Collector Returns Art Italy Says Was Looted." *New York Times,* January 18, 2008, 1.

Praetsch, Martin. "Van Gogh from the Sweatshop." *Spiegel Online,* August 23, 2006.http://www.spiegel.de/international/0,1518,433134,00.html (accessed March 4, 2009).

Radnoti, Sandor. *The Fake: Forgery and Its Place in Art.* Oxford: Rowman and Littlefield Publishers, 1999.

Renfrew, C., "Trade in Illicit Antiquities: The Destruction of the World's Archaeological Heritage." Cambridge: McDonald Institute for Archaeological Research, 2001.

Robson, E., L. Treadwell, and C. Gosden, ed. *Who Owns Objects? The Ethics and Politics of Collecting Cultural Artefacts.* Oxford: Oxbow, 2006.

Rothfield, Lawrence. *Antiquities under Siege: Cultural Heritage Protection after the Iraq War.* Lanham, MD: Rowman and Littlefield Publishers, 2008.

Shenzhen Government Online (2008), "Culture and Arts." 2008. http://english.sz.gov.cn/lis/lis1/200708/t20070827_230706.htm (accessed March 4, 2009).

Simpson, Elizabeth, ed. *The Spoils of War: World War II and Its Aftermath: The Loss, Reappearance, and Recovery of Cultural Property.* New York: Harry N. Abrams, Inc., 1997.

Smith, Judith E., and Wen C. Fong, eds. *Issues of Authenticity in Chinese Painting.* New York: Metropolitan Museum of Art, 1999.

Soudijn, M. et al. "Some Perspectives on the Illicit Antiquities Trade in China." *Art Antiquity & Law* 8, no. 2 (2003).

Spencer, R. D., ed. *The Expert versus the Object: Judging Fakes and False Attribution in the Visual Arts.* Oxford: Oxford University Press, 2004.

"Spitzer Reaches Settlement with Gallery Selling Fake Art on the Internet." Press release of January 24, 2001. New York: Department of Law, 2001.

Stibbe, C. M. *Agalmata: Studien zur griechisch-archaischen Bronzekunst. Babesch.* Supplement, 11–20060165–9367. Dudley, MA: Peeters, 2006.

Sutton, Peter. "Rembrandt and a Brief History of Connoisseurship." In Spencer, *The Expert versus the Object,* 29–38. Oxford: Oxford University Press, 2004.

Thompson, Clive. "How to Make a Fake." *New York Times,* May 24, 2004.

Tijhuis, Edgar. *Transnational Crime and the Interface between Legal and Illegal Actors: The Case of the Illicit Art and Antiquities Trade.* Nijmegen: Wolf Legal Publishers, 2006.

Toman, Jiri. *The Protection of Cultural Property in the Event of Armed Conflict.* Hants, England: Dartmouth Publishing Company, 1996.

"Traders of the Lost Art." *Irish Times,* December 19, 2006, 12.

Trendall, A. D. *Red Figure Vases of South Italy and Sicily: A Handbook.* London: Thames and Hudson, 1989.

Trendall, A. D., and A. Cambitoglou. *The Red-figured Vases of Apulia.* Vol. 1, *Early Apulian.* Oxford: Oxford University Press, 1978.

———. *The Red-figured Vases of Apulia.* Vol. 2, *Middle and Late Apulian.* Oxford: Oxford University Press, 1982a.

———. *The Red-figured Vases of Apulia.* Vol. 3, *Indexes.* Oxford: Oxford University Press, 1982b.

———. *First Supplement to The Red-figured Bases of Apulia.* Bulletin Supplement, vol. 43. London: University of London, Institute of Classical Studies, 1983.

———. *Second Supplement to The Red-figured Bases of Apulia.* Bulletin Supplement, vol. 60, part 1. London: University of London, Institute of Classical Studies, 1991.

———. *Second Supplement to The Red-figured Bases of Apulia.* Bulletin Supplement, vol. 60, part 2. London: University of London, Institute of Classical Studies, 1992.

———. *Second Supplement to The Red-figured Bases of Apulia.* Bulletin Supplement, vol. 60, part 3. London: University of London, Institute of Classical Studies, 1993.

UNESCO. *States Parties to the Convention for the Protection of Cultural Property in the Event of Armed Conflict 1954.* The Hague, http://portal.unesco.org/la/convention.asp?KO=13637&language=E, 2007.

Usborne, Kenneth. "Great Impressionist? New York Art Dealer Faces Trial for Forgery." *Independent* (London), March 12, 2004.

Vickers, M., and D. W. J. Gill. *Artful Crafts: Ancient Greek Silverware and Pottery.* Oxford: Clarendon Press, 1994.

Von Bothmer, D., ed. *Glories of the Past: Ancient Art from the Shelby White and Leon Levy Collection.* New York: Metropolitan Museum of Art, 1990.

Walton, Kenneth. *Fake, Forgery, Lies and eBay.* New York: Simon & Schuster, 2006.

Wanstall, Ken, and David Roxan. *The Rape of Art: The Story of Hitler's Plunder of the Great Masterpieces of Europe.* New York: Coward-McCann, 1965.

Watson, Peter. *Sotheby's: The Inside Story.* London: Bloomsbury, 1997.

Watson, Peter, and Cecilia Todeschini. *The Medici Conspiracy: The Illicit Journey of Looted Antiquities from Italy's Tomb Raiders to the World's Great Museums.* New York: Public Affairs, 2006.

White, S. "Building American Museums: The Role of the Private Collector." In K. Fitz Gibbon, *Who Owns the Past?* 165–77. New Brunswick, NJ: Rutgers University Press/American Council for Cultural Policy, 2005.

Yang Ren Kai. *Genuine and Fake Illustrated Dictionary of Chinese Calligraphy and Paintings in Every Dynasty.* Shenyang Shi: Liaoning Picture Press, 1997.

Index

About the Contributors

Noah Charney grew up in New Haven, Connecticut, and earned advanced degrees from The Courtauld Institute of Art and University of Cambridge. He began as an art historian, specializing in seventeenth-century Roman art and architecture and sixteenth-century Italian Mannerist painting and iconography, before shifting focus to the study of art crime and its history. Charney is the founding director of ARCA, the Association for Research into Crimes against Art, a nonprofit think tank and consultancy group on issues in art crime (http://www.artcrime.info). His work in the field of art crime has been praised in such forums as the *New York Times Magazine*, *Time* magazine, BBC Radio, National Public Radio, *El Pais*, *Vogue*, *Vanity Fair*, and *Tatler*, among others. He has appeared on radio and television as an expert on art history and art crime, including BBC, ITV, CNBC, and MSNBC. Charney is the author of numerous articles and a novel, *The Art Thief* (2007). He is editor-in-chief of *The Journal of Art Crime*, a new twice-yearly peer-reviewed academic journal published by ARCA. Charney's forthcoming nonfiction books include a complete history of art crime, an illustrated history of forgery, and a monograph on the world's most frequently stolen masterpiece. Charney has taught art history and the history of art crime as a distinguished visiting lecturer in numerous venues and nations, including the United States, London, Cambridge, Ljubljana, Florence, Rome, Madrid, and Amsterdam. His most recent post is as a visiting lecturer at Yale University in the spring of 2009. He lives in Europe with his wife.

Dennis Ahern is the Head of Safety and Security for the Tate Galleries, including the Tate Modern, the world's most visited museum. He has been working within the safety and security field since 1978. He began his career as a police officer with Her Majesty's forces, where he saw active duty in a variety of areas including counter terrorist and counter intelligence operations. In 1999, he joined Tate, initially as part of the project team for Tate Modern as the safety and security manager. In his role as Head of Safety and Security, he manages and coordinates a challenging and varied risk process, including safety, personnel and property security, fire safety, legal compliance for licensed public venues, business continuity and the insurance structure for Tate. He regularly lectures on art protection, risk and security, both nationally and internationally. He is a regular contributor to the specialist training for the police and security services in the UK, and consults for a variety of nonprofit cultural institutions and organizations worldwide, including ARCA, where he is a founding trustee. Dennis is a long-standing member of American Society of Industrial Security, ASIS International and qualified as a certified protection professional in 2001. He is a member of the Royal Society for Health and Safety and the member of the International Institute of Risk Management. In 2004 he was awarded Security Manager of the Year in the UK's security excellence awards.

Anthony Amore is the Director of Security for the Isabella Stewart Gardner Museum in Boston, Massachusetts, where he is responsible for both the day-to-day security of the institution and museum's investigation into the 1990 theft of 13 priceless works of art—the largest property theft in U.S. history. Prior to joining the Gardner Museum, Mr. Amore spent 14 years with the federal government in the law enforcement and security field. Most recently, he served with the U.S. Department of Homeland Security's Transportation Security Administration as a key adviser to the Federal Security Director at Logan International Airport in Boston. He also served the TSA as the Assistant Federal Security Director for Regulatory Inspections, responsible for the enforcement of federal transportation security laws and regulations at the aforementioned airports. Mr. Amore was the primary author of key documents, such as the agency's first local strategic plan; the study that helped shape the reorganization and regionalization of the national agency; and an analytical study of the effectiveness of the federal screening program. He was also the agency's first Assistant Federal Security Director to introduce behavioral observation training with the TSA workforce. In 2002 and 2003, Mr. Amore was nominated by his superiors for a Service to America Medal.

Judah Best is a nationally known lawyer who specializes in the representation of companies and prominent individuals under federal criminal investigation. He represented former Vice President Spiro T. Agnew and negotiated Mr. Agnew's *nolo contendere* plea. Among his clients have been Enron Corporation, the Democratic National Committee, Mobil Corporation, senators, and congressmen. He is a Fellow of the American College of Trial Lawyers and a former Chair of the American Bar Association's

Section of Litigation. As a relief from his active legal practice, Mr. Best is an ardent collector of American art, and his collection ranges from works created in colonial times to the mid-1950s. He is active in the Smithsonian American Art Museum, located in Washington, DC, and currently serves on its Board of Commissioners. Because he believes that art should be enjoyed by the public, he is in the process of donating works from his private collection to the Smithsonian Museum. As he puts it, "I enjoy taking friends to the Smithsonian and explaining the historical context of paintings on exhibit. I particularly enjoy the look on their faces when they realize that I am talking about a painting I previously owned." Judd Best also speaks about one of his pet subjects: stolen art. He recently lectured on this subject in Bilbao, Spain, home of the splendid new Guggenheim Museum.

Toby Bull lives and works in Hong Kong, China. He is a qualified art authenticator and holds a degree in Fine Arts Valuation (as well as two other degrees). Since 1993, he has worked for the Hong Kong Police Force. Currently a Senior Inspector of Police and posted to the Marine Division, he has extensive experience in mounting antismuggling and anti-illegal immigration operations along the Sino–Hong Kong southern water boundary. His lifelong love of antiques led him to obtaining academic qualifications in this field, which, coupled with his professional security background, soon sparked an interest in the world of art crime. He is an Associate Member of the Association of Certified Fraud Examiners and is also a registered volunteer with the Beijing Cultural Heritage Protection Center (CHP)—an officially recognized Chinese NGO whose core competency lies in cultural heritage laws and policy. Over the past few years, he has traveled the globe attending various art crime conferences and professional courses. He recently wrote a paper on the problems of fake Chinese antiquities in the marketplace, as well as the illicit antiquity trade flowing out of China and into Hong Kong—a condensed version of which is reproduced here.

Duncan Chappell, a lawyer and a criminologist, is a Professorial Fellow at the University of Wollongong's Center for Transnational Crime Prevention, and an Adjunct Professor at the University of Sydney's Faculty of Law and at Simon Fraser University's School of Criminology in British Columbia, Canada. His previous professional positions include those of Director of the Australian Institute of Criminology, and President of the New South Wales Mental Health Review Tribunal. His current research interests include art crime as well as issues associated with occupational violence, and mental illness and the criminal justice system. His most recent publications include *Violence at Work* (3rd ed., 2006), written jointly with Vittorio Di Martino , published by the International Labour Office

(ILO) in Geneva. He has been a frequent consultant to national and international bodies including the United Nations, Commonwealth Secretariat and the ILO, as well as holding senior academic posts in Australia, Canada, and the United States.

Bojan Dobovšek is the Assistant Professor of Criminology and Criminal Investigation and Vice Dean at the Faculty of Criminal Justice, University of Maribor, Slovenia. He is a member of Commission for the Prevention of Corruption as representative of Judiciary branch of power, a representative of Slovenia in GRECO, and a trustee of ARCA. He is the author of several books and numerous publications on corruption and organized crime, considered the leading expert in Balkan organized crime. His ongoing research projects include: corruption in state institutions, corruption networks, organized crime and terrorism, methodological obstacles in measuring corruption, analyses of conventions on corruption, and art crime investigations. He is author of draft recommendations for OECD projects entitled Anti-Corruption Networks for Transition Economies, and the Istanbul Anti-Corruption Action Plan for Armenia, Azerbaijan, Georgia, Kazakhstan, the Kyrgyz Republic, the Russian Federation, Tajikistan and Ukraine.

Dick Drent is the Director of Security of the Van Gogh Museum (VGM), having accepted this function in January 2005, with a mission and a mandate to improve the security level of the security in this museum to an absolute high standard. Before the VGM, he worked in field of Law Enforcement in the Netherlands for 25 years, including 12 years with the Dutch National Police Agency, as a coordinator in the National Undercover and Sensitive Operations Unit. Together with some former law enforcement colleagues, he is the codeveloper of the ORRI method in museum security training, a method discussed in his essay. He is also a trainer on special skills training in the security business and in law enforcement.

Derek Fincham specializes in the public and private law relating to arts and antiquities. He maintains a Weblog on art and antiquities policy, the Illicit Cultural Property Blog (http://www.illicit-cultural-property.blogspot.com), which has been cited by the *New York Times* and the BBC. He is also a contributor to the London School of Economics Cultural Heritage and Art Law Initiative (http://www.lawandculture.co.uk). He currently holds a teaching fellowship at the Loyola University New Orleans College of Law. He earned his PhD in law from the University of Aberdeen in Scotland, and a JD from Wake Forest University, where he served as an editor on the Intellectual Property Law Journal and was awarded a Public Interest Grant for work with the North Carolina Volunteer Lawyers for the Arts.

David W. J. Gill is Reader in Mediterranean Archaeology at Swansea University, Wales, UK. He is a former Rome Scholar at the British School at Rome and was a member of the Department of Antiquities at the Fitzwilliam Museum, University of Cambridge. He has published widely on archaeological ethics with Christopher Chippindale. He is currently completing a history of British archaeological work in Greece prior to the First World War.

Ann Hartley is Assistant Attorney General, Financial Litigation Division, Office of the Attorney General of Texas since 1987. She holds a JD with Honors from the University of Texas School of Law and a BA in Sociology from Rice University.

John Kleberg is a retired Assistant Vice President at The Ohio State University, where he was instrumental in organizing the program described as well as having administrative responsibility for security, police, and other business and finance operations. He also has been a law enforcement administrator, trainer, and educator in Ohio and Illinois. His undergraduate degree is from Michigan State University, graduate degree from the University of Illinois and postgraduate work at The Ohio State University and Kent State University. He is the author of numerous articles on campus safety and security issues and consults on campus security issues including campus museums, libraries and galleries.

Stevan P. Layne, CPP, CIPM is CEO and Principal Consultant for Layne Consultants International and Founding Director of the IFCPP. He is a former police chief and institutional security director. Mr. Layne has been involved with providing protection advice and assistance to over 500 cultural institutions, federal, state, and municipal agencies, and both public and private entities. He is the author of the *Cultural Property Protection Manual*, the *Business Survival Guide*, and numerous articles on protection of cultural property. He is a keynote presenter and seminar leader for several national organizations and a popular presenter at museum related conferences. Steve resides in Florida with associate offices in Colorado, California, Massachusetts, Vermont, and Illinois.

Silvia Loreti was born in Rome, and took her BA and MA in art history at the Courtauld Institute of Art in London. She has served as a teaching assistant at the Courtauld Institute, leading discussions on modern art theory and the classical tradition, and is currently completing her PhD there under the supervision of Christopher Green. Her dissertation, on the relationship between primitivism and classicism in avant-garde theory, with a focus on the work of Picasso and de Chirico, has been prepared in Paris, where she has been based since 2005.

Travis McDade is Head of Rare Books and Assistant Professor of Library Administration at the College of Law at the University of Illinois. He teaches Legal Research at the law school and Rare Books, Crime and Punishment—a course of his own design—at the Graduate School of Library and Information Science. He researches and writes in the area of rare book, map and manuscript crime and is the author of *The Book Thief: The True Crimes of Daniel Spiegelman.*

Dafydd Nelson is a competition law journalist with MLex news agency in Brussels. He holds an LLM in European Community Law from the London School of Economics and Political Science and has a keen interest in how law is applied in the art world. Dafydd spent a year and a half working for Norton Rose LLP in London as Best Practice Manager, where he was deeply involved in money laundering regulations and state economic sanctions. Dafydd also worked in the Banking and Finance division of Eversheds Solicitors, where particular attention needed to be paid to sources of finance from foreign jurisdictions for money-laundering purposes.

Erik Nemeth, an independent scholar in Santa Monica, California, explores the interrelation of cultural property and international security. In publishing on the intersection of art history, illicit markets, and intelligence studies, he focuses on the evolving relevance of the art market to foreign policy. Following a decade in the software development industry in the United States and the former Eastern bloc, Erik pursued graduate studies in neuroscience. Dissertation research in retinal physiology provided an introduction to neuroaesthetics, which turned his attention to the art world, and a curiosity about art crime developed into research on the connection between security-intelligence and looted art. Erik has published in *Terrorism and Political Violence* and in *International Journal for Intelligence and CounterIntelligence* and will present at the 2008 conference of College Arts Association. He currently works for the Getty Research Institute in Research Databases while also serving as a research associate for ARCA. Erik holds a BA in Computer Science and a PhD in Vision Science, both from the University of California at Berkeley

Richard W. Oram is Associate Director and Hobby Foundation Librarian at the Harry Ransom Center, University of Texas as Austin. He is currently chair of the Security Committee of the Rare Books and Manuscripts Section of the Association of College and Research Libraries/American

Library Association and was formerly Section Chair. He holds a PhD in English Literature from Cornell University and a master's in Library and Information Science from the University of Texas at Austin.

Colonel Giovanni Pastore has been the Vice-Commandant of the Carabinieri Division for the Protection of Cultural Heritage, widely considered the world's finest art police, since 1995. He commands the 12 Carabinieri art police divisions within Italy. Pastore was trained at the elite military academy in Modena. He studied art history, law, and security, and excelled in horsemanship. Over his long career, he has been decorated with numerous medals both in Italy, including the equivalent of a knighthood, and by grateful nations abroad, in appreciation for his professional service. He is proud to be one of the founding trustees of ARCA.

Kenneth Polk is Professor of Criminology at the University of Melbourne. Although now retired from most teaching duties, he continues to do research, mostly on issues related to art crime. His other research in recent years has dealt with aspects of violence, including two books on homicide—*When Men Kill* (1994), and *Child Victims of Homicide,* with Christine Alder (2001). His postgraduate degrees were from Northwestern University and UCLA, and he has held visiting positions at Cambridge University, the University of Leuven, the University of Amsterdam, the University of Mexico (UNAM), and the University of Hong Kong, among others.

Dorit Straus, the Worldwide Fine Art Specialty Manager at the Chubb Group of Insurance Companies, joined Chubb in 1982. Prior to Chubb, she studied archeology at Hebrew University in Jerusalem, Israel, lectured on Biblical Archeology and worked at various museums. (The Jewish Museum, The Peabody Museum of Ethnography at Harvard University, and the Museum of Contemporary Craft in New York, now known as the Museum of Art and Design). Dorit has underwriting expertise in Property, Casualty, and Entertainment as well as fine art. Dorit was a key member of OBJECT ID of the Getty Institute, which established universal criteria for describing works of art. She speaks on art and insurance at international venues including seminars on risk management for museums and cultural institutions at Shanghai University, the keynote speaker at fine art risk management seminar sponsored by the government of Taiwan, a featured speaker at a conference at Dresden, Germany, and a panelist at a seminar on art theft at Cambridge University, United Kingdom.In February 2008, she lectured about art fraud to the Israeli Insurance Industry in Tel Aviv. Dorit would like to thank Joshua Straus for his assistance in preparing her chapter.

John Stubbs is the author of a PhD on "The Rhetoric of the Farfetched and its Bearing on Shakespeare" (2005) and a biography of the English poet and churchman John Donne, *Donne: The Reformed Soul* (2006), for which he was awarded a Royal Society of Literature Jerwood prize for nonfiction, the Irish Writers' Centre/Glen Dimplex New Writer of the Year Award 2007, and nominated for The Guardian First Book Award, The Sunday Times Young Writer of the Year Award, and The Costa Biography Award.

A. J. G. Tijhuis works as a lawyer in Amsterdam. Besides that, he lectures at the Criminology Department of VU University and is connected to the Netherlands Institute for the Study of Crime and Law Enforcement in Leiden. He has been studying the illegal art trade since 2001. He has published a number of articles on, among other topics, the illicit antiquities trade in China, the task force to fight illicit trafficking in cultural property stolen in Iraq, the connection between art and drugs trade, and the illicit art and antiquities trade as criminal market. In 2006, he published his PhD, which focussed on the interface between the licit and illicit art and antiquities trade.

Judge Arthur Tompkins has been a District Court Judge in New Zealand for 11 years, having been appointed in 1997. His appointment followed 10 years in private practice in Auckland as a commercial barrister. He gained his bachelor's degree in Law from Canterbury University, in Christchurch, New Zealand, in 1983, and subsequently graduated Masters in Law, with First Class Honours, from Cambridge University, England, in 1984. He has taught the Law of Evidence, and presented at numerous conferences and workshops on a variety of topics, including expert evidence, the intersect between law and science in the courtroom, and most extensively in relation to forensic DNA and forensic DNA databanks, in New Zealand, China, England, Ireland, and France. He is an Honorary Member of Interpol's DNA Monitoring Expert Group, and an elected Fellow of the Cambridge Commonwealth Trust.

ARCA

The Association for Research into Crimes against Art (ARCA) is an international think tank and research group on contemporary issues in art crime. This nonprofit organization studies issues in art crime, and work as consultants on art protection and recovery issues brought to them by police, governments, museums, places of worship, and other public institutions. In addition to consulting, ARCA works to promote awareness of the severity and true nature of art crime. This work includes media relations, publishing, lectures, and academic programs.

In addition to this book, ARCA has established the first peer-reviewed academic and professional journal in the study of art crime and cultural property protection: *The Journal of Art Crime.* This twice-yearly journal will continue the work begun with this book. ARCA welcomes submissions and subscription interest. ARCA has also established the first academic program in the field, an independent master's program in Art Crime Studies. For more information on ARCA, its projects, and how you can help to fight art crime, please visit http://www.artcrime.info.